Maternal Pasts,
Feminist Futures

LYNNE HUFFER

Maternal Pasts, Feminist Futures

Nostalgia, Ethics, and the Question of Difference

STANFORD UNIVERSITY PRESS

Stanford, California   1998

CIP data appear at the end of the book

FOR BETSY, MY MOTHER

ACKNOWLEDGMENTS

This book is a weave of voices. Having acknowledged that, I am tempted to say: "You know who you are." Nonetheless, I want to try to express my gratitude to the many, many people whose advice, generosity, intellectual challenge, kindness, moral uplift, and material support have contributed to the completion of this project.

First, I would like to thank Domna Stanton; although at the time I was not ready to pursue this project, it was in conversations with her during graduate school at the University of Michigan that the idea of this book first began to take shape. For advice, support, and helpful comments on different parts of the book I would like to thank John Brenkman, Karl Britto, Cathy Caruth, Cathy Cohen, Benjamin Elwood, Beth Huffer, Kevin Newmark, Elizabeth Rottenberg, Neil Saccamano, and Anette Schwarz. I am especially grateful to Carla Kaplan, who has been a faithful and enduring friend, colleague, and reader of drafts in all their stages over many years. A special word of thanks also goes to Nicole Brossard for her gracious and encouraging reading of Chapter 5.

Perhaps the most important tangible gifts I have received are places to write without the distractions of everyday life. First, I would like to thank Deb and Henry Townshend for opening up their home in Pomfret, Connecticut. I would also like to thank the Camargo Foundation for its support of my work through a residential grant in Cassis, France. I am especially grateful to Anne-Marie Franco and Michael Pretina of the Camargo Foundation, and to Annie Rouzoul, resident of Cassis and dear friend. I want to thank all of my colleagues at Camargo, especially Joyce Brodsky, Barbara Cooper, and Cole Swensen.

I want to express my appreciation to Yale University for providing the leave time necessary for writing, both through a Morse Fellowship (1992–93) and a Senior Faculty Fellowship (1995–96). I would like to thank Alyson Waters of *Yale French Studies* for her brilliant editing, and Noah Guynn for the editing he has done over the years, both at *Yale French Studies* and on the final version of this manuscript. I also want to thank Helen Tartar of Stanford University Press for her encouragement and her commitment to this project.

A special word of gratitude goes to my mother, Betsy McConnell, to her partner, Gillian Edwards, to my sister, Beth, to my niece, Lisi, to my brother, John, to my sister-in-law, He Hong, to my father, Bill, to his wife, Brooke, and to my brothers Andrew and Patrick, for their support, encouragement, and love. Michelle LaPerrière has given me friendship, strength, and endless inspiration, in addition to gracing the world with her beautiful art; Shepard Parsons shared spiritual guidance, peach pancakes in Pomfret, and new forms of family; and Charis, who was born as I was finishing this book, fills my life with joy. A deep word of gratitude goes to my partner, Tamara Jones, whose love, energy, intellectual challenge, and presence in my life over the last two years of the writing of this book gave me the confidence and the strength to finish. And finally, I want to offer thanks to Serene Jones, the person most closely involved in this book; her friendship, wisdom, and courage are here in every page.

L.H.

CONTENTS

Mom   1
Introduction: Maternal Pasts   6

Nostalgia: The Lost Mother

1 Blanchot's Mother   35
2 Lips in the Mirror: Irigaray's Specular Mother   55

Nostalgia and Ethics: Approaching the Other

3 Imperialist Nostalgia: Kristeva's Maternal *Chora*   73
4 Luce *et veritas*: Toward an Ethics of Performance   96

Toward Another Model

5 From Lesbos to Montreal: Brossard's Urban Fictions   117

   Afterword: Feminist Futures   134

   Notes   143
   Bibliography   179
   Index   195

Maternal Pasts,
Feminist Futures

Mom

When I was in college, my mother came out as a lesbian. This book, at its core, is about my coming to terms with *that*. Let me explain. I'm quite certain that my mother's presence is somehow inscribed throughout these pages. However, her particular place here as *my* mother is probably not obvious to anyone but me. Indeed, this book is not "about" my lesbian mother; it's not even about lesbian mothers in general. Nonetheless, at the heart of this project stands the figure of my lesbian mother. So I find myself, from the start, faced with something of a paradox: my mother is both here and not here. And perhaps, despite the conundrum, this is actually a good place to start. After all, what I'm really mapping in this book is presence and absence—visibility and invisibility, voice and silence—in the complex relation between lesbians, mothers, and daughters.

Before I go further, let me assure you: this is not yet another version of that frighteningly ubiquitous story about the literary critic turned autobiographer. This is not a narrative about my inner child, or about my personal psychic drama in the halls of academe. So let me try, for a moment, to define what this book is. Put succinctly, it is a feminist reading of the mother as a figure of nostalgia in the work of four French-speaking writers: Blanchot, Irigaray, Kristeva, and Brossard.

Like any product of human endeavor, this book is a construction *in* time. Over the course of writing, I made a conscious decision not to completely mask the changes that inevitably occur. The individual stitches are part of the story, and I want the seams to show. Against that backdrop, this work records, albeit in an oblique and refracted way, a span of my own individual, comically caricatural narrative. When I began writing I was a married, heterosexual homeowner with a golden retriever. Since that time, I have passed through a stage best described as lonely and in pain, to my present state as a happy, cat-loving lesbian with new commitments to sexual, racial, and economic justice. Other changes mark my intellectual life. My approach to reading what I soon learned to call "texts" began in graduate school with a heavy dose of French structuralism and poststructuralism; later, at Yale, I was briefly warmed by the dying embers of hard-core deconstruction. Having absorbed some of that heat, I now, eerily, feel chilled by words like *différance* and *catachresis*. This is not to say that I've rejected everything that came before; rather, I'm constantly sifting through the ashes for something to be coaxed into warmth and flame. And what shall I call this thing that I do now? Feminist theory with a queer, deconstructive spin, or should I just add myself to that eclectic soup known as cultural studies? I'll leave the question of labels for another venue and another time—at least for now—and go back to tending my fire.

In terms broader than those outlined above, the chapters in this book reflect a shift from a concern with general principles to the particular struggles of actors grounded in a specific place and time. Along the same lines, the questions I pose move from a focus on the rhetorical structure of language as a self-enclosed system to an interrogation of language as it is embedded in social institutions and practices. Significantly, what unifies these chapters is a commitment to feminism as an ongoing, unending process of struggle. The way that feminism is shaped and articulated has shifted across time, sometimes dramatically. But like the exposed seams I refuse to hide, I throw those shifts into a positive light: for me, they reflect the perpetually transformative and self-critical impetus of feminism at its best. We won't get anywhere if we think, finally, that we've found the answer, if we fail to move, if we become transfixed by our own unchanging reflection in the mirror. When we look in the mirror do we just see ourselves, or do we see someone different, still caught in the mirror but beginning to break free?

This differently reflective, speculative look in the proverbial mirror brings me back full circle to that other question, which is, of course, my lesbian mother. Symbolically, lesbians and mothers in this culture have something in common: both function as figures of absence, invisibility, and silence. What can we learn from that recognition, especially when the face we recognize as our own is a blank?

This book begins with mothers and ends with lesbians; along the way, it interrogates the literary, epistemological, and ontological structures through which presence and absence, visibility and invisibility, voice and silence, are produced. Taken together, those structures are governed by what I will call a logic of replacement. This logic comes out of a particular Western, deconstructive tradition of thought that looks at language as the differential play of presence and absence. Within that tradition, the logic of replacement can be described as a system whereby a term—the word or the sign—can come to the fore only by effacing another term—the thing or the referent—that it ostensibly sets out to name. If we further contextualize that logic of replacement within a psychoanalytic tradition of thought, the play of presence and absence can be articulated in the vocabulary of gendered subjects. My focus begins from within that psychoanalytically informed linguistic structure in order to talk about the absence and presence of the mother-daughter dyad. To put it in the terms I used before: the daughter—the linguistic sign—can come to the fore only by effacing the mother—the referent—she ostensibly sets out to name.

Significantly, this logic of appearance and disappearance, of moving toward something only to erase it, describes the nostalgic structure that this book both uncovers and critiques. A nostalgic structure both creates and obliterates a lost object; in the terms I've laid out here, nostalgia requires an absent mother. So what happens when that mother is doubly absent or invisible, when she literally and symbolically turns out to be a lesbian?

Although, as I stated earlier, this is not a book *about* lesbian mothers, that question lies behind all the other questions I attempt to answer in my readings of Blanchot, Irigaray, Kristeva, and Brossard. How do we think the mother beyond the familiar logic of oppositions between complementary halves—paternal and maternal, presence and absence? How do we sketch out a different model, one that moves from a relation of annihilation and replacement to one of mutuality and coexistence? Irigaray says at the end of her poetic tribute to her mother, "And the One Doesn't Stir Without the Other": "And what I wanted from you, Mother, was this: that in giving me life, you still remain alive."[1]

How does a daughter write about or even to a mother without consigning the mother to the absence, invisibility, and silence on which a certain conception of writing traditionally depends? How does she do *that* and, at the same time, undo the patriarchal logic through which the concept of mother exists at all? How does a daughter "kill the womb,"[2] as Nicole Brossard puts it, and also make way for maternal life emerging in some other form? What happens when that form is lesbian?

To the extent that patriarchy defines all women as mothers, either potential or real, it is not surprising that some radical thinkers—like Monique Wittig, for example—would do away with the term altogether. But while Wittig can leave the word "mother" out of her lesbian feminist lexicon,[3] for me the process has not been so simple. Maybe it's because my mother *is* a lesbian that I can't bring myself to simply blot her out in the name of a postpatriarchal lesbian utopia. As much as I wanted to go "Beyond the Mother"—my original title for this book— I know now, more than ever, that such an attempt at escape or transcendence is not just jumping the gun, so to speak, but is in fact intrinsic to the "mother problem" itself. Escape and transcendence are ultimately nostalgic and therefore obliterating gestures ... which brings me back, once again, to my lesbian mother.

For better or worse, and despite any number of theoretical maneuvers I might make here or in subsequent chapters, my lesbian mother is still here. She gave birth to me—her daughter—and raised me to be born, again and again—a lesbian's lesbian daughter. I'm still trying to grasp the play of presence and absence in that relation. There's a play in *that* structure which has yet to be articulated, and this book is a beginning, in all its forms. Throughout these pages, even in the most closeted moments of arcane abstraction, my mother is still there ... wishing, no doubt, that I might finally write something that actually speaks *to her*. Perhaps I succeed, if only for a moment, in Chapter 5 ("From Lesbos to Montreal"), the most recently written, "lesbian" chapter. Perhaps not. I suspect that with this book she will be, yet again, both proud and disappointed that it's not a book she would have any particular interest in reading if I were not, in fact, her daughter. Maybe that conflicting disappointment and pride are also inscribed in our culture's maternal script. But if that's where we are—my mother and I—then so be it: that's where we'll have to start. We can only ever start where we are, in this place and time: lesbians, daughters, and mothers. *Maternal Pasts, Feminist Futures* traces our presence: here, where we find ourselves.

Maternal Pasts

> All this time that she remains in the story, in his-tory, she can
> earn her living only by disturbing the symbolic field. Modify-
> ing the first clause, the instrument of reproduction, her only
> tool. The dissolution of forms, like an end of the world played
> out on the stage of the flat belly. Her uterus set beside her like
> a backpack.   —NICOLE BROSSARD, *L'Amèr*

I began by invoking the figure of my lesbian mother. In fact, there's a
bit more to this story of women than that: I also have a sister. Alas, I
must admit, the place she inhabits in the landscape I'm mapping is even
less visible than that of my mother. And yet, my sister's latent presence
here promises the possibility of other maps, for reasons that I hope will
become clear by the end of the book. For now, let it suffice to say that,
symbolically, mother and sister stand at opposite poles of the gendered
relational structures this work describes. On one end stands a conservative structure of mother-love in which nostalgia both creates and effaces the object of desire. On the other end stands a more liberatory
structure of sister-love in which mutually affirming subjects of desire
coexist. It is my hope that by tracing the confining boundaries of the
maternal map, the book will open up future sisterly spaces for thinking
about relations between women: friends, lovers, feminists in struggle.

So I began this project by asking my sister what she would want to
know in reading the introduction to a book called *Maternal Pasts, Fem-*

inist Futures. And she replied: "Well, to begin with, what does it have to do with anything?" One of the reasons I love her so much is that she's so direct. Unfortunately, I've had trouble responding to the skeptical curiosity embedded in her question—which I'd rather not have to answer. And yet, as usual, she's right on the mark: what *any* book has to do with anything is precisely what the introduction is supposed to spell out.

We all have mothers. Unfortunately, that will hardly suffice as an answer to my sister's question. As she or anyone else can see by simply glancing at the subtitle—"Nostalgia, Ethics, and the Question of Difference"—this is not a book about real mothers in the everyday sense of the term. Rather, to begin with, I look at the mother as a powerful cultural symbol, a symbol so powerful that it shapes the dominant structures of Western thought. When I speak of the mother as a symbol, I mean that the mother is a term—a complex cultural construct—which exists in relation to other terms. Together those terms form a nexus of semantic connections from which we make sense of the world. This book asks the question: what is the relationship between the mother and the conceptual constructs that frame our understanding of the world? How can we theorize that relationship?

Beginning

We can begin by critiquing the mother. Okay, says my sister, but just what does that mean? To talk about the mother in relation to the world is certainly impressive, but can you try to be a bit more specific? All right, I say, I'll give it a try. First of all, in the Western tradition the mother is a symbol of beginnings; as the one who gives birth, she occupies the place of the origin. Metaphorically speaking, everything begins with the mother. Second, because the mother marks the place of the origin, she also marks the place of return: in giving birth, the mother simultaneously assures the eventuality of death. Symbolically, the maternal origin does not mark a beginning whose outcome is uncertain; rather, the mother as origin represents the circle of life whose ultimate *telos* is death. As Simone de Beauvoir puts it in *The Second Sex*:

The Woman-Mother has a face of shadows: she is the chaos whence all have come and whither all must one day return; she is Nothingness. In the Night are confused together the multiple aspects of the world which daylight reveals: night of spirit confined in the generality and opacity of matter, night of sleep and of nothingness. In the deeps of the sea it is night: woman is the *Mare tenebrarum*, dreaded by navigators of old; it is night in the entrails of the earth. Man is frightened of this night, the reverse of fecundity, which threatens to swallow him up. He aspires to the sky, to the light, to the sunny summits, to the pure and crystalline frigidity of the blue sky; and under his feet there is a moist, warm, and darkling gulf ready to draw him down; in many a legend do we see the hero lost forever as he falls back into the maternal shadows—cave, abyss, hell.[1]

In this general sketch of the mythical meanings attached to the maternal figure, two points become clear. First, the mother is associated with an inaccessible origin; second, the structure of the maternal origin is a self-enclosed circle: its beginning is also its end. In the dominant Western tradition Beauvoir describes, the mother represents the place whence we came and to which we return. Correspondingly, she also symbolizes the very foundation for everything we come to see, know, and be. She is the ground upon which the world of meaning is constructed; she is, in Beauvoir's words, the "opacity of matter" and "the entrails of the earth" upon which "the sky," "the light," and "the sunny summits" are erected. In that sense, the mother as origin is the condition of possibility of meaning itself.

At its widest level, then, this book is about the construction of systems of meaning in relation to a maternal figure. That focus may seem overly abstract to some readers; still, it is precisely by looking at those "abstract" structures of meaning that I want to elucidate the purpose of this book. To return, once again, to my sister's original question—so what does this book have to do with anything?—well, to put it simply, this work has to do with *meaning-making*: the way we make sense of the world.

I want to emphasize that the mother is not the *only* symbol of beginnings in the tradition I'm invoking here, although, as Beauvoir argues, she certainly constitutes an important, even exemplary figure of origins. Nevertheless, my argument in this book does not depend on claiming a unique or exclusive role for the mother as origin. Rather, the maternal figure functions for me as a heuristic device for uncovering and dismantling nostalgic structures of thought. Other figures may also occupy the place of the origin: a case in point is the example of Sappho in Chapter 5. And it is precisely by examining the myth of the lost mother that more general conclusions can be drawn for thinking about other originary structures of meaning.

What does it mean, then, to talk about the mother as origin? And how precisely does the maternal origin function in the making of meaning? First, it is important to remember that, within a deconstructive tradition of thought, meaning itself has no origin, no absolute ground, no place of beginning from which all other meanings stem. Ferdinand de Saussure's insight about language as a system of signs that signify *in relation* to each other is pertinent here. According to Saussure, meaning is not absolute but differential: signs acquire meaning in their difference from each other.[2] And yet, in the psychoanalytically informed, deconstructive tradition of thought that has come to be known as "French theory," the term "mother" is not just one sign among many signs in an endless relay of differentially constructed meanings. Rather, as the origin, the mother becomes an originary sign, a ground of meaning, the place of beginnings to which the chain of relational meanings ultimately returns.

Second, and just as crucially, that chain of relational meanings functions within a political and ideological context. In that sense, the semiotic construction of a world of meaning around an inaccessible maternal ground has consequences that are not abstract at all, but in fact play themselves out in concrete relations of power. Specifically, the mother as origin occupies a position in the ideological and political systems through which *gendered* meanings are constructed. Not only is a world of meaning structured in relation to a maternal origin, but those meanings are given value according to the oppositional relations of gender. Further, as Beauvoir points out, across our cultural grid of gendered values, men occupy the positive and the neutral positions while women occupy the negative.[3] It follows, then, that there are connections to be made between the gendered distribution of values and the coding of the mother as the lost origin. The mother, too, occupies the negative position; she is, in fact, the most extreme expression of the construction of the feminine as negativity: absence, invisibility, meaninglessness, silence, loss.[4] In other words, as the ground of meaning, the mother can only ever be the empty foundation of meaning: she is never meaning itself, but only that which allows meaning to come to be. The political and ideological implications of such a position seem clear: she is never an agent, a subject of meaning, or a wielder of power, but rather a figure of negativity; as Beauvoir puts it, she is chaos, shadows, cave, abyss, hell. Behind the powerful men who represent that which is most valued and privileged in Western culture lies the doubled figure of both their birth and death, the source of their being as well as the specter of their negation: behind the hero lies the maternal void.

Backpacking

Given that dynamic of masculine presence and maternal absence, it is my hope that in the charting, uncharting, and recharting of this maternal map, the very logic of gender can be pushed to its breaking point. How might this happen? Let's look at this chapter's epigraph. Nicole Brossard's image of the uterus as backpack works, for me, as a figure for the disruption and transformation of the logic of gender. Indeed, writing a generation after Beauvoir and from a different place on the Francophone map—namely, Quebec—Brossard both repeats and disrupts the gendered system so forcefully articulated in *The Second Sex*. Brossard remaps what Beauvoir had already charted as one of Western culture's most powerful scripts: woman = mother = womb. "First we must ask," Beauvoir writes on the opening page of *The Second Sex*, "what is a woman? '*Tota mulier in utero*,' says one, 'woman is a womb'" (xv). The symbolic importance of the woman = mother = womb equation highlights the leap that turns the mother into the origin of all that is: from Homer's celebration of "the earth, firmly founded mother of all" to William Blake's praise of the earth as "the matron Clay" (Beauvoir, 163), the maternal womb is associated with mud, nature, the earth as source of life. In other words, the very world itself is a mother, or, as Richard Klein puts it: "the world is a dream in the body of the mother."[5]

Because their symbolic position as body, as womb, and as world relegates women to an inferior status vis-à-vis men, Brossard wants to bring about an end of that world: "like an end of the world played out on the stage of the flat belly." For Brossard, the world as woman is fecund and round, round like the belly of a pregnant mother. Everything begins in the rounded belly. Like a sentence generated from its own internal logic, the world of meaning is born out of a maternal beginning, what Brossard calls "the first clause, the instrument of reproduction." But if, symbolically, women both *generate* the world and *are* the world, the world is not something that they can possess. If woman-as-mother-as-womb is the world, that world is there for the taking. In fact, men created it so that they could take it: the world is *man's* dream in the body of the mother.

So when Brossard deflates that rounded dream, man's world becomes a stage on which other symbolic possibilities can be performed. If man's world-to-be-taken is always round like a pregnant belly, we must also be able to imagine other forms—like a flat belly, for instance—in order to play out an end of man's world. In that "dissolution of forms" Brossard modifies the masculine world perspective that creates the equation woman = mother = womb and, in so doing, challenges the very logic of gender, figured here as round versus flat. If gender gives us a world whose meaning is "round," round like the swell of a belly, it is precisely that roundness which allows men to be "flat" and to conquer our rounded world. Brossard debunks that exclusionary and essentialist meaning by making a new world that is *both* round and flat, like a backpack that can be empty or full. ("Round and flat," Jeanette Winterson writes, "only a very little has been discovered.")[6]

Let me be clear: I am not out to "destroy" the mother. Rather, my project is to trace the structures through which maternal meanings are produced and, in doing so, to unpack and challenge those meanings. In the example I'm pursuing here, one such meaning reduces woman to an organ: "*Tota mulier in utero.*" Challenging and transforming that essentializing definition of woman-as-mother-as womb can mean, as it does for Brossard, symbolically turning the womb into a backpack. In that gesture, biology becomes something that can be emptied or filled, put on or taken off at will. Further, by placing the womb beside her,

Brossard's symbolic mother moves beyond a binary logic of front and back or round and flat, where to challenge gender would mean simply to reverse things. Instead, the dualistic logic of front versus back opens up toward a third, restructuring possibility: "her uterus set beside her like a backpack."

Brossard's uterus-as-backpack can thus work as a figure for the theoretical approach that frames *Maternal Pasts, Feminist Futures.* The uterus-as-backpack conveys, among other things, the inadequacy of mere reversal—front to back, round to flat, man to woman, father to mother—in disrupting the logic of gender. If the world is a dream in the body of the mother, I want to look at the stuff of that dream. The hero's dream might just be the mother's nightmare. And if that's the case, exposing the nightmare and shaking it up might give us a very different world.

Backtracking

This book begins at a critical juncture: the point of connection between nostalgia, the mother, and the structure of origins in Western thought. I approach this thematic knot of questions from a particular theoretical, historical, and political locus: the place on the map where feminism begins to take hold as a sustained body of thought. More specifically, the pretext of my inquiry begins with the rise of North American feminist criticism in the 1970's and, in particular, the importance of the mother in that project. When I began this work in the late 1980's, I was responding to what I and others identified as a trend in the first two decades of feminist literary criticism and theory. As I saw it then, the attempt on the part of North American feminist critics during the 1970's and 1980's to replace a paternal body of "great" works with a maternal corpus of texts was founded on the questionable myth of the lost mother, the mother-as-origin described above. Particularly in the field of feminist literary criticism, this maternal figure held forth a utopian promise of mother-daughter bonding for the female progeny who would come to write in order to rediscover her. Indeed, the gesture that replaced the paternal authority of the male tradition with an equally powerful female model of literary authorship was, and to some extent still is, one of the grounding concepts of American feminist literary theory.[7] Thus my argument began as a challenge to this logic of reversal: the reconstruction of a specifically female heritage of writing, I said, is necessarily based on a structure of nostalgia that, rather than displacing traditional paradigms of literary authority, in fact reinforces and repeats them. My starting point was to rethink the symmetrical opposition between paternally and maternally coded literary genealogies and, in so doing, to open up readings that would no longer be structured exclusively by those oppositions.

In the course of its writing, this project grew in directions that I had not foreseen. Nonetheless, its genesis in a critique of reversal and the nostalgic structure which frames that logic remains pertinent to the book in its final form. Going back to the place where this book began also helps me to situate its focus in the context of related work that has been done in the fields of feminist theory, literary criticism, and philosophy. First, the challenge I pose to the logic of reversal is neither unique nor new; there is, by now, a vast body of deconstructive work which looks at gender on the level of that logic of binary oppositions.[8] By the same token, to question nostalgia as a liberatory structure is hardly original; again, a number of theorists have paved the way for ongoing work in this area.[9] Indeed, the bibliography of this book is a testament to the importance of those feminist thinkers and writers concerned with the relationship between political change and the structures of meaning that both guide and constrain our thinking.

More specifically, my own focus emerges out of the conversation that began in the mid-1980's between "French" and "American" feminisms.[10] That Franco-American conversation has spawned a body of critical and theoretical work, especially in the United States, that continues up to the present moment. I am not interested in repeating the myriad permutations of that conversation here. In fact, my intervention into the topic of feminism and the mother is not comparative in nature, and the writers I engage are all part of a French-speaking tradition. While my approach is clearly French-oriented, my political stance is firmly rooted in a North American feminist tradition.

Against that backdrop, I do want to make some claims of my own. And although it is precisely my own critique of nostalgia that would never allow me to believe in originality, much less to claim it for my-self, there are aspects of my argument that differ from those of the theorists on whose work I build. By focusing on the nexus of issues mentioned above—nostalgia, the mother, and the structure of origins—I develop an argument about Western constructions of gender that has not yet been thoroughly articulated. In that argument, I move from nostalgia toward the articulation of an ethical model of relation. Further, the theoretical approach I'm taking has unabashedly political implications. The ethical relation forces us to consider a concept of community that is politically effective but does not homogenize the differences within the collective *we*. Thus by working *through* the abstraction of theoretical structures, this book also reaches toward something that is both real *and* new: another logic or another form that feminists and progressive intellectuals might find useful. Ultimately, my purpose is to ask questions not only about language, ideology, and gender, but also more generally about the structures of thought that uphold an oppressive social system. It's hard to know exactly what shape might emerge out of all those questions, but for now I'll just stick with Brossard's backpack: it's symbolic but real, visionary but concrete, abstract but also quite useful.

Nostalgia

I want to look more closely at the question of nostalgia, particularly in its connection to the mother and the origin described above. First, and most important, nostalgia has a structure. Specifically, a nostalgic structure is a system of thought that begins with the idea of return, from the Greek *nostos*: "the return home." This movement of return takes many different forms, depending on who is thinking nostalgically and what the context of that thinking might be. Crucially, the Greeks with their *nostos* might hold out the promise that, yes, you can return whence you came, but nostalgia happens because you can't go home again. As John Brenkman puts it: "home takes shape and becomes meaningful through the back-forming imagination. It marks a yearning to return to where you never were."[11] What looked like home is an illusion of home, a mirage that disguises a blank, what Beauvoir calls the "Nothingness" of the "Woman-Mother."

It is useful here to examine the way feminist theory analyzes gender and patriarchy in the context of a nostalgic structure. In addition to producing economic, sexual, social, and cultural forms of male domination, patriarchy also privileges men over women as thinkers, knowers, and speakers.[12] That unequal dyad of man over woman produces a logic of analogous pairings such as thought over body and spirit over matter. Further, as we saw in the woman = mother = womb equation described by Beauvoir and elaborated by Brossard, because women bear children, in a male-dominated system woman is symbolically reduced to her corporeal, material form as a reproductive body: "the instrument of reproduction, her only tool." Under patriarchy, to be a woman is to be a mother.

The privileging of man over woman as a thinking subject connects the logic of gender with the search for origins that lies at the heart of a nostalgic structure. Because thought involves a quest for knowledge, thinking is an activity of seeking that is motivated by desire. As patriarchy's privileged seeker of knowledge, man must construct an other-to-be-known as the object of his desire. Further, gender inequality creates man as subject and woman as object and silent other; as Beauvoir writes, "she is the incidental, the inessential as opposed to the essential. He is the Subject, he is the Absolute—she is the Other" (xix). Finally, because gender ideology reduces woman to mother, the object of man's search becomes, metaphorically, the lost mother. As a result, this form of nostalgia becomes a dominant structure of thought in a system that privileges men over women.

The Freudian psychoanalytic construct of the family triad both illustrates and reinforces the philosophical structure of nostalgia described above. Freud harnessed the myth of Oedipus as the founding narrative of psychoanalysis which, as such, has become a normative model of masculine subjectivity.[13] In that psychoanalytic narrative, the son becomes the father's rival in a triangular plot whose object of desire is the lost mother. The son, like the "hero" mentioned by Beauvoir, is plagued by a nostalgic desire—to return to the mother—whose eventual outcome is self-destruction. Just as Oedipus's acts of killing his father and marrying his mother lead to his demise, so the psychoanalytic story of the son's longing for the mother contains a message of doom.

And while, for Freud, overcoming that longing, or the "Oedipus complex," is an essential stage of normal masculine psychic development, the desire itself never disappears, but is simply transferred to another feminine object. As popular wisdom says, that's why so many men end up marrying their mothers. The truth behind the cliché lies in a patriarchal gender ideology that says: woman = womb = mother. In that system, the successful shift of object choice from mother to wife doesn't amount to much, since the initial structure which accounts for masculine heterosexual desire remains in place.[14] Nostalgia—a longing for that which is lost—fixes the structure as the normative paradigm for human psychic development.[15]

Of course, nostalgia anchors the system but also exposes the ruse of a gender construct based on the triadic psychoanalytic model. Indeed, man's nostalgic quest is a sham because the son can never return to the mother. To do so would be to embrace death, the *Mare tenebrarum* of myth and legend. In real life, patriarchy requires the repeated *failure* of the son to unite with his lost other. By repeatedly missing his maternal object of desire, the son sustains himself as an endlessly desiring subject. In this way, the object of desire—the ever-disappearing woman-as-mother—guarantees the existence of the subject of that desire—the ever-questing son. Man thus comes to exist by differentiating himself from that which he is not: the blank space, the unreachable mother, his silent and invisible other.

Feminist theory shows how a nostalgic structure works to perpetuate patriarchal oppression, but nostalgia also functions *within* oppressed groups struggling for liberation. For example, scholars in African, Francophone, and African-American studies have pointed to a nostalgic longing for "mother Africa" among people within the African diaspora who find themselves in a white racist culture.[16] Of course, the generalizing terms I use here risk masking the significant differences in the culture, politics, and identities of those for whom Africa might represent a lost origin. My purpose at this point is not to explore those differences, but to suggest that there is a structural similarity, whose form is nostalgic, between seemingly divergent movements and systems of thought. Another parallel example of a nostalgic structure would be the myth of Sappho, which highlights the lesbian nostalgia for a Greek source of woman-loving art and culture that would challenge traditional heterosexist models.[17] Finally, as mentioned earlier, a number of feminist critics have noted the nostalgic structure underlying the desire to retrieve a lost canon of literary foremothers to counter the male-dominated tradition. I want to focus for a moment on this last example in order to explore further the question of nostalgia in relation to feminist strategies of liberation.

The Freudian narrative of the Oedipus complex has been rightly criticized by feminist critics as a story that excludes women as subjects of desire. Indeed, while Freud mentions a parallel Electra complex, he does not develop the idea; further, as many have pointed out, simply reversing the Oedipus myth to include women hardly gives us an accurate model of female psychic development.[18] Freud gives us cause to question the applicability of the Oedipus complex to either boys or girls as a universal story of development and individuation. As Brenkman puts it: "The gender critique shows that the Oedipus complex does not arise from the inner logic of desire and the biological necessity of sexual reproduction, but rather from the imperatives of social reproduction, the cultural forms of gender differentiation, and compulsory heterosexuality. The male model, too, therefore, is thrown in question" (178). Nonetheless, the Oedipus model provides the scaffolding for many of the guiding concepts of American feminist literary theory, precisely because the Oedipus myth articulates a structure of nostalgia that feminists have found useful in developing alternative models of female subjectivity and desire.

One of the clearest formulations of the link between the Oedipus myth and those feminist strategies that reinterpret the myth in terms of a female subject is an essay by Mary Jacobus, "Freud's Mnemonic: Women, Screen Memories, and Feminist Nostalgia." In her article, Jacobus reads Freud's Oedipus story as the "screen" that is constitutive of the feminist desire for a return to the mother. More specifically, Jacobus argues that Freud's construction of Oedipus as the founding narrative of psychoanalysis is grounded in an act of "forgetting," one that forms the basis of the Freudian understanding of sexual difference. Jacobus convincingly demonstrates that the Oedipus story "screens" the story of the pre-Oedipal phase, which she identifies in mythological terms as Hades' rape of Persephone, or the separation of the daughter from the mother through a patriarchal act of violence.[19] More important, Jacobus points out that this repressed story of femininity which Freud "forgets"—what she calls the "dark side of the oedipus complex" (132)—came to constitute one of the main narratives of contemporary feminist theory, manifesting itself, through an "implicit psychic utopianism," as a nostalgia for the lost pre-Oedipal bond between mother and daughter. In other words, in learning to remember and long for the mother, *we* feminist daughters in essence came to remember what Freud forgot.

The "screened" story of Demeter and Persephone has thus attained the status of a feminist myth of origins, a "universal feminist 'memory'" (Jacobus, 133) of a prior psychic and physical wholeness that has, because of the intrusion of patriarchy in the form of the father, been irretrievably lost. The matrilineal fiction, which, according to Jacobus, grounded much of the American feminist theory of the 1970's and 1980's, suggests that the dismembered and violated pre-Oedipal body can, through the process of female remembering, eventually be rediscovered and reconstructed as whole.

Jacobus goes on to expose the limitations of this feminist nostalgia for a pre-Oedipal oneness with the mother by arguing that memory itself can only be understood as a retrospective construction of that which never existed. Like theory, memory is constituted through a necessary forgetting of the fiction, or myth, that founds it.[20] Thus, Jacobus argues, "memory itself is only a myth. There is no unified, self-complete, undivided theory, or, for that matter, memory: both theory and memory fold back on themselves to reveal a rift—something that is not self-identical" (135). This rupture reveals the fallacy of positing a pre-Oedipal moment as pure, unitary, and unmediated. As Jacobus puts it: "There never was a prior time, or an unmediated relation for the subject (whether masculine or feminine), except as the oedipal defined it retroactively . . . No violent separation can be envisaged, except with an aura of pathos, because separation is inscribed from the start" (135).[21]

So what does this feminist critique of feminist nostalgia have to do with maternal pasts and feminist futures? This is the point where a moment of contention within feminism can open toward a more constructive vision.[22] In that spirit, my critique of feminist nostalgia lays the groundwork for where this book is headed—namely, toward a different model that can be figured as lesbian desire. That different vision is articulated most fully here in the final chapter on the holographic *we* in Nicole Brossard (Chapter 5). Significantly, while Jacobus, like many others, critiques feminist nostalgia, she recuperates it for the feminist project of "remaking, or making over, the past" (138). For Jacobus, feminist politics becomes a process of remembering. Unlike the feminist critics she challenges, Jacobus is not interested in refinding an illusory pre-Oedipal wholeness; for her, memory is a "patchwork rather than a seamless web" composed of the found objects or mnemonics "in which a woman 'finds herself' where she is not" (138). So despite her debunking of the myth of wholeness that would reunite mother and child, Jacobus continues to privilege the psychoanalytic structure of loss and return for what she calls "feminist politics in its retrospective, nostalgic mode" (138).

Although I, like Jacobus, begin with a critique of feminist nostalgia, I am unwilling to follow her in its recuperation. Nostalgia can be figured as either a patchwork quilt or an unbroken web, just as it can be harnessed for either liberatory or oppressive aims. The fact remains that the structure underlying nostalgic thinking reinforces a conservative social system. Because nostalgia requires the construction of a blank space, a lost origin to be rediscovered and claimed, it necessarily produces a dynamic of inequality in the opposition between a desiring subject and an invisible other. Further, in a nostalgic structure, an immutable lost past functions as a blueprint for the future, cutting off any possibility for uncertainty, difference, or fundamental change. Because nostalgia is necessarily static and unchanging in its attempt to retrieve a lost utopian space, its structure upholds the status quo. As Carla Kaplan puts it: "At the heart of nostalgia . . . is resistance to change" (*Erotics*, 295).[23]

For me, the story of nostalgia—like Freud's story of the son, like Jacobus's story of the daughter—is interesting not only for what it tells but also for what it leaves out. Jacobus finds her model of the mnemonics of "feminist politics in its retrospective mode" (138) in a poem by

Adrienne Rich, "Transcendental Etude." In that poem, Rich evokes the found objects or "finest findings" (76) from which Jacobus then constructs her vision of a nostalgic if fragmented feminist politics. Jacobus reads the "bits of yarn, calico and velvet scraps," the "small rainbow-colored shells," the "skeins of milkweed," "the darkblue petal of petunia," "the dry darkbrown lace of seaweed," "the shed silver/whisker of the cat," and "the finch's yellow feather" (Rich, 76–77) as "the personal detritus of memory which compose a woman's life" and "in which, as women, we both find and lose our forgotten selves" (138). What a nostalgic structure cannot include, and what Jacobus (to say nothing of Freud) fails to see, is the possibility of a desire for another woman who is *not* the mother. In her failure to see that other desire, Jacobus reflects a similar blindness in feminist theory that has only recently begun to change. And even in the current barrage of titles that could be classified as "lesbian theory," very few contest the maternally coded structures that make a *non*-maternal, woman-to-woman, subject-to-subject model of desire a virtual impossibility.[24] Where that woman-to-woman, subject-to-subject form of desire *does* emerge is in Rich's poem, in a movement that begins with nostalgia as "homesickness" and concludes with its implicit rejection. Rich's image of "two women" meeting, "eye to eye" (and I to I)—as strangers, as lovers, as coexisting subjects of desire—provides a poetic glimpse into a structure no longer governed by the heteronormative workings of nostalgia. Indeed, the "*strangeness*" celebrated in Rich's poem has nothing to do with *nostos*:

> *Homesick for myself, for her*—as, after the heatwave
> breaks, the clear tones of the world
> manifest: cloud, bough, wall, insect, the very soul of light:
> *homesick* as the fluted vault of desire
> articulates itself: *I am the lover and the loved,*
> *home and wanderer, she who splits*
> *firewood and she who knocks, a stranger*
> *in the storm*, two women, eye to eye
> measuring each other's spirit, each other's
> limitless desire,
>   a whole new poetry beginning here.[25]

French Feminism

In the preceding discussion of nostalgia and feminism, I have focused almost exclusively on North American feminist criticism and theory. However, that focus is only one part of the story behind this project. In fact, the thinker who has probably most influenced my theoretical approach here is Luce Irigaray, a philosopher and theorist who is most commonly known in the United States as one of a "Holy Trinity" of "French feminists," the other two being Hélène Cixous and Julia Kristeva. Both the term "French feminism" and the name Irigaray work as important markers of this book's contextual borders. However, in acknowledging that context I also introduce problems, and while it is tempting to gloss them over or not bring them up at all, the difficulties themselves are instructive for the process of assessing and sorting through the relationship between feminism and nostalgia.

Put simply, the problems raised by Irigaray and "French feminism" have to do with definitions and, more pointedly, the politics of naming and the institutionalization of knowledge. So what *is* French feminism, anyway? When faced with this question I want to shake my head and say I don't know; instead, I'm more likely to respond by saying something about the writings of various French intellectuals on the questions of woman, the feminine, and the other. I might then go on to talk about the "Trinity" and to criticize it for being reductive, elitist, and overly simplistic. And I might further point out some of the differences between Kristeva, Irigaray, and Cixous, and raise the question of their relation to feminist movements. Irigaray, for example, only reluctantly allies herself with organized feminism; Kristeva and Cixous actively denounce it. Nonetheless, the work these writers produce has come to be known as "French feminism." To be sure, I can, and do, challenge that limited and inaccurate definition of "French feminism," adding other French thinkers and activists to the list as well, names like Simone de Beauvoir, Monique Wittig, Christine Delphy, in addition to non-French Francophone writers like Nicole Brossard and the Algerian historian and novelist Assia Djebar. In doing so, I problematize "French feminism" by talking about the process of canonization and the hegemony of the North American academy in the institutionalization of knowledge. I talk about sexuality and race and national boundaries, about the politics of translation, about invisibility, exclusion, and marginalization. But after all of that talk, what I *really* want to say is that, in my opinion, the concept of "French feminism" has outstayed its welcome: it no longer works, so it is time to move on.

Beyond my own attempts to reassess "French feminism," there is an important body of scholarly work that looks at the concept with a critical eye.[26] For example, Christine Delphy, a French sociologist and feminist activist, has argued that what present-day academics call "French feminism" is the sheer fabrication of Anglo-American scholars. That is not to say that activists and theorists who are both French and feminists do not exist; Delphy herself is one of them. But, Delphy argues, the particular brand of thought called "French feminism" has very little to do with either feminism or France. " 'French Feminism,' " Delphy writes, "was created by a series of distortions and voluntary or involuntary errors about what was happening in France from the mid-seventies on. . . . 'French Feminism' is . . . a highly consensual object in the sense that the only debates about it focus on its relevance to Anglo-American concerns."[27] Delphy suggests that Anglo-American scholars have created and celebrated "French feminism" in order, among other things, to rehabilitate psychoanalysis and an essentialist understanding of gender.[28] Whether in the form of Cixous's breast milk, Kristeva's semiotic womb, or Irigaray's labia, "French feminism" privileges a concept of *difference*—as opposed to a rights-based argument for *equality*—that tends to both highlight and reify biological differences between men and women.

What seems crucial here for looking at the relationship between French feminism and nostalgia is the focus on the body. Indeed, although nobody quite knows what it means, "writing the body" has, for many, become synonymous with the idea of French feminism.[29] This celebration of the female body has been important for the recognition and naming of a form of desire that is not based on a masculine model. Further, as the phrases "writing the body" or *écriture féminine*[30] suggest, the celebration of female desire creates a space for theorizing and performing alternative forms of artistic expression. This focus on the connection between female sexual desire and female expression points to the influence of a seemingly open, orgasmic, fluid French body on North American feminist theory. To be sure, the image of a puritanical, sensibly shod American feminist who discovers *jouissance* in an encounter with her sexy, stiletto-heeled French sister is too much of a caricature to be taken seriously. Nonetheless, caricature or not, it is undeniable that in recent years American feminist theory, especially in the humanities, has become obsessed with the body: gendered, racialized, sexual, cybernetic, or performative, "the body" is now being rethought, dismantled, deconstructed, and scrutinized, just like "the subject" a decade ago. And whether the influence is acknowledged or not, it is also undeniable that this focus on the body has developed, in part, from an interest in those texts that have come to be known as "French feminism."[31]

In looking at this phenomenon, I want to make a distinction between the maternal body that emerges in Kristeva or Cixous and the body that takes shape in Irigaray. Despite the stylistic, intellectual, and political differences between Cixous and Kristeva, both celebrate a decidedly maternal body, whether through the Cixousian gesture of writing with breast milk or the Kristevan act of dashing off poems whose sounds and rhythms are generated in the womb. Of course, both Cixous and, even more tellingly, Kristeva tend to privilege the "body writing" of poets who just happen to be men. This move, many claim, is what gets them out of the essentialism trap, because *anyone*, male or female, can write with breast milk or wax poetic to the beat of the womb. Of course, as Delphy points out, this move toward male writers could also legitimately be criticized as sexist and androcentric. Be that as it may, in the work of both Kristeva and Cixous, the "body" of body writing is more symbolic than real, representing more a subjective relationship to systems of language than the flesh and blood of real bodies. Most important, their implicit reclamation of a lost or invisible bodily attribute—breast milk or womb—as a *symbol* of some greater, discursive loss is a quintessentially nostalgic move.

The case of Irigaray is different. Although Irigaray's corporeal metaphors of mucus and fluids seem to invite similar accusations of maternal nostalgia, her work holds far more potential than that of Kristeva or Cixous for the feminist theoretical project that is trying to articulate a different model.[32] I should point out here that the question of the body in Irigaray is closely connected to ongoing debates about the problem of essentialism in "French feminism," where accusations of essentialism tend to be centered around the biological metaphors found in "French feminism's" evocations of the maternal body. Domna Stanton, for example, has eloquently critiqued the maternal metaphor in Cixous, Kristeva, and Irigaray.[33] And I agree with Stanton and others that, especially in the texts of her middle period, Irigaray privileges a maternal body. However, Irigaray's early work is worth revisiting. I'll be more specific: it's those lips that keep tempting me, that I want to go back to, that are begging to find their place on this map.

Irigaray's lips have come to represent, for me, the complex non-metaphorical, nondualistic logic that characterizes Irigaray's most radical thinking. In this admittedly biased, perhaps lesbocentric preference for lips, I am not alone. When my students read Irigaray, the thing they inevitably come away with is the lips. Similarly, Jane Gallop argues for the nonmetaphorical potential of the lips in the context of Irigaray's "body politic"; along the same lines, Maggie Berg celebrates the ironic play in Irigaray's "lipeccentric" rewriting of the Lacanian phallus.[34] And Christine Holmlund finds "Irigaray's association of lips with a lesbian sexuality" to be "richly evocative."[35] "Imagine," Holmlund continues, "lips on lips, above and below. No longer is genital sex in the service of reproduction the only option for women" (298). Indeed, there is nothing specifically maternal about lips, and to attribute maternal meanings to Irigaray's lips is, in my opinion, to misread her.[36] So despite Irigaray's later meanderings into dangerously amniotic and even heterosexual spaces,[37] it is in the figure of her nonmaternal lips that, symbolically, I find the most liberatory potential of her thought. Like Holmlund, I *choose* to focus on the lips because I too find that it is "useful and necessary to insist on Irigaray's references to sexual practices *among* women" (Holmlund 298). Irigaray's lips are lesbian, overtly nonreproductive, and therefore antinostalgic. Like the "stranger" in Adrienne Rich's poem, they articulate a connection to another woman who is *not* the mother. To go back to Beauvoir's equation between woman and womb, Irigaray's lips are radically unwomblike; they are more like Brossard's backpack: open *and* closed, flat *and* round, empty *and* deliciously full.

Performativity and Ethics

Let me pursue, for a moment, the issue of Irigaray's influence on contemporary theory in the United States. Generally speaking, at least two distinct lines of feminist thought have developed, mostly in the humanities, that can be traced, in part, back to Irigaray's work. The first is the burgeoning field of performative theory; the second is a smaller body of work whose focus is the question of ethics. The performative strand, exemplified by the work of Judith Butler, harnesses the well-known Irigarayan concept of mimicry, or mimesis, in order to subvert any notion of a coherent identity.[38] The ethical strand develops the extralinguistic implications of Irigaray's thought in order to rethink the social relation.[39] By looking at the permutations of Irigaray's ideas in these two bodies of thought, I want to critique the former in favor of the latter and, in so doing, suggest ways to develop a model of language that would be accountable to ethical considerations.

One of the hallmarks of contemporary, "postmodern" thought is the destabilization of knowledge and the subversion of a coherent subject as the source of that knowledge. We have learned that knowledge, and the truth it speaks, is in fact contingent, formed and articulated according to particular histories and specific regimes of power. Nowhere has this process of destabilization been more apparent than in the field of gender studies. If gender is a construct, the theory goes, it is also an act, the performance of a fiction that we have come to believe in as natural and real. Further, if we are men and women because of the repeated acts that produce us as gendered beings, we can subvert those identities by harnessing and repeating those gendered acts. This performative theory of subversion draws directly on Irigaray's concept of mimesis, articulated most famously in *This Sex Which Is Not One*: "To play with mimesis is thus, for a woman, to try to recover the place of her exploitation by discourse, without allowing herself to be simply reduced to it . . . to make 'visible,' by an effect of *playful repetition*, what was supposed to remain invisible."[40] Just as Irigaray emphasizes the transformation of invisibility into visibility through repetition, so performativity highlights a shift from marginality to empowerment through a similar act of repetition. Further, when we acknowledge that link between performative theory and Irigarayan mimesis, it also becomes clear that the scope of Irigaray's influence on contemporary theory extends beyond gender and includes sexual models of identity as well.[41] Seen in this light, Irigarayan mimicry constitutes a crucial foundation for a plethora of recent work, including "queer" theory, that builds on the explosion of identity created by the performative subversion of gender.

What is the relationship between performative theory and the question of nostalgia at the center of this book? First, performative theory begins with the idea that there is no origin; rather, as Butler argues, gendered, racial, and sexual identities are based on an *illusion* of original meaning which, on closer analysis, reveals itself to be the product of the repeated "regulatory practices" (*Gender Trouble*, 16) that make us believe in those identities as natural and prediscursive. Thus, like Irigaray's mimetic lips, performative theory is fundamentally antinostalgic, for there is no origin of identity to which we can return. All we can do is move forward, "taking up the tools where they lie" (*Gender Trouble*, 145) and repeating what is already there. Judith Butler's use of the example of drag illustrates this point. Rather than trying to replace or compensate for the loss marked by the illusion of an absent mother, performativity celebrates, redeploys, and multiplies that loss. For Butler, drag is an exaggeration of femininity and thus a parodic subversion of any essentialist notion of gender identity. If, for the sake of argument, we agree with Butler that drag is the hyperbolic performance of the feminine, we could also conclude that drag is a hyperbolic performance of loss, since, as in the myth of the lost mother, the feminine symbolizes absence, invisibility, meaninglessness, and loss. But whereas a nostalgic structure wants to retrieve the loss in order to fill it with a content, drag wants to simply repeat it; in doing so, the argument goes, femininity exposes its origin as an illusion and makes loss visible *as* loss. To use Irigaray's terms, that which was invisible becomes visible through "playful repetition." Thus unlike the structure of return, recuperation, and wholeness that defines nostalgia, a performative structure is built on repetition, proliferation, and fragmentation.

So if performativity is antinostalgic, why can't it provide us with the model we're seeking? My argument with performativity is essentially this: unlike the Irigarayan mimesis on which it draws, performative theory fails to consider the key ethical questions that must be asked about any communicative act. What this means, more concretely, is that performative theory refuses to acknowledge the social bond underlying any deployment of language. And in order to acknowledge and consider that social bond, we need first to ask about the ethical relation. How does the subject speak to the other? How does the first person account for and think the second person who would hear her, draw her up short, put her into question? How does the subject speak her relation to a *thou*, her ethical relation to an other?

These questions suggest that despite its antinostalgic structure, performative theory provides an inadequate map for tracing and understanding the connections between language, identity, and the social bonds that constitute the ethical and political sphere. Once again, it is here that Irigaray can prove to be helpful. While Irigaray's concept of mimesis has provided performativity with some of its basic theoretical tools, Butler and others have failed to recognize the ethical component of Irigaray's model. That ethical component emerges most clearly in the figure of the two lips. In her closing essay of *This Sex Which Is Not One*, "When Our Lips Speak Together," Irigaray inscribes an ethical model of speech that differs considerably from the performative model, despite the affinities between them. As I argue at length in Chapter 4, Irigaray uses the two lips to theorize and to perform a relational model of subjectivity that would allow for the irreducible difference of the other. In so doing, the lips come to symbolize an ethical model of social and discursive relation in which the performative subject is heard, drawn up short, and put into question by an other. Thus both the self-proliferating loss of performative theory and the self-recuperating loss of nostalgia are inadequate. Only an ethical model can embrace the possibility of transforming an unequal self-other dyad into a relation of coexistence, where self and other meet "eye to eye" (and I to I) to become mutually affirming subjects.

Throughout this introduction I have pointed to the problems with nostalgic thinking, and suggested that we move toward a different model. The difficulty, of course, is imagining what that model might look like. Although one could reasonably argue, as I did above, that performativity is antinostalgic, it has become clear that a critique of nostalgia alone is not enough. We must have a constructive vision to guide that critique. For me, that vision begins with thinking about the ethical relation, a sisterly relation to another who, to use the terms of this book, is not the mother. But the vision only begins there, for it must be fleshed out with a concept of community, a multiplicity of ethical relations that, together, constitute the *we*. That *we*, to be sure, is difficult to conceptualize. How do we theorize the irreducibility of the other in the context of a larger community? How do we negotiate the political necessity of community when the very identity of that community threatens at every moment to annihilate the particularity and difference of those through whom the community is constituted? The challenge of those questions could be rearticulated in Irigaray's terms: it is the challenge of *difference* within the *sameness* of the *we*.

Mapping

This final section lays out the organization of the book. I use the metaphor of mapping here because, over the course of this writing, my exploration of the maternal figure in literature and theory increasingly took the shape of a geographical exploration. I noticed that the vocabulary describing the mother is often spatial: the Blanchotian underworld, the Irigarayan cave, the Kristevan womb, the Brossardian island. Further, this maternal topography evokes images of enclosure, constriction, and spatial confinement, places from which most of us might like to escape. At the outset, I too must have wanted to rise above it all, climbing like Beauvoir's hero "to the sky, to the light, to the sunny summits." I wanted to transcend gender, to go beyond the mother. But as Brossard's uterus-as-backpack reminds us, you can't simply step beyond the womb as if it never existed. You have to use it and, in using it, transform it. And then, one day, it's sitting there beside you and it no longer looks like a womb.

So instead of transcending the mother, I decided to try to map her, to get to know her a little better. This project of mapping is, paradoxically, both extremely general and, in its own way, quite specific. In uncovering the workings of maternal nostalgia in Blanchot, Irigaray, Kristeva, and Brossard, I also uncover a logic of replacement whose implications extend well beyond the works of these particular writers. Indeed, I argue that nostalgic thinking is a fundamental but often invisible structure that undergirds Western thought. In close readings of the four authors under consideration, I look at the particularities of how such a structure articulates itself. At the same time, I sketch out the implications of those close readings by contextualizing my critique of nostalgia within the frame of a politics of liberation.

The first section of the book, entitled "Nostalgia: The Lost Mother," critiques nostalgia by mapping its workings in specific texts by Blanchot and Irigaray. Chapter 1, "Blanchot's Mother," provides a foundation for the critiques that follow by focusing on nostalgia in Maurice Blanchot's *The Space of Literature* (1955; translated 1982). For the purposes of my analysis, Blanchot's influential theory of literature serves as a model for theories of language that posit an absolute distinction between literary and nonliterary discourses. Significantly, Blanchot's claim that the world of things is radically separated from the world of representation hinges on a nostalgic structure of loss. Further, Blanchot's formulation of the autonomy of literary space depends on the gendering of this nostalgic structure, where the lost origin is figured as a feminine object of desire. In fact, it is precisely the loss of the feminine object that, for Blanchot, distinguishes literary from nonliterary communication. My analysis of Blanchot focuses on his use of the myth of Orpheus and the story of Oedipus to dramatize loss as the disappearance of Eurydice and the mother, respectively. Thus the centrality of gender to Blanchot's nostalgic structure exposes the political underpinnings of a purportedly neutral theory of literature that has been foundational for postmodern theories of language and representation.

While Chapter 1 explores nostalgia through the literary problems associated with the act of writing, Chapter 2 analyzes the epistemological issues that are linked to the act of knowing. This second chapter, "Lips in the Mirror: Luce Irigaray's Specular Mother," examines Irigaray's reading of the mother in *Speculum of the Other Woman* (1978; translated 1985). In *Speculum*, Irigaray critiques psychoanalysis and philosophy as two master codes through which gender and the quest for knowledge are articulated within a nostalgic structure. By opening with Freud and ending with Plato, *Speculum* links the psychoanalytic quest for subjecthood as the loss of the mother with the Platonic quest for truth as transcendent illumination. My reading of Irigaray connects the psychoanalytic logic of sexual difference with the philosophical logic of model and copy, where Freud's story about the anatomical origins of gendered meanings frames Plato's construction of the cave as an originary womb (*hustera*). In focusing on those parallels, this chapter shows how Western epistemologies tend to subsume differences into a universalizing truth, what Irigaray calls the structure of the "same." Further, "Lips in the Mirror" foregrounds Irigaray's implicit critique of nostalgia by considering the liberatory potential of the figure of the two lips. In that context, the lips come to represent a supplemental, anti-nostalgic marker of difference excluded by the Freudian and Platonic systems.

The second section of the book, "Nostalgia and Ethics: Approaching the Other," explores nostalgia, gender, and the ethical concept of the other in Kristeva and Irigaray. Chapter 3, "Imperialist Nostalgia: Kristeva's Maternal *Chora*," critiques the political implications of Julia Kristeva's influential theory of the semiotic. Most fully articulated in *Revolution in Poetic Language* (1974; translated 1984), this theory draws on the Greek concept of the *chora*, or space, which Plato in the *Timaeus* compares to a mother, receptacle, or nurse of becoming. Because Kristeva's construction of the maternal metaphor rests on a concept that undergirds Plato's philosophy of being, I raise questions in this chapter about the ontology of sexual difference on which Kristeva's theory of the semiotic is grounded. Although Kristeva makes specifically political claims about the revolutionary force of the semiotic, the nostalgia and the ontological essentialism that frame her theory make it more conservative than many of her interpreters would like to admit. Further, the philosophical system that structures Kristeva's theory of poetic subversion also opens her to an ethical critique of ontology's symbolically imperialist thrust. Using Levinas, I argue that ethics, unlike ontology, theorizes the primacy of sociality, an always prior responsibility to the other that Kristeva's theory fails to address.

Chapter 4, "Luce *et veritas*: Toward an Ethics of Performance," returns to Irigaray in order to ask about the implications of her work in the development of performative theory. To be sure, as I argued earlier, performativity offers a model of language and subjectivity that is no longer governed by a nostalgic structure. However, the blindness to ethical questions displayed in Kristeva's theory of the semiotic characterizes performative theory as well. More specifically, this chapter reads Irigaray in relation to the work of Judith Butler. Despite the apparent affinities between performativity and Irigarayan mimesis, I argue that Irigaray inscribes an ethical model of speech that would contest Butler's performative act. Invoking once again the figure of the lips, I highlight their implications for a nonnostalgic concept of ethical relation.

Although Irigaray's lips begin to hint at the possibilities of a different model, the book's final section, "Toward Another Model," develops a fuller, more constructive vision of what it would mean to move beyond nostalgia. Chapter 5, "From Lesbos to Montreal: Nicole Brossard's Urban Fictions," explores Brossard's work in relation to the question of lesbian writing. This chapter examines the problem of a maternal origin by addressing the nostalgia implicit in the Sapphic tradition of lesbian writing. I argue that Brossard's work distinguishes itself from this Sapphic tradition by demystifying nostalgia rather than celebrating it. Further, not only does Brossard uncover and subvert the nostalgic structures through which a concept of origins is produced, she also provides a different, visionary model for thinking about the relationship between subjectivity and language. Unlike the logic of absence and replacement that defines nostalgia, Brossard offers an inclusive, plural, holographic model. Rather than mapping a mythical mother, the Brossardian hologram provides a method of mapmaking that is able to mark the real traces of those whom the world has rendered invisible and silent.

Finally, in the "Afterword" I sketch out the theoretical constraints that must inform our feminist visions of the future. Unlike the nostalgic traps of the past, these feminist futures must engage the problem of the ethical relation to another. Like Brossard's cartography of invisibility and silence, ethics points us toward new paths across a map fraught with the political conflicts and cultural erasures that are a result of centuries of oppression and violence. In the face of that sedimented history, ethics calls each of us to speak and to listen, even in our invisibility and silence. Through the ethical exchange of that speaking and listening, an invisible *I* at the heart of a *we* can begin to move into a future of visibility and liberation. The subject emerging as the *I* of that *we* strives continually to speak and to form herself through the ethical relation that binds every *I* to another. In that way the *we* can begin to take shape and voice in the opening of our infinite differences. If "the world is a dream in the body of the mother," the plurality of differences in the ethical relation offers one way out of that trap. And, I hope, finding our way out of the mother trap will give us different maps for the different landscapes of our collective feminist futures: a "whole new poetry beginning here." Where else can *we* begin, but here?

Nostalgia:
The Lost Mother

Blanchot's Mother

all the male poets write of orpheus
as if they look back & expect
to find me walking patiently
behind them. they claim i fell into hell.
damn them, i say.
i stand in my own pain
& sing my own song.

—A L T A , "Euridice"

I have to admit, the first time I read Maurice Blanchot's *The Space of Literature* (1955, translated 1982) more than a decade ago, there was much that I just didn't get. Strangely, though, the book fascinated me— not because I understood it, but because its pages were haunted by the unfulfilled yearning of ghosts. Blanchot's story of literary space spoke to my own romantic sensibilities; and despite—or perhaps because of— its mysterious, elliptical language, I felt a shudder when I read it. Now, rereading Blanchot for the umpteenth time, I still shudder, but for different reasons. I haven't completely escaped Blanchot's spell, but as my own libidinal yearnings have changed, I have learned to demystify the mythical romance that frames his tale of poetic communication.

That demystification began, for me, with the realization that much of Blanchot's haunting power comes from his implicit appeal to nostalgia. Nostalgia, I thought, is inherently conservative: nostalgia wants us to retrieve the past, to return to the good old days when men were men and women knew their place. So if that's the case, I mused, perhaps there's a link between the romantic frame and the nostalgia that drives it. Blanchot's appeal to the myth of Orpheus is certainly romantic ... but there's more to it than that. OK, I surmised, it all seems to come back to Blanchot's mother. She's the one he's really writing about.

This chapter gives some analytical shape to those musings from my days in graduate school. My purpose here is to explore the nostalgic structure underlying Blanchot's concept of literary space. In so doing, I ask the following questions: To what extent is Blanchot's nostalgic model necessarily founded in heterosexual desire? Is that model paradigmatic of literary communication, as Blanchot seems to claim? What is the role of the mother in that nostalgic structure? Finally, is Blanchot himself, like Orpheus, engaged in a heroic quest to bring his own work into being? Who, ultimately, is his Eurydice?

Orpheus

Indeed, the myth of Orpheus and Eurydice is a good place to start. In *The Space of Literature*, Blanchot retells the story of Orpheus, the tragic poet engaged in a heroic quest for his lost lover, Eurydice. Using the myth of Orpheus and Eurydice to describe the concept of literary space, Blanchot draws on the conventional frame of a heterosexual plot to give his theory of poetic communication the shape and movement of a romantic narrative. Here's the story:

Orpheus, a brilliant musician who sings and plays the lyre, becomes listless and silent with inconsolable grief at the death of his wife, Eurydice. Eventually wandering into the Underworld, where Eurydice has come to dwell, Orpheus once again begins to play. Enchanted by his music, the guardians of the Underworld grant him the favor of retrieving Eurydice under one condition: that he lead the way up to the light of day without looking back at his beloved wife. But just as Orpheus approaches the end of his journey, he is overcome with desire for Eurydice and, turning to gaze at her face, loses her forever.

The Orpheus myth is central to Blanchot's concept of literary space. As he states in the epigraph to *The Space of Literature*, every book has a "center" that, like Eurydice, is harder to reach the more closely it is approached. In *The Space of Literature*, Blanchot explicitly tells us that the book's center—the point toward which "the book is headed"—is the section entitled "The Gaze of Orpheus." There Blanchot links the moment of Eurydice's disappearance to the movement of limitless desire that brings a literary work into being. This moment in the Orpheus myth thematizes Blanchot's project in *The Space of Literature*: to describe the operation through which the negativity of loss opens toward a promise of poetic communication. Eurydice's disappearance symbolizes a loss that is recuperated by the compensatory gift of Orpheus's song. "Orpheus's error," Blanchot writes, "seems then to lie in the desire which moves him to see and to possess Eurydice, he whose destiny is only to sing of her. He is Orpheus only in the song."[1]

"He is Orpheus only in the song." Blanchot uses Orpheus to describe the coming into being of the literary work as an infinite movement between terms. Just as Orpheus approaches Eurydice only to lose her, so artistic communication is the movement of one term in relation to another. Simultaneously, one term appears as the other disappears. The first, disappearing term is the object that inspires the artistic expression, while the second term is the artistic representation of that object in the form of an image. Described in the vocabulary of the myth, Eurydice is the object or source of inspiration, and Orpheus's song is the image that represents her. Thus his song comes into being at her expense: the more he is heard, the more absolutely she is lost. In fact, in order for the image to appear, the real object that it names *must* disappear. To state the same process in semiotic terms, Eurydice is the referent that disappears behind the sign—Orpheus-as-song—which comes to name the referent, to give it "form, shape, and reality in the day" (171). Such is the price of representation, the abyssal loss at the heart of writing.

To speak of the abyss at the heart of writing is, admittedly, to engage in a discourse of which many of us have grown weary. When Foucault wrote, in a 1966 essay on Blanchot, that "we are standing on the edge of an abyss that had long been invisible," he was saying something new.[2] That "something new" was the decentering of the subject of thinking and writing, Barthes's "death of the author"[3] or, as Foucault put it in the Blanchot essay, the recognition that "the being of language only appears for itself with the disappearance of the subject" (15). We've heard about this, *ad nauseam*. We've also heard, since the early 1980's, about the feminist response to the celebration of the decentered subject.[4] As feminist critics have noted, theories that decenter the (masculine) subject paradoxically privilege the feminine by turning her into a seductive figure of absence. To put it simply, they celebrate woman by effectively making her disappear.[5]

Curiously, in that unfolding drama about the gendered articulation of a decentered subject, Blanchot's voice is scarcely heard. And yet, most critics agree that Blanchot's work is crucial to the theoretical developments that have come to be known as "French discourse," a rubric that generally describes thinkers as divergent as Barthes, Foucault, and Derrida. P. Adams Sitney points out that in the late 1940's, *Yale French Studies* described Blanchot as "the most important critic in France." And Geoffrey Hartman asserts: "When we write the history of criticism for the 1940 to 1980 period, it will be found that Blanchot, together with Sartre, made French 'discourse' possible." Similarly, Timothy Clark professes that Blanchot's 1949 essay on Mallarmé in *La Part du feu* is "a kind of crude harbinger of deconstruction."[6] Indeed, Blanchot's influence on twentieth-century French thought can hardly be overstated; as Sitney makes clear, however, Blanchot (compared with Barthes, Foucault, or Derrida) has been relatively neglected by the American intellectual establishment. It is not so surprising, then, that while certain feminist critiques of "French theory" are by now well known, very little critical work has engaged Blanchot from a feminist theoretical perspective.[7]

So despite my reluctance to gaze yet again into Blanchot's abyss of writing, that is precisely what I'm doing here—not simply because few have done so through a feminist lens, but also because engaging Blanchot opens up new perspectives on the history of modern French thought. Indeed, the concepts developed in *The Space of Literature*—as well as in *Faux pas* (1943), *La Part du feu* (1949), *Le Livre à venir* (1959), and *L'Entretien infini* (1969)—are fundamental to the destabilization of discourse and subjectivity that marks much late-twentieth-century theoretical discourse. Crucially, Blanchot links the production of a decentered subject to the production of a literary work. Unlike later theorists influenced by his ideas, and most notably Derrida, Blanchot theorizes the specificity of literary space by distinguishing between poetic and other forms of communication.[8] In so doing, he pushes to the extreme a form of thought that insists on the radical breach between the world of things and the world of representation. In Blanchot's work, that breach is epitomized by the coming to being of the literary work; according to Blanchot, in poetic communication the divorce between word and thing is absolute. And with the unmooring of the sign from its referent comes the epistemological crisis of what Lyotard calls our "postmodern condition": a loss of the belief in absolute truth.[9]

This loss of truth, then, is a corollary to the postulation of the decentered subject. Further, the radical skepticism underlying that philosophical stance has also led to a collapsing of the boundaries that distinguish literary from nonliterary discourses, epitomized, again, by the work of Derrida.[10] Given that context, my interest in Blanchot lies in the connection between gender and a distinct literary space. The gendered structure of literary space is also, and at the same time, a nostalgic structure: nostalgia is characterized by the loss of a feminine object of desire. And it is precisely that gendered form of nostalgia which distinguishes literary from nonliterary communication in Blanchot. Blanchot's nostalgia, therefore, constitutes a conceptual map to be traced and eventually reconfigured with feminist theoretical tools. This chapter challenges Blanchot by interrogating the boundaries of sexual difference within which he postulates the breach between sign and referent: the gap that separates Orpheus from Eurydice.

Oedipus

Although the Orpheus story is essential to Blanchot's description of poetic communication, there is another story at work in *The Space of Literature* as well. This second story reinforces and complicates the first one, and its structure repeats the movement between appearance and disappearance sketched out in the story of Orpheus. The second myth is the psychoanalytic drama of the son and his mother. In Freud's Oedipal version of the story, the son must move beyond the incestuous desire he feels for his mother by leaving her behind in the world of childhood, thereby entering adulthood and the world of men. Like the Orpheus myth, this story is played out as a heroic quest involving love and irrecuperable loss. Also like the Orpheus story, the Oedipal story is inscribed in the frame of a romantic plot driven by heterosexual desire. Just as Orpheus must lose Eurydice in order to appear as a tragically poetic hero, so the son must lose his mother in order to attain heroic status.

In *The Space of Literature*, the psychoanalytic story of Oedipus appears only implicitly through its structural parallels to the Orpheus story.[11] Blanchot never names the Oedipal son, except as "the fascinated child" (33) consumed by his deadly attraction to the maternal face. Unlike the Orpheus story, which Blanchot explicitly locates at the book's center, the Oedipal story seems at first to play a marginal role in Blanchot's theory of literary space. The mother and son appear only once in the main body of the text, in the section entitled "The Essential Solitude," and once again in an Annex entitled "The Two Versions of the Imaginary." Nonetheless, like the story of Orpheus and Eurydice, the romantic narrative of the son and his mother is crucial to Blanchot's concept of poetic communication.

Both the Orpheus and Oedipus myths describe a movement of separation and return that forms the skeletal structure of nostalgia. Moreover, in both myths the point of loss is a feminine object of masculine desire: in the Orpheus story, that object is Eurydice; in the story of the Oedipal son, it is the mother. That parallel points to the gendered articulation of the nostalgic structure underlying Blanchot's model of literary communication. Correspondingly, Blanchot's two stories of nostalgic longing not only explain the specificity of literary communication as a structure of loss; they also, significantly, reveal a collapse of the figure of feminine absence into Eurydice and the mother. That collapse, symbolized by the moment of Orpheus's gaze, forms the center of Blanchot's theory of poetic communication.

Orpheus: Take Two

One of the difficulties of Blanchot's use of the Orpheus myth is its deceptively straightforward plot. Superficially, the movement of literary communication appears, like the Orpheus myth, to follow a simple story line from separation to return, from loss to its recuperation. However, a closer look at both the myth and Blanchot's appropriation of it suggests that the story is more complex than this. Crucial here is the distinction Blanchot makes between everyday and poetic communication. Although each involves a moment of loss, only poetic communication becomes a self-perpetuating process where, like a whirling dog chasing its own tail, loss pursues itself. It is precisely that infinite structure of loss which links Blanchot's concept of poetic communication to the problem of nostalgia at the heart of this book. More specifically, the continual movement between infinite loss and the infinite promise of restitution defines both the subjective experience of nostalgia and the rhetorical structure of trope.

In the Orpheus story as Blanchot retells it, everything begins with Eurydice. As the initial loss for which Orpheus must grieve, Eurydice is the origin of Orpheus's song, his source of inspiration. In that sense, Eurydice's death marks both an absence and the birth of desire provoked by that absence. Orpheus is the poetic subject whose task it is to bring absence into light as representation. The figure par excellence of the poet's muse, Eurydice thus produces the movement of poetic expression: "For him [Orpheus] Eurydice is the furthest that art can reach. Under a name that hides her and a veil that covers her, she is the profoundly obscure point toward which art and desire, death and night, seem to tend" (171). As an abyssal absence, Eurydice thus simultaneously reveals and hides herself. Coming to the fore through the artifice of appearance ("sous un nom qui la dissimule"),[12] Eurydice shows herself in Orpheus's song. And retreating into her disappearance behind the curtain that screens her ("sous un voile qui la couvre" [225]), Eurydice vanishes behind the song. Thus Blanchot describes the lost object's self-disclosure in poetic communication: its appearance as disappearance is the paradoxical coming to being of the literary work.

The paradox of Blanchotian writing lies precisely in the imperative to transform absence into its substitute as figure; in order for Orpheus to refind Eurydice he must replace her absence with its figural representation: the sign replaces the referent it names. However, that process of figuration through which Orpheus would refind Eurydice also guarantees that he will never refind her; he will only see her as she disappears behind the figure that will replace her. Following the con-straints imposed by the guardians of the Underworld, Orpheus can only see Eurydice again by not seeing her, by turning away. He cannot face Eurydice in her absence; rather, he must give that absence a false face through the gesture of turning away, or troping her.

At this point in the process Blanchot has simply described the movement of figuration that defines any linguistic act: when we utter a word to describe a thing, we no longer see the thing. Like Orpheus, we turn away from the Eurydice-thing and, in so doing, replace her with a linguistic utterance. We know she is still there behind us, so to speak, but the rules of semiotics can't allow us to see her and speak her at the same time. To speak means necessarily to turn the thing into a trope or figure. Thus Eurydice, the referent, becomes an utterance with a meaning (signifier/signified): the sign that is her replacement.

While that gesture of replacement is fundamental to the linguistic act, it is *not* the nostalgic center toward which *The Space of Literature* is headed. Rather, the book's center—"The Gaze of Orpheus"—recounts the moment of Orpheus's *transgression* of the rules of semiotics de-scribed above. Having turned *away* from and thus troped Eurydice, Or-pheus does the one thing he is forbidden to do: he turns *toward* Eury-dice to face the loss itself ("looking this point in the face" [171]) and, in that *second* turning, loses her forever. So it is not in Eurydice's death, but in Orpheus's attempt to both retrieve *and* see her as figure—in her disappearance a *second time*—that Eurydice is lost forever.

For Blanchot, then, poetic communication is a transgressive linguis-tic act that involves an extra turn of the tropological screw. In describ-ing Orpheus's extra turn, Blanchot points to what is commonly charac-terized as the heightened metaphoricity of poetic language, a language that removes itself from the world of things to create a suspended world of its own. Paradoxically, what is already a figure becomes even more of a figure; in turning *toward* Eurydice—the poetic thing—Orpheus forces her into a shape now further removed from the thing itself. Thus, with that moment of *secondary* loss, Blanchot marks the suspended time and space of poetic appearance: the "death sentence" that is also a "sus-pended sentence" condemning the literary work to the continual but impossible pursuit *of itself* through the figural replacement of absence.[13]

It is precisely this concept of secondary loss that constitutes literature's nostalgic structure. Crucially, just as the heightened metaphoricity of poetic language requires an extra turn of the trope, so the specifically *nostalgic* desire that produces literature requires an extra turn. In terms of nostalgia, that second turning produces memory. Without the detour of memory—Orpheus's second turn—a structure of loss cannot be nostalgic. Nostalgia requires memory, just as poetic language requires the troping of trope that is the extra turn.

Thus, secondary movement introduces memory into the nostalgic structure underlying literary communication in Blanchot. Orpheus's second look reveals that the work, chasing its own tail, can only ever retrieve *itself*. Eurydice—the beginning, or origin of the work—is only there as a distant memory, a linguistic construct, a figure. When Orpheus turns toward her, she is already dead, replaced as a trope: "for is there ever a work? Before the most convincing masterpiece, where the brilliance and resolution of the beginning shine, it can also happen that we confront something extinguished: a work suddenly become invisible again, which is no longer there, has never been there. This sudden eclipse is the distant memory of Orpheus's gaze; it is the *nostalgic* return to the uncertainty of the origin" (174; my emphasis).

Orpheus's second look is a nostalgic look toward the work's origin, precisely because that origin is long gone, or, rather, was never really there. Paradoxically, in that nostalgic turn toward the origin, Orpheus guarantees that he will fail to see it. He can only ever see it as a memory, a fiction of his own making. Thus Orpheus's memory is an eclipse: a recalling that blinds itself in the very gesture of looking back, a nostalgic return to an inaccessible origin. Eurydice, whose replacement as memory stands in for the origin, was never really there to begin with. For Blanchot, her interest lies only in her death and disappearance. And it is precisely in that guise of absence—as death and disappearance— that Eurydice remains the imperious and forever unattainable source of the literary work.

Thus literature records the memory of Eurydice: in other words, literature remembers that which is merely a product of its own desire, which is to be itself, as literature. Again, Orpheus is Orpheus only in the song. This point is crucial in Blanchot's construction of literature's self-removal from any contextual reality: according to Blanchot, the secondary communication of literary language makes none of the truth-telling claims of mimetic representation.[14] Literature does not contain images that reproduce reality as its figural copy; nor does it mimetically reflect empirical experience—giving life to that which is dead—by recalling it and filling it with poetic form. Blanchot's conception of poetic communication emphasizes the *gap* between the world and literary representation, where poetic language merely gives a false appearance to the disappearance of reality, or death of the object. Consequently, according to Blanchot, poetic language makes no claims to being an accurate or truthful imitation of the world. Rather, in poetic communication, language reproduces itself in its own image, in a self-reflective system of mediation. As Blanchot puts it: "Doesn't language itself become altogether image? We do not mean a language containing images or one that casts reality in figures, but one which is its own image, an image of language" (34n3). Literature is the space where language becomes an image of itself, where language speaks as an image of words.

Thus unlike the objective, concept-building discourses of philosophy, history, or the sciences, the literary work constitutes itself in a negative relation to meaning, value, and truth. Its structure is circular: initiated by a loss requiring a replacement, literary fiction-making at the same time creates the absence requiring a replacement, that is, its own origin as loss. Orpheus loses Eurydice *because* he turns to face her; at the same time, he *must* turn to face her in order to lose her. Eurydice *is* that loss, and without the secondary turning that causes her to disappear forever, there would be no work to speak her *as* loss. Correspondingly, Orpheus exists only as the song which speaks that loss. As such, he is no more than the dispersed subject of a movement that both produces and requires its own inaccessible origin in loss. And that origin can only exist as the fictional construct, or memory, of an origin.[15] Thus the necessary but illusory source of the literary work was, from the start, a figural replacement: a woman who, in appearing, must disappear.

So, for Blanchot, the gaze of Orpheus lays bare the illusion of the origin of the literary work, highlighting literature's self-removal from truth in the very gesture of seeking it. In other words, in producing and laying bare the illusion of the origin, literature brings itself forth as deception, as fiction, as "untruth." Correspondingly, the nostalgic longing for an origin which drives that process is itself the product and the cause of an illusion whose ground is nothing but itself. In the moment of the gaze back toward Eurydice, Orpheus perceives no real object or figure because all he sees is the reflection of his own looking as movement. What Orpheus perceives then, is a reality that is rendered poetic because it is *twice* mediated, *twice* deferred, *twice* removed from itself as truth. Further, because it is illusory, that poetic space is also duplicitous: it is the depth behind every poetic image, and thus a limitless source from which to draw inspiration, and nothing but the image itself, a reflection of itself as mere words. The look thus creates its own origin, the fascinating depth of memory. Like an image ricocheting in a hall of mirrors, literature remembers and longs for itself.

Blanchot's concept of literary space could thus be described, in philosophical terms, as the appearance of truth in its veiling; to look at truth in order to face it means, at the same time, to lose the possibility of seeing it. Philosophically, at least since Plato, truth is linked with seeing: the more we see, the closer we get to truth. For Blanchot, however, truth is always the reserve of the visible, the dark edge of the knowable, the thing we can't see. Thus the conditions of possibility of poetic communication and the conditions of possibility of seeing the truth are linked, through the structure of Orpheus's gaze, by the conditions of possibility of vision. To look at the visible—Eurydice-as-figure—means to look at the possibility of visibility itself. And that means to be blinded, for one cannot see oneself looking, except in a mirror, and then one is no longer seeing the looking itself.[16] To look at visibility—the possibility of vision—means, paradoxically, to look at the impossibility of seeing. Literature thus exposes the trap of truth: the closer we get to it, the more we lose it, because the only way we can say it is by holding up the reflective screen of language, the mirror in which all we see is ourselves.

Thus literature is the space where speaking is only the image of speaking and where seeing is only the look in the mirror. So when Orpheus tries to bring Eurydice into the light of day, he must do so, in turning away, through the metaphorical operation of not-seeing, that is, through the detour of figuration. And when he transgresses the law in order to turn to face her, he can only see through memory, which is necessarily self-reflective, a mirroring of his own gesture of looking. His song, then, is the look in the mirror, language reflecting itself as image. Thus in the very gesture of looking at Eurydice-as-truth, at the very possibility of his own seeing, Orpheus forever loses her (that truth, that possibility of seeing). This explains further why Blanchot emphasizes the gap between literature and truth, the necessity in literature to "belong to the shadow of events, not their reality, to the image, not the object, to what allows words themselves to become images, appearances—not signs, values, the power of truth" (24). For Blanchot, literary language does not signify or carry meaning, does not refer, and does not function within a system of values where it would make claims as truth. In other words, the loss that constitutes literature's nostalgic structure— the loss of Eurydice, the loss of the origin—means not only that literature cannot tell the truth (that is, fiction as the opposite of veracity) but crucially that literature is literature *because* it lays bare its self-recognition as untruth.

Oedipus: Take Two

Literature's self-recognition as untruth brings us back to the realm of self-reflective illusion dramatized by the Orpheus myth. That realm of illusion is also the space where the drama of the mother and son unfolds. Just as the Orpheus story takes place in a shadow-world, so the equally romantic story of the Oedipal son occurs in a space of self-mirroring images. This space—the space of literature—is what Blanchot calls the milieu of fascination: "where what one sees seizes sight and renders it interminable, where the gaze coagulates into light, where light is the absolute gleam of an eye one doesn't see but which one doesn't cease to see since it is the mirror image of one's own look" (32–33). Fascination names the in-between space of the second look, a self-blinding, self-mirroring turning to see: "the gaze turned back upon itself and closed in a circle" (32).

For Blanchot's Oedipus, this "limitless depth behind the image" (32) is described as the realm of childhood, the maternal place to which the son—like Orpheus to Eurydice—nostalgically returns:

If our childhood fascinates us, this happens because childhood is the moment of fascination, is itself fascinated. And this golden age seems bathed in a light which is splendid because unrevealed. But it is only that this light is foreign to revelation, has nothing to reveal, is pure reflection, a ray which is still only the gleam of an image. Perhaps the force of the maternal figure receives its intensity from the very force of fascination, and one might say then, that if the mother exerts this fascinating attraction it is because, appearing when the child lives altogether in fascination's gaze, she concentrates in herself all the powers of enchantment. It is because the child is fascinated that the mother is fascinating, and that is also why all the impressions of early childhood have a kind of fixity which comes from fascination. (33)

Here again, as in the Orpheus myth, Blanchot's theory of literary space turns on the disappearing appearance of a feminine figure, this time in the guise of the mother. In this way Blanchot sets up a parallel between Eurydice and the mother as the figures of loss and illumination that constitute the "elemental deep" (34n3) through which the literary work comes into being. In that context, both Eurydice and the mother are examples of the feminine figuration of the fiction of truth:[17] the far edge of the sayable, "the furthest that art can reach" (171). Like Eurydice, or like truth, the mother appears, but only as dissimulation: "under a name that hides her and a veil that covers her" (171). Once again, literature is literature because it lays bare its "feminine" other, its self-recognition as untruth.

Why should we care about Blanchot's mother in her role as feminine other? Indeed, most readers of Blanchot have focused on Eurydice's role in Blanchot's theory of literary communication. But the link between Eurydice and the mother is crucial; using not only Eurydice but also the mother, we can unmask the *collapse* of the feminine at the heart of nostalgia. It is precisely that collapse which allows us to interrogate the theoretical and political implications of Blanchot's aesthetic theory. In other words, Blanchot's collapse of woman into mother allows an interrogation of the ways in which gender and nostalgia are linked in literary communication.

The unmasking of the link between gender and nostalgia puts into question Blanchot's well-known concept of neutrality. Blanchot uses the term "neutrality" to describe the self-reflective realm of poetic communication that displays its own removal from a world of meanings and relative values. Further, he specifically uses the figure of the mother to mark the "neutral" (33) space of pure reflection in which that poetic communication occurs. However, the mother reveals that there is more to Blanchot's neutrality than meets the eye.

The mother is the "neutral" marker of a space of pure reflection in which poetic production occurs, the absence that constitutes the irreducible ground of figuration as movement. As such, she marks meaninglessness itself, "a bit of non-sense, an X,"[18] the interruption or suspension of signification that constitutes the Blanchotian literary space. To put it in terms used earlier to describe Orpheus and Eurydice: the mother marks literature as the tropological movement that recognizes itself as mere self-reflection and, therefore, is itself pure mediation, or language as a mere mirroring of itself. A deceptive placeholder[19] that signifies nothing but the illusion of mediation as a referential mirror, the mother is the self-reflective realm of fascination that displays its own removal from a semiotic grid of relational values. Thus Blanchot describes the mother in terms of neutrality: "neutral, impersonal presence, . . . the immense, faceless Someone" (33).

However, that apparently neutral, nonfigural maternal absence is at the same time described by Blanchot as a figure: "Perhaps the force of the *maternal figure* [*la figure maternelle*] receives its intensity from the very force of fascination. . . . She [the mother] concentrates in herself all the powers of enchantment" (33; my emphasis). Thus the mother is a figure and a nonfigure. She carries the force of meaning within a semiotic system of values constituted, at least in part, through a family structure in which gender functions as the binary opposition between paternal and maternal poles. At the same time, she is removed into a ghost-world of nonsignifying relationality. She is the lost object with a face toward which the child nostalgically longs to return, and the nonhuman loss itself, the irreducible blank that, like Eurydice, was already lost from the start.

In this way, the woman-as-mother of Blanchot's literary space remains superficial and deep, the disappearing point that is the acme of light and the vortex of darkness: "light which is also the abyss, a light one sinks into, both terrifying and tantalizing" (33). She is the marked "thing" that must be there for anything to happen at all, and the neutral "nothing" whose existence is an illusion. As Derrida puts it in a different context: "The mother is the faceless figure of a *figurant*, an extra. She gives rise to all the figures by losing herself in the background of the scene like an anonymous persona. Everything comes back to her, beginning with life; everything addresses and destines itself to her. She survives on the condition of remaining at bottom [*au fond*]."[20] That foundational but empty condition of language as mediation, its inaccessible but necessary ground, is the "anonymous, impersonal being" (Blanchot, 31) who can only appear in her feminine transformation as Eurydice or the mother. She is the paradoxical reminder of both survival and death, the *sur-vie* of surfaces that allows existence and creativity to continue, and the infinite depth of disappearance that swallows life and force behind an inescapable deception of appearances.

The key to understanding this maternal contradiction between figure and nonfigure, signification and nonsense, lies in its implications for Blanchot's central concept of the operation of writing itself. As the space of pure relationality, the mother is the condition of possibility of language, the structure of the between that both allows a tropological system to keep turning and reveals the illusory apparatus undergirding that system. As "the relation the gaze entertains" (33), the maternal image is that formless, indifferent space of suspension, the interval that underlies the very possibility of figuration. Blanchot's mother—"the fascinating . . . mother . . . of early childhood [*du premier âge*]" (33)—is neither an original space nor an originary time, but is rather the continual movement of a relation between terms: the gap of the hyphen, of the *inter-dit*. However, in Blanchot her appearance as a figure vested with meaning marks the inevitable humanization of the movement of loss which itself is the condition of possibility of writing. As Blanchot puts it: "In this way the image fulfills one of its functions which is to quiet, *to humanize* the formless nothingness pressed upon us by the indelible residue of being" (255).

Like Eurydice, the mother is the appearance of disappearance itself; as such, she constitutes the link between the structures of nostalgia and trope in Blanchot's delimitation of literary space. It is important to remember here that the paired figures of Eurydice and Orpheus, the mother and son, are ways of naming the process through which literary communication happens. More precisely, that mythic structure of loss and figuration could most accurately be described as the movement of a relation. In that movement, something withdraws and, in that withdrawal, allows something else to come to the fore. Thus, Eurydice withdraws and, in that withdrawal, allows Orpheus to come to the fore. Similarly, the mother withdraws and, in that withdrawal, allows the son to come to the fore. That relation of disappearance and appearance constitutes the movement of figuration. In *The Space of Literature*, the heterosexual couplings of Eurydice-Orpheus and mother-son thus function—in the terms of a binary logic of complementary halves—as the internally divisible but inseparable markers of a nonhuman relational movement. The feminine half of those harmonious couplings—Eurydice or the mother—names the void or lack—the loss—at the center of the relation through which those apparently symmetrical opposites are produced.

The workings of the relational structure described above govern the mutually reinforcing structures of trope and nostalgia. In both, the unattainable center of those movements of turning and return remains an irrecuperable void or point of loss. The result is a "poetics of pure figure"[21] where language is completely self-reflective and removed from meaning or truth.

However, even Paul de Man would admit that this notion of a purely poetic language completely severed from its referential ground is "properly inconceivable" (*Allegories*, 49). Yet such a reference-free notion of language emerges in Blanchot's theory of literary communication. Blanchot explicitly links the paired stories of Eurydice and the mother to an "elemental deep" (34) that has nothing to do with signs that signify in the world. However, in order to appear, this limitless, formless, feminine, and maternal ground of babble—"the giant murmuring" (27)—must construct its own limits by opening into the form of an image—"language opens and thus becomes image" (27). That image both speaks and makes meaning. The illusion of a poetics of pure figure reveals itself as a rhetoric of value and meaning. Blanchot's space of literature is not in the uncharted void of outer space; it is always and necessarily tied to its referent: a space on a map of the world.

The Politics of Sexual Difference

If it is true, then, that a reference-free language is "properly inconceivable," there is much that could be said about the political implications of Blanchot's aesthetic theory. Despite Blanchot's repeated insistence on the specificity of literary space as removed from a referential system of truthful correspondence between word and thing, meaning must and does occur. One such meaning is the transformation of the void at the center of figuration into the voice of a speaking subject. As we have seen, that void is feminine—Eurydice, the mother—and that voice is masculine—Orpheus, the son. The purportedly neutral workings of figural language rely on an ideologically charged, value-laden structure of meaning embedded in the politics of sexual difference. Those politics, to put it simply, erase the feminine so that the masculine may speak.

So despite Blanchot's removal of literature from the realm of truth, the workings of language have everything to do with truth and meaning. Moreover, because that meaning occurs in a context of relative value, the truth it tells is never ideologically neutral. Blanchot exposes that valuation in the stories he chooses to relate: the story of Eurydice and the story of the mother. Both those stories thematize the movements of nostalgia, a nostalgia whose heterosexual, binary structure functions as a model for understanding Blanchot's central concept of figuration. The disappearing appearance of object-into-image that for Blanchot characterizes poetic communication *requires* the collapse of woman-into-mother as blank or void at the point of that disappearance. Correspondingly, the speaking that remains takes the form of a presence and a voice that articulates a meaning. That voice describes the contours of literary space. It may speak in the *name* of silence, but it is not silent.[22] The ones in whose name the voice speaks are the ones who are silent: Eurydice, the mother.

In thinking about Blanchot's text as itself a gendered fiction of literary communication, I find it imperative, then, to interrogate his concept of neutrality as it relates to the nostalgic structure of trope. Further, that interrogation not only opens up the question of value and meaning from which Blanchot attempts to remove the concept of liter-

ary space, it also points to the necessary but unacknowledged masculinization of the Blanchotian poetic subject. The valorization of that
masculine subject has implications for the purportedly decentered subject of a theoretical text—the one by Blanchot—that is generally re-
garded as a paradigmatic twentieth-century model of literary authority.
However decentered, disappearing, and dispersed he might be, Blanchot's "celui qui écrit"—"he who writes" (21)—nonetheless *requires* a
structure of sexual difference anchored in meaning, value, and truth in
order to exist at all. "To write on, to talk on women, on the corpses of
dead women," Hélène Cixous has said, "is one of the recurrent motives
in Blanchot's texts."[23]

Eurydice and the mother reveal, through the necessity of their own
disappearance, that invisible logic of the subjective masculinization of
Orpheus or the son, the "silent" discursive subject who, despite this silence, ends up speaking, signing his name, and thus authorizing a text
with the power to communicate in a world of signs.

It is true that Blanchot himself accounts for the way literature ultimately comes to communicate in the world. For Blanchot, however, it
is precisely the purported neutrality of the structure of the "neutral, di-
rectionless gleam [*lueur neutre égarée*]" (32) that makes possible the transformation of hovering suspension into the promise of the communication of meaning. Blanchot describes that transformation as the filling
up, through reading, of the radical opening of the origin with the life of
the world and history: "filled with the world's life and with history's"
(205). Thus the in-between space of pure reflection—"that which, in
the work, was communication of the work to itself, *the origin blossom-
ing into a beginning*"—becomes anchored in the world of mimetic representation: "in the image of this world of stable things and in imitation of this subsisting reality." In this way the in-between of pure relation is stabilized into the containment of meaning—"the 'empty'
movement takes on content"—and, as a result, "becomes the communication of a given thing [*de quelque chose*]" (205).

This is how Blanchot accounts for the fact of reading and interpretation. It is through reading that the literary space disconnected from
meaning becomes a movement toward signification, value, and truth.
Most important, in that process the poetic subject disappears, swal-

lowed, like Eurydice, into the violent opening of neutrality. And in that neutrality, according to Blanchot, the world settles into its place of endless interpretation, like a package wrapped in an anonymous reading. No longer a subject, the Orphic voice becomes the pure opening of song: "he is Orpheus only in the song."

However, Blanchot's description of a fragmented and dispersed Orphic voice in fact hides its own foundation in the binary and gendered structure of the origin and its loss. That structure is the structure of nostalgia. The lost origin—Eurydice, the mother—is recuperated, as loss, into a form that is not only thoroughly human but, like humanism itself, decidedly masculine as well. Moreover, that trembling neutrality describes a logic that attempts to go beyond dialectical thinking toward the pure neutrality of a poetic economy. Still, the seeming invincibility of the system's purportedly neutral logic is also the mask marking the system's failure. Blanchot's neutral system of literary communication uses a structure of sexual difference in order to describe itself as neutral. In other words, it uses a value-laden discourse to describe the absence of value or truth. The neutral poetics of figure that, for Blanchot, is the outcome of loss, nostalgic longing, and the impossible return is not at all neutral. Released from the irrecuperable void of Eurydice's fall, that Orphic neutrality comes to speak as a voice in which *we*, the reader, see *ourselves* reflected.

That *we*, to be sure, is a masculine one. Correspondingly, the fall of Eurydice is a feminine condition from which *we*, after all, must be delivered. It is precisely the production of the *we*—the "celui qui écrit"— that reveals the binary, gendered logic underlying what appears to be a space of neutrality.

So, again, why should we care about Blanchot's mother? Despite the radical opening that, through reading, releases literature from the self-reflective circle in which it is trapped, the gendered structure Blanchot's theory requires produces an equally radical *containment* of meaning. That containment is the homogenization of the feminine as origin, disappearance, and elusive silence. From a feminist perspective, then, the opening of reading is already constrained by an always prior closing of the feminine at the moment of enunciation. The world that fills Blanchot's "neutral" literary space is already dualized, binaristic, gendered.

And in that gendered constraint, interpretive possibilities—other possibilities of speaking—are lost, so to speak, from the start.

I can't provide a ready-made map showing what it might look like to do things differently, but surely we can start by moving in other, nonnostalgic directions. Let's begin with the assumption that Eurydice and the mother aren't lost at all; they've just been lost to *us* because *we* can't hear them. Let's assume they're present after all. I imagine they're pissed off. I imagine them resisting, refusing their collapse as well as their effacement. So what would happen if we took them seriously? What would happen—to Blanchot, to literature, to theory—if the feminine opened up, if the feminine became feminist, if Eurydice and the mother began speaking to each other?

CHAPTER 2

Lips in the Mirror:
Irigaray's Specular Mother

ideal republic
Language ripples our lips
— SUSAN HOWE, "Pythagorean Silence"

It's so hard to be present.

Most of us live in the past and the future. Today, in the last decade of the twentieth century, our collective shift away from the present expresses itself in terms of a "post"-time: ours is the so-called age of postfeminism, poststructuralism, post-Marxism, and postmodernism. The new, we are told, is no more than the past repeated, but in a form that is false, inauthentic, a copy.

As a result of this supposed loss of the new and the true, we have both mourned and celebrated the cracked and shifting ground of epistemology and representation. The very project of cultural production, traditionally fed by a faith in originality, is put into question by a culture of repetition and sameness where anonymous subject positions replace creative agents. The production of meaning, in its postmodern sense, is a repeatable, infinitely reproducible process whose agent—the author—has disappeared. With the death of the author comes the death of meaning; with the death of meaning comes the loss of truth. Thus to speak the truth is to borrow a voice whose truth has already been spoken. To speak is to repeat the already said.

These defining traits of our postmodern age have been so often repeated that they themselves have become descriptors that lack any substantive meaning. However, there is more than cliché to this story. Not everyone has come to see newness as an impossibility; not everyone has given up on truth. Eclipsed by the shadow of all those dead authors are those who have never claimed to kill the creative subject or the particular truth that subject might speak. Feminists and other progressive intellectuals have been especially important to this project of thinking about truth as particularity in an analytic context where meanings are racialized, gendered, and socially situated.[1] Unfortunately, philosophers have often ignored and even derided that progressive intellectual stance precisely because, unlike traditional philosophy, it pays attention to particularity, difference, and change. Despite postmodernism's rhetoric about dismantling truth, philosophy continues to privilege generality and universality in the name of truth. A Western, white-dominated, masculinist version of the truth becomes canonized and celebrated, like a Platonic ideal, in a self-perpetuating, normative structure. That truth-telling system is what the French philosopher Luce Irigaray—a feminist thorn in philosophy's side[2]—has famously called "the same."[3]

Using Irigaray as a guide, I want to challenge philosophy on its own terms, but from a standpoint of feminist critique that ultimately hopes to dismantle the philosophical structure of the same. Like Irigaray in *Speculum of the Other Woman*, I want to ask how that challenge to philosophy can be articulated around the question of gender. But I also want to push the feminist Irigaray of the 1970's beyond herself by placing some of her most important, early feminist insights in the context of the present, labeled by many as our postfeminist era. In the seeming indifference of today's gender play and gender trouble, how can we ask about woman? Or, stated slightly differently, in refusing to buy the postfeminist label, can we return to woman and find different interpretations of the already said? In other words, can the ongoing feminist project of thinking gender—in the characteristic "post"-movement of thought thinking itself—open up its own possibilities, *as* thought, to the self-critical changes necessitated by that rethinking?

Indeed, it seems crucial, now, in this age of conservative backlash, to ask those feminist questions. My aim here is not simply to repeat the already said. Rather, I want to rethink the texts where questions about gender have been articulated, but where they have been denied the full potential of their liberatory possibilities. Irigaray's work is particularly suited to that purpose, as the ongoing interest in her philosophy makes clear.[4] So let's ask, yet again, from a philosophical perspective: What is a woman?[5] How can we read, represent, and know her?

One way to think about these questions is to look again at the linkages between systems of knowledge and the construction of the feminine. Specifically, and more locally, the institutionalization of psychoanalysis and philosophy within the academy has produced two master codes through which the interpretation of sexual difference has yoked itself to a more general rhetoric of epistemological and representational crisis. It is not surprising, then, that a number of thinkers have raised crucial questions, particularly from the standpoint of feminist critique, concerning the ways in which those two discursive fields have named as feminine the limits of their knowledge. Crucial to my project is the way in which philosophy and psychoanalysis together articulate the related questions of woman, knowing, and the telling of her story through a metaphorical system in which the mother functions as a central trope. Without going into the specific political and ideological forms the collapsing of woman and mother has taken, we can ask about the relationship between them through the reading of two exemplary texts—Plato serving for philosophy and Freud for psychoanalysis— which articulate that connection. Asking about woman then becomes asking about the mother, from the double perspective of both philosophy and psychoanalysis. So, to repeat the same questions, but with a different turn: What is a mother? What does it mean to read, represent, and know her?

This return to the mother through a double reading of psychoanalysis and philosophy mirrors and interprets my exemplary "French feminist" model, Luce Irigaray's *Speculum of the Other Woman*. Irigaray's pairing of the Freudian and Platonic texts in the first and last chapters, respectively, delineates the paradigmatic construction of those systems of knowledge and sexual difference around the maternal figure. More specifically, *Speculum* links the Platonic quest for truth as transcendent illumination with the psychoanalytic quest for subjecthood as the loss of a maternal origin. This pairing of the philosophical and psychoanalytic models of sexual difference reveals a parallel structure of origins that, whether expressed as an epistemological ground of speculative thought or as a psychic explanation of human development, functions according to a logic in which sexual difference is reduced to a repetition of "the same." Both structures are nostalgic and pivot on a maternal locus of absence articulated either, in Freudian terms, as a primordial lost object of desire or, in the Platonic system, as the shadowy reserve of the shining light of truth. In other words, the nostalgic structure of origins is constitutive of the structure of sexual difference. *Speculum*'s inverted speculation begins with Freud to end with Plato's story of the cave. So doing, *Speculum* rewrites the psychoanalytic enigma of woman ("What is a woman?") as a question that already anticipates its answer in the form of a philosophical parable of truth: Plato's myth of the cave. Freud's story of "becoming woman"[6] ends, from the start, in the Platonic freezing of becoming as being. In that movement from becoming toward the freezing of being, a collapse occurs, the collapse of the possible difference *between* women—between woman and mother, for example, or between mother and daughter—into a nondifferentiated sameness. That sameness reduces the feminine to an equivalency between woman and mother.

How, then, might the story of becoming woman become a true story of difference? That question of difference and the writing of texts points to the reasons for rereading, within its own mimetic logic, Irigaray's miming of those two exemplary paternal texts, Freud for psychoanalysis and Plato for philosophy. My own rereading of Irigaray is motivated by the specific strategic goals of a feminist practice that resists the indifference of a purportedly postfeminist era. It is also spurred by a more generally theoretical agenda. Taken together, both strategy and theory involve precisely the politics of difference and the horizons of understanding the writing of literature and history. More specifically, as a paradigmatic figure of the ground or origin from which difference is constructed, the mother not only links psychoanalysis and philosophy but also connects the strategic concerns of feminist practice with theoretical questions about knowing and seeing, epistemology and representation. As a figure of difference caught in a logic through which the disruptive potential of that difference is effaced, the mother provides a way for thinking about the potentially *asymmetrical* relationship between strategy and thought, between political positions and theoretical moves. That asymmetry exposes the cracks in the logic through which the very terms of that analogous opposition between acting and understanding are constituted. Submitting the maternal figure to critique, then, not only puts into question the structures of sexual difference that define the domain of strategic feminist intervention but also disrupts the symmetrical logic of mimesis through which difference itself is reduced to fit an equation of analogical substitution. Is there a way to push beyond the metaphorical thinking that replaces difference with the same? If so, what role does the mother play in that movement?

My own particular reading of *Speculum's* maternal figure works here, then—as Plato works for Freud, or Freud and Plato for Irigaray—to exemplify, "for example, or as an example,"[7] a strategic feminist textual practice of difference through which the logic of mimesis is exposed and subverted. The model for that different practice—Irigaray's oft-cited strategy of mimicry—both repeats, as reiteration, and puts into question, as interruption, the verbal edifice that constitutes identity (Freud) and truth (Plato) around a feminine figure of absence.[8] That absence can only appear in its veiling as figure; moreover, as Derrida has famously shown in his reading of Nietzsche,[9] the feminine shape of that figural construction places woman at the liminal juncture where the quest for truth faces its own impossibility as unknowledge. More important for my analysis, it is precisely through the economy of metaphor that the feminine shape of this impossible truth produces the collapse of woman and mother.

As replaceable terms marking the category of the feminine-as-absence (the lost origin), woman and mother expose the logic of identity through which difference is subsumed into a totalizing truth. *Speculum* intervenes, as an exemplary feminist interruption, at the point of collapse where woman and mother are hinged as impossible metaphors of truth. Irigaray returns to the Platonic cave in order to read it, *this* time, as the impossible figure of an impossible truth. So doing, she exposes the asymmetry that threatens a mimesis whose illusory symmetrical logic links the economy of metaphor and the economy of sexual difference. That logic of model and copy, in its connection with a logic of sexual difference, constructs the potential difference *between* model and copy, mother and daughter, as a repetition of sameness. The collapse of the potential movement of difference *becoming* (Freud's "becoming woman") into the freezing of being as form (Plato's edifice of truth) is based on an opposition between nature and culture; between maternal, womanly, biological beginnings and their dialectical overcoming through the work of representation or cultural production.[10]

More specifically, Irigaray uses Plato to read the Freudian primal scene—that first conception between ovum and sperm—not as an origin, but as the mimesis of an already mimed, more originary nature that remains inaccessible. Through Plato's parable of the cave as a space of fictional illusion, the primal scene becomes a copulation of puppets against a screen of projection. Thus the "nature" of human origins and sexual difference, the natural model of biological conception, is constituted in relational, metaphorical terms, as the flat retracing of a three-dimensional model that is always more originary, more organic, and more elementary: copied on the model of elementary organisms.[11] The three-dimensional materiality of the Platonic space-time of origins is therefore already a false reproduction, an exemplary copy that provides a model from which we can only recommence an exploration.

This exposure of biological beginnings in "the uterine cavity" (*Speculum*, 279) as a product of figuration or metaphorization similarly exposes the mimetic logic that constructs woman and mother as the same, as nature. The feminine, maternal form of that nature is a metaphorical and necessarily impossible projection of a ground-as-earth, into the shape of a den, matrix, or womb (*hustera*).[12] Mother-as-nature, the biological matrix from which life begins, becomes from the start the grotesquely false imitation of the pregnant body caught within the frame of representation. Those who would, as seekers of truth, come forth into knowledge from this womb of beginnings are therefore trapped, as prisoners of the rhetorical deception of the cave, in the mimetic play of a logic of identity: "The men all stay there in the same spot—same place, same time—in the same *circle*, or circus ring, the *theatrical arena* [*enceinte théâtrale*]¹³ of that representation" (*Speculum*, 245).

In this way, Irigaray shows how the deceptively three-dimensional cavern-as-hustera is reduced, through the process of copying, or mimesis, to the two-dimensional plane of a circus ring, theatrical scene, or frozen lake of reflection: a place where any transformation, including the biological change and swelling of the pregnant body, is revealed as a flat illusion. Going back to Freud, she further uses this logic to show how Freud collapses difference into sameness, through the formula: becoming woman = "being (like) my mother" (*Speculum*, 42; translation modified). What happens, therefore, is that any possibility of maternal difference becomes assimilated into the substitutions of metaphorical thinking, so that the mother herself is always off-stage, as the forbidden remains of knowledge. Invisible and obscene, the maternal figure is the unknown object, or inaccessible origin, that is both produced and forbidden by the truth-speaking law of philosophical and psychoanalytic knowledge. Thus the maternal *hustera* is both constructed as a presence and denied as a dark spot or a hole, simultaneously figured and left behind as the "behind" (*Speculum*, 339) through which representation is made possible. She is the "behind (of) the mother" (340) that both lies behind and is left behind in every mimetic performance of truth. Thus the mother can only "appear" in disguise; as formlessness itself, she can exist only through the borrowing of forms given to her by the paternal, truth-telling system. She becomes a performance of nature, an act of the maternal event of copulation, pregnancy, and birth, that in fact never really happened.

This is the logic through which the philosophical and psychoanalytic systems of knowledge construct themselves as universal truth. What is crucial here is the following recognition: the totalizing power of this self-identical system of truth contains within itself the very mechanism of its failure. Through the process of turning, or troping,¹⁴ the metaphorical reductions of a self-identical system of truth reduce woman to a repetition of the same: becoming woman = being (like) my mother. But Irigaray points toward the possibility of a supplementary turning, what she calls a "hysterical tropism" (*Speculum*, 274) or "one last turn [*volte de plus*]" (41). So what can happen in that extra turn? More of the same, or something different? Irigaray suggests that the extra turn of "hysterical tropism" can crack open the dark hole, or blank, that collapses *women* in their *difference* into the sameness of an analogical equation. Those differences between women require a different model of representation in order to articulate themselves *in their difference*. What they need, in other words, is a different model of rhetorical relation: another way to speak.

It's hard to know how to describe that other-than-metaphorical relation, since the system of description we have at our disposal is itself metaphorical. But one way to think about a different rhetorical model is to draw, again, on the terminology of psychoanalysis. In anthropomorphic terms, the model of the "extra turn" might be imagined as an opening relation between woman and mother. The different operation of that other relation would involve another (dare I say *lesbian*) desire that, in its *extra* turn, would destabilize the Platonic edifice of truth. Still beginning in the logic of copy and model on which representation depends, the relation would shift because of the opening of difference *within* sameness. And that introduction of difference into the analogical equation which reduces women to a repetition of the same would create an opening for different possibilities of saying and knowing. It would move beyond the false difference of the heterosexual "copular effigy"[15] where woman-as-mother is forced and frozen into a forgotten, off-stage labor. So while we cannot draw a map of this new model, it would apparently necessitate a rethinking of the relationship between difference and representation. Or, to switch for a moment to a political terminology, it would affirm the liberatory movement of difference and change. Difference would articulate itself in its difference.

An example serves to illustrate the collapse that results from metaphorical substitution, and the way that collapse is linked with the construction of sexual difference. In the chapter on Freud, Irigaray points out that the Freudian emphasis on the nature of male and female genitalia is, like the copulation of elementary organisms mentioned earlier, illusory as a literal ground of sexual difference. More specifically, she describes the Freudian role of the clitoris: it is a copy of man's representation of woman's desire.[16] Freud's story of female sexual development posits the clitoris as an earlier stage of a linear progression; he describes clitoral libido as the spark for the later, more fully developed vaginal libido. The logic of mimesis posits the penis as the model and the clitoris as the copy. But then, seemingly out of nowhere, Freud unveils the vagina. This exposure of the construction of feminine libido as the copying of the penis forces one to ask: What is, exactly, the libidinal counterpart of the penis? Is it the clitoris? Or is not the vagina the penis's more oppositional, more feminine other? It becomes clear here that the symmetry of the anatomical logic of binary opposition is disrupted by, or at the point of, the clitoris. The passage toward "becoming woman" is revealed as a movement not only from model (penis) to copy (clitoris) but, more importantly for sexual difference, from a first to a second copy, from an active clitoris to a passive, receptive vagina.

In that supplementary turn or move, the clitoris falls away. Thus vaginal libido—the constructed truth of feminine desire—becomes the metaphorical replacement of another, unknowable (clitoral) event, the now forever lost third term of a dualistic, reproductive construction of human sexuality. This exposes the spot where a feminine libido—the clitoral "event" or origin that is lost—would but cannot be. "Woman" becomes a hole, and the phrase "feminine libido" mere words that signify nothing.

What would happen to the concept of the model—exemplified by Plato through the parable of the cave—if its logic were rewritten in the articulation of a different, clitoral desire? If the clitoris is the lost "event" of feminine libido, could it be set in motion again, its supplementarity harnessed in an effort to reopen the collapse of difference into sameness, where "becoming woman = being (like) my mother," means being a receptive vagina-as-hole? If woman is the lost "event" of the origins of sexual difference, might it be possible to set her into motion again through a self-reflexive recitation, or rubbing, at the metaphorical spot (the clitoris) where that loss occurred? In that different model as rubbing, might something different—between woman and mother—move and open toward something other?

These questions suggest that the point of the clitoris—the difference of feminine libido—goes beyond the blank of words that mean nothing. If "the expression 'female libido' means nothing" (*Speculum*, 43;

translation modified), it is because our language of tropes cannot say them. "How can I say it?" Irigaray repeatedly asks.[17] My answer is: keep rubbing. If you keep rubbing the clitoral spot that seems to remain lost on man, something else is bound to happen. Something else is bound to happen, and Irigaray calls it lips. Keep rubbing, and before you know it, you'll find there are lips kissing: kissing themselves and each other. So perhaps the words "feminine libido," which mean "nothing" in a specular economy of sameness, are the terms of an *asymmetrical* relation between clitoris and lips. These terms, then, rubbing and kissing, might pass through the mirror of representation in an *extension* of metaphorical meaning.[18] Those irreducibly Irigarayan lips neither speak nor figure through a metaphorical economy, but come together in their opening, in the rupture of the homological equations of sexual sameness: "Some lips always able to open themselves."[19] Like the woman and mother who come together in that movement, the terms of the relation—between clitoris and lips, between lips and lips—are connected in their difference: "These rubbings between two who are infinitely close" (*This Sex*, 79; translation modified).

So where do we go from here? From this place of self-critique that spirals into crisis, are we forever bound to repeat ourselves? Are we destined to return, to go back to the beginning—in yet another projection of trope toward freezing—to this essay's opening question, to the closure of the Platonic question of *eidos*, about the *what* of transcendent truth as form? Shall we ask, yet again, in an endless enumeration, the metaphysical question: "What is a woman?"[20]

Indeed, Irigaray herself has something to say about that particular form of philosophical speculation. For her, not surprisingly, the *what* of woman is precisely the question *not* to ask. As she puts it in *This Sex Which Is Not One*, in a series of interviews about *Speculum*: "*What is a woman*? I believe I've already answered that there is no way I would 'answer' that question. The question 'What is . . . ?' is the question—the metaphysical question—to which the feminine does not allow itself to submit" (*This Sex*, 122). However, in yet another mimetic turning of thought, couldn't we ask: Luce, is not your truth-telling *interdiction* the metaphysical gesture par excellence? After all, your interdiction—"That they [women] should not put it, then, in the form: 'What is woman?'"

(*This Sex*, 78)—is aimed exactly at *us* women. Isn't this particular pro-hibition—that women should not ask what a woman might be—a funny way to forbid the self-reflexive turning that, libidinally, we might call masturbation? After all, as Irigaray herself puts it, "woman can touch herself, 'within herself,' in advance of any recourse to instruments. From this point of view, to forbid her to masturbate is rather amusing" (*This Sex*, 133). Consequently, isn't the question's "metaphysical" status as an-other inter-diction (a discursive place from which we women should be excluded) reason enough for its rearticulation here?

Not, of course, that despite all that rubbing, we can ever answer the question. Any more than we can know about, see, or speak those lips. But perhaps in amusing ourselves by asking *anyway*—about the *eidos* of truth, about its feminine form as formlessness (lips), about the lips or women (*elles*) that are always simultaneously here and "there" (*This Sex*, 77)—we can say ourselves in the form of a question that can never close itself off completely as form. As a necessary but impossible, per-haps masturbatory, *we*-question, *our* mimetic rearticulation can become something other than the stasis of a posthysterical saying, "sadly repeti-tive, . . . [without a] possible historiography" (*Speculum*, 61).[21]

So, we too can practice a disruptive "move back through the 'mas-culine' imaginary, that is, our cultural imaginary" (*This Sex*, 162) by passing into and through the mirror of mimetic speculation, finding ourselves "both implicated by it and, at the same time, exceeding it" (*Speculum*, 147). This essay has shown that the simultaneous construc-tion and effacing of "becoming woman" is integral to the logic of spec-ular mimesis. The mother is both a shadowy place of origin *and* an in-finite process of future becoming; she is both the cave as nature *and* the cave as an infinitely reproducible cinematic projection. As Irigaray puts it, she "will herself be the place where origin is repeated" (*Speculum*, 41). The feminine is therefore both eclipsed and eclipsing in the specu-lar economy Irigaray describes: woman is both a silent ellipsis projected toward a future form of expression *and*, as that ellipsis, a coming to ex-pression that will never arrive. Woman as mother is both the place of mechanical repetition that leads nowhere *and*, at the same time, the pos-sibility of a repetition that *would* bring difference, the extra turn of an alternative future.

But, to return to this chapter's opening question, what about the present? Right now, in the present of this time and this writing, our little clitoral trope has been rubbed into kissing lips. Can lips laugh while they're kissing? Can we laugh in our difference, but not know how to say it? I don't know, "from that excess, 'first' I laugh" (*Speculum*, 147), Irigaray replies. So we rub, and we kiss, and now we're laughing in the mirror. We're trapped here, in the speculum, but there's also something else going on: rubbing, kissing, laughing, rupture. We insert ourselves here—as a laugh, a *risa*—into the serious project of specula-(risa)tion.[22] And Irigaray concurs: "Besides, women among themselves begin by laughing" (*This Sex*, 163).

More seriously, now, perhaps by rejecting the rigid opposition between work and play, between the ontological labor of *becoming* into *being* and the libidinal play of *jouissance*, that masturbatory self-amusement (whose interdiction is impossible and thus equally amusing) might transform the work of mimesis into another story. If the play of mimesis constitutes a "playful repetition" (*This Sex*, 76) of a paternal truth whose seriousness is all too deadly, then, in all seriousness, let's replay it.[23] Let's practice the difficult "retraversal" of the mimetic retelling of a linguistic event—the *what* of a (feminine) truth that never occurred—which makes its appearance in an eidetic structure. Let's replay it, again, and turn up the voltage with "one last turn" (*Speculum*, 41), thereby pushing the *plus de*, or more of truth, to (and beyond) its limit. In other words, if the metaphysical question par excellence is precisely, "What is a woman?," then let's ask it again—as rubbing, kissing, laughing lips—in a different practice, or practice of difference, of another woman "becoming."

Is this business of lips serious or funny? Or, more pertinent, perhaps, to our current postmodern condition: is it politically responsible to play (however seriously) such games? Perhaps, in at least a partial response to that closing question, the nagging *we* of *this* particular reading—the one that keeps popping up, huffing and puffing, only to laughingly disappear offstage—can be brought into the possibilities of its own performance. For it is precisely that vaguely designated and unknowable *we* that said, from the start, that the story of difference would be doomed to failure before it even got going: "But let us say that *in the beginning was the end of her story"* (*Speculum*, 43). But who are we to say such things? And who are *we* (yet another "we") to keep asking such (im-pertinent) questions?[24]

These *we*-questions are all too painfully relevant to the crisis of our current condition, the disruptive point of turning that feminist intellectuals have both inherited and participated in building. And indeed, as Irigaray puts it, we are "without a standard or yardstick [*étalon*]" (*This Sex*, 174), as well we should be: there neither is, nor can be, a measure, display, or model of the right thing to do. We are the multiple forms of a question whose answer is impossible, the nonfigural opening of lips that remain "without models, standards, or examples" (217). The problem, indeed, is that there is no absolute form of a *we*, any more than there are lips or a language to say them. "Without lips, there is no more 'us'" (208), "we are no more" (211). Which is precisely why we must continue to speak: with difficulty, in our catachrestic extension as lips, as a perpetually self-critical *we*.

In the system of exchange through which our language and our labor construct the columbarium of science, we must keep ourselves in circulation and, at the same time, ask the question which resists the terms of that profit-making exchange: *"But what if these 'commodities' refused to go to 'market'?"* (*This Sex*, 196). Would the *sans étalon* of our resistance also rupture the mimetic model that constitutes the very terms of our political refusal? Would that rupture "forever disrupt," as Irigaray asserts, "the order of commerce" (*This Sex*, 197), whose economic syntax both constructs and excludes us? Even further, how do we know when it's serious or funny? How do we know what we're doing when our own gesture of resistance threatens to turn itself into yet another (metaphorical) payoff as profit? Would our resistance to the stasis, sameness, and freezing of the *semblant*[25] keep itself from freezing *as* resistance?

Of course, we cannot know anything "once and for all" (*Speculum*, 280). Which is all the more reason for making the (perhaps) uncertain political gestures of another syntax, another model, another turning of our "sad poets"[26] into a different economy of laughter. We cannot know the other form of that other, never-ending story. Most important, we cannot allow our desire for a happily-ever-after—"once and for all"—

to leave us, once again, in the collapse of an empty mimetic enumeration. Rather, our desire for difference—for the *entre-elles* of rubbing, kissing, laughing lips—must be tempered by the knowledge that desire can't do it all. It is tempting to read Irigaray's sexy rhetorical play as an invitation to privilege desire and pleasure as the tools as well as the utopian outcome of sexual liberation. But in its emphasis on the *structure* of mimesis, *Speculum* highlights the systemic nature of an oppressive, oculocentric culture. Simply replacing vision with a celebration of touch and sensual pleasure is not the answer, for any gesture toward difference is necessarily inscribed within a logic and a politics whose structure is given from the start, despite the force of our libido. It's in the *play of the structure* that our work—however uncertain it might be—must happen, and again, continue to happen.[27]

In continuing to ask those self-negating metaphysical questions (what is a woman?), we may, at the same time, work toward affirming that unknown *we* into a different "economy of abundance" (*This Sex*, 197). Indeed, in that double gesture of affirmation and negation lies the challenge of a self-critical questioning which, postdialectically, also points to something new. It may well be true that, as Irigaray puts it with the élan of a certainty, "our abundance is inexhaustible" (213). But the *other path* (*Speculum*, 362) of any utopian promise must continue to appear in the mode of a conditional that remains diachronically linked to the past. This is our challenge: to move onto that path while acknowledging, responsibly, the blind spots and the failures of the "might have [aurait pu]" (361, 362), what we might have been able to do.

It's still so hard to be present. We never quite know what we're doing, so we nostalgically look to the past or dream about the future. If we decide to resist, here and now, we can't be sure that we're doing the right thing. Let's take, for example, the revolt of the prisoners described by Irigaray at the end of *Speculum*.[28] If we women decide, like Irigaray's cave-dwellers, to kill the philosopher-king, we may discover that we have simply killed what was "already dead: the poor present of an effigied copula." We may just be doing the same old thing, replaying a history of violence where, in Irigaray's reading, the imprisoned cave-dwellers "tear themselves apart." The repetition of that violence—the denial of difference—is symbolized for Irigaray by "a murder that has probably already taken place" (*Speculum*, 364). Irigaray explains: "When Freud describes and theorizes, notably in *Totem and Taboo*, the murder of the father as founder of the primal horde, he forgets a more archaic murder necessitated by the establishment of a certain order in the city, the murder of woman as mother."[29]

The memory of that other past—the murder of the mother—comes to us "in the conditional tense of a myth" (*Speculum*, 364), in the story of Orestes and the killing of Clytemnestra.[30] But, as Irigaray reminds us, "mythology hasn't changed" (*Corps-à-corps*, 17). We cannot repeat *that* murderous past by disguising it as freedom and projecting it into the future. Rejecting the violence of that mythology means moving from a nostalgic culture of mother-love to a liberatory love between "sister-women" (*Corps-à-corps*, 31). To return to our beginning in this chapter's epigraph: we may never, thank God, know the "ideal republic" first philosophized by Plato and poetically reinvoked by Howe. But we can start, in the present, in a language that "ripples," to find the force of our rubbing, kissing, and laughing lips: to discover, as Irigaray puts it, "the singularity of our love for *other* women."[31]

Nostalgia and Ethics:
Approaching the Other

Imperialist Nostalgia:
Kristeva's Maternal 'Chora'

The world is a dream in the body of the mother.
—RICHARD KLEIN

Luce: "The myth of the cave, for example, or as an example, is a good place to start."[1]

Echo: " ...to start... start... start... "

Julia: Where are you, Luce? Is it you? It's so damp and dark in here ... I can't see a thing. What was that you said about starting with myth?

Echo: " ...myth?... "

Julia: Luce, is that you? All I can hear is an echo repeating what you've already said.

Luce: But it *is* just an echo, not something I said, I assure you. Or perhaps the echo is you, repeating me, mocking what you suppose I have already said.

Echo: " ...already said... "

Julia: Me, an echo? Repeating you? Why would I do that? To say what you've already said? Really, despite what they all say, my work has nothing to do with yours. Okay, so we both read Plato, talk about the mother, go on and on about her subversive potential. But really, that's about it.

Luce: Yes, I agree. But what can we do? To the others we're basically saying the same thing. They call us "French feminists"! Feminists?... You, a feminist? Those Americans, always bent on defining reality for the rest of us. Does the word "imperialism" come to mind?

Julia: Well, I rather like the U.S. They've been good to me. Invitations, receptions, a position at Columbia... And my name is practically a household word, to say nothing of my ideas. Take the *semiotic*, for example, along with the *chora*. I've single-handedly put Plato's *Timaeus* back on the map. And you, you're still stuck on the *Republic*. A bit overread, wouldn't you say?

Luce: At least I expose it for the sham that it is, which is more than I can say for your take on Plato. A concept of being based on the mother as an originary space of creation... Do you really buy that? I suppose you also believe that this ugly cave is really the *hustera*, just good old "mother nature" waiting to reproduce. And they have the nerve to call *me* an essentialist!

Julia: Well, I don't know. I still think the mother is pretty compelling. By the way, have you ever seen a Bellini painting? Or listened to Pergolesi's "Stabat Mater"?[2]

Luce: It's all an aesthetic illusion, just like the cinema at the back of the cave. As far as I can see, they keep creating a mother in order to annihilate us. If you stick with Plato, you'll end up just like her, you know. We are, after all, one and the same: becoming woman = "being (like) my mother."[3] And if you think you'll get to be a philosopher-king and, at the same time, a subversive poet, well, you've got another think coming. You still don't get it, do you? The whole thing gets inverted and what do we become? A stillbirth in Plato's womb. I've said it before, and I'll say it again (I know, I'm always mimicking, repeating myself—incessant repetition is what *I'm* famous for): "let us say that *in the beginning was the end of her story*"[4]... I wonder if I'll end up like Echo...

Echo: "like Echo... Echo... Echo... "

The imaginary dialogue staged above takes place in a cave, the space of maternal origins. Yet from the start, confusion sets in: who is the original author of each utterance? Irigaray? Kristeva? Plato? Echo? Indeed, Echo's mimicking voice disrupts the conversation, making it difficult to locate the origin of the words that Luce and Julia speak. By extension, this uncertainty about linguistic origins puts into question the very concept of origins itself. Reinscribing once again the myth of the feminine, Echo's disembodied words mark her absence as a subject of speech.

In classical mythology, as in the dialogue, the myth of Echo is ultimately the story of a woman disappearing. Echo is a nymph condemned to repeat the final syllables of speech uttered by others. When Echo falls in love with Narcissus, she tries to woo him by repeating his words; he responds, however, by spurning her. Echo retreats to the woods in shame, hiding in the shadows, her body wasting away until only her echoing voice remains.

In many ways, Echo's story recalls the heterosexual myth of the masculine poet and his feminine other analyzed in Chapter 1, "Blanchot's Mother." Just as Eurydice's disappearance kills Orpheus but also allows him to live on as a self-reflective poetic voice, so Echo's disappearance leads to Narcissus's death by liquefaction in the pool where he sees himself reflected. Significantly, the Narcissus death scene ends with the image of a flower—"a funeral flower or a flower of rhetoric"[5]—which takes the place of Narcissus's liquefied body. So while the myth tells us that Echo's voice remains, her voice becomes the feminine other of a masculine poet who, like Orpheus, emerges immortalized: "an imago, a figure, a rhetorical flower."[6] Echo's voice—the story of woman—remains only as repetition, the shadowy underside of a tradition that celebrates itself through the tragedy of Narcissus.

Are women, like Echo, figuratively disembodied, destined simply to repeat the words that were already spoken by a narcissistic poet or philosopher-king? Let's look, again, at what Luce and Julia have to say about this question toward the end of their conversation. If, as Irigaray claims, the mother comes to nothing in the epistemological apparatus of Plato's *Republic*, might she fare better in the ontological frame of the *Timaeus*?[7] The *Timaeus*, after all, provides the key concepts of Kristeva's maternal thinking. More specifically, Kristeva's construction of the maternal metaphor through her appropriation of the Platonic *chora* raises questions about the ontology of sexual difference on which it is grounded. In articulating her influential theory of the semiotic, Kristeva returns to the mother not only to talk about the feminine but, crucially for my purposes, to announce a subversive form of aesthetic practice that would revolutionize the social, economic, and political structures of modern society.

To be sure, Kristeva's return to a maternal myth exposes the differences between her notion of the feminine as a destabilizing, even pulverizing force in language and Irigaray's concept of the feminine as relational, pliable, and fluid. Indeed, these differences have been analyzed and explicated by a number of scholars.[8] However, less attention has been paid to the explicitly political claims put forward in Kristeva's theory of the semiotic. Those claims, while purportedly serving a progressive agenda, in fact conform to a conservative ideology of individual possession and imperialist expansion. Kristeva's theory of liberation through language is therefore ultimately inimical to what I, and many others, would call a liberatory politics: a politics based in the primacy of sociality and the ethical relation. Without such a concept of ethics and the primacy of the social sphere, no politics of collective resistance to the forces of oppression can ever be squeezed out of the Kristevan semiotic. As Luce puts it in her conversation with Julia: "You, a feminist?"

The fictional interchange provides a point of departure for this critique of the political implications of the Kristevan mother. That dialogue forms a two-part structure which encompasses a series of corresponding oppositions: between Luce and Julia, between epistemology and ontology, between the *hustera* and the *chora*, between the *Republic* and the *Timaeus*. Plotting the mother across those comparisons allows us to frame the Kristevan mother in the context of a nostalgic structure of return. Just as Luce returns to the cave in order to expose the cinematic apparatus through which a maternal origin is created, so Kristeva makes a journey of return toward a structure of origins.

Further, that dialogue between Luce and Julia both recalls Irigaray's reading of Plato and opens the way toward the political questions that Irigaray seems to have left behind. Although the focus here will remain on the *chora* and the ontological structure from which Kristeva extracts it, we must nonetheless return initially to the epistemological questions raised by Irigaray in her reading of *The Republic*. Indeed, to begin again with that other beginning here, in a chapter about Kristeva, means to point to the *necessity* of a movement of return in asking, yet again, about the mother. The shift from the epistemological questions raised by philosophy and psychoanalysis (Irigaray) to the social and ethical questions raised by politics (Kristeva) appears to describe a movement beyond the mythical womb of representational illusion. However, such a progression requires a return to the fictional space of the maternal body that the realm of the political ostensibly will have left behind.

The 'Hustera' and the 'Chora'

Kristeva introduces the Platonic concept of the *chora*, or "space," to set up her famous semiotic/symbolic opposition, first described in *Revolution in Poetic Language*.[9] In *Revolution*, Kristeva coined the term "semiotic" (*le sémiotique*) to describe the unsayable, untheorizable space that interrupts and displaces the order of language based on the paternal phallus, which Kristeva (following Lacan) calls the "symbolic" (*le symbolique*). Although the symbolic is marked by paternal interdiction as the Lacanian "Name" and "no" of the father (*le nom / non du père*), the maternal semiotic is associated with the pre-Oedipal phase prior to the formation of the subject through an entry into language. Through analogy, Kristeva links the semiotic to the Platonic *chora*: just as the *chora* precedes the formation of the universe in Plato's ontology, so the semiotic precedes the formation of the human subject in Kristeva's psychoanalytic model.

Paradoxically, the semiotic *chora* exists both as a locus prior to the symbolic (as that which precedes language), and as a concept that can only define itself in opposition to the symbolic, as that which, understood synchronically, emerges and breaks open an already established linguistic system. The *chora* thus precedes and subverts the epistemological structure on which it is founded and which it requires for its very articulation. Further, as the foundation for Kristeva's political claims about the revolutionary force of poetic language, the *chora* organizes the entire conceptual system through which that radical force is theorized. The *chora* therefore forms the core of a corpus whose aim is to describe a subversive force in language that both threatens coherent meaning and is constitutive of the process through which meaning occurs.

In order to uncover and thereby unleash the force that both constitutes and disrupts signification in language, Kristeva returns to what she identifies as the source of that force, an ontological preorigin of meaning. That preorigin is the *chora* as it appears in Plato's *Timaeus*. In the *Timaeus*, the *chora* functions as the space of becoming out of which the possibility of being comes. Kristeva thus appears to move beyond Irigaray in her exploration of Platonic origins, to a more originary, ontological preorigin of language. The story of creation in the *Timaeus* presents itself as a precondition for the very possibility of representation and the subsequent rise to truth through reason narrated in *The Republic*; the *chora*, therefore, would both chronologically and conceptually precede the logic of copy and model around which the *hustera* was constructed. Indeed, in Plato's story of being, the *chora* is presented as the condition of possibility of creation itself, the necessity upon which the truth-speaking logic of Plato's universe is founded. In that regard, it constitutes a more originary ground than the *hustera* analyzed in the previous chapter.

However, just as the Kristevan semiotic precedes and disrupts the symbolic, so the *Timaeus's* articulation of a prerational origin occurs because the mimetic logic of the *hustera* on which the ideal republic builds itself is already in place. That paradox is made manifest in the fact that the *Timaeus* comes after *The Republic* in the chronological trajectory of Plato's works. Although in logical terms the ontological system would precede the epistemological one, both Plato and Kristeva need the *hustera* before they can begin to talk about the *chora*. In fact, the *Timaeus* opens with Socrates' recapitulation of the principles outlined in *The Republic* the day before, and the entire discussion of the *chora* occurs in the context of recalling that dialogue about politics, language, and the construction of the state. Thus the presymbolic *chora* depends on a prior writing in order to be written as a story of origins; although it ostensibly precedes the possibility of writing,[10] it can only occur as an afterthought, as part of a structure of recalling. In this structure, remembering what came before is only ever possible as the deferred articulation of a past that is irretrievable and, paradoxically, already written.

So when Kristeva returns to the preoriginary beginnings of meaning, she obscures the fact that those beginnings lie not in the chaotic formlessness of a space before being, but in the womblike space of representation and knowing, the theatrical scene of Plato's cave. Her return to ontology and the story of the *chora* constitutes a return to the moment which, in the Platonic narrative that leads from creation to truth, comes *after* an earlier story of representation. In order to narrate the becoming of being, the *Timaeus* needs a story of knowing that is already in place. That story is *The Republic* in its rise to power through the philosophical construction of ideal truth. And that transcendent movement toward the Platonic ideal begins, as Irigaray shows, from the myth of the *hustera* and the representational culture which produces an illusion of nature in the form of a maternal other.

Thus the language that speaks the politics of the state governed by reason and transcendent truth requires, after the fact, a more originary matrix than the *hustera* itself, a preoriginal ground out of which the very possibility of that language can occur. But that prior *chora* can only happen textually as an aftereffect, as the necessity upon which, retrospectively, the logic of the *hustera* is based. The *chora* thus functions as language's ground: always deferred, impossible but necessary, its condition of possibility.

The 'Chora' in the 'Timaeus'

What is the *chora*? As it is presented by Kristeva and, more symptomatically, a number of her most influential interpreters, the *chora* at first appears to be virtually equivalent to the *hustera*, a womblike repository of maternal essence.[11] However, rather than constituting a figural model of femininity-as-mother in the shape of an enclosed and immutable receptacle, the *chora* is more precisely thought as space in its extension. As we have seen, in the *Timaeus* the *chora* is a matrix of creation, or, more specifically, the space of becoming out of which Plato constructs a philosophy of being. The perceptual frame that governs the epistemological system of the *hustera*—an apparatus of vision wherein knowing the truth means *seeing* it—requires a prior logic of place or positioning within which that perception can occur. Whatever is perceived must be perceived somewhere; the relation between perceiver and perceived thus needs a concept of space in order for that relation to happen. The *chora* and, with it, Plato's ontology, provides his epistemology—an already written ideal republic—with just such a concept of space, one in which the relations of perception that constitute representation can take place.

As space, then, the *chora* is a kind of place but, as Derrida asks, "What is place?"[12] What is a place that exists before being, that has no place to call its own because it is the very condition of possibility of anything taking place at all? Indeed, things take place precisely because the *chora* is not a place and has no place or form that is proper to it. As limitless, formless space in its extension, the *chora* exists because it displaces itself in order to make space. It makes space for stories that would not end in their beginning, for events that, in the movement of their telling, can take their place. "A viewless nature and formless, all-receiving" (*Timaeus*, 179), the *chora* is a place-maker, the movement which makes possible the taking place that is language, the holding of place by marks or figures. The *chora* itself is not a figure,[13] but, rather, as Heidegger points out, constitutes itself as space by ceding space; it is that which separates, deviates from everything that is particular, effaces itself, receives and makes space (*Platz macht*), like the imprinting of wax with figures.[14] Neither wax nor figure, the *chora* cannot occupy space. A verb rather than a noun, the *chora* is a function—the function of iteration—which produces the opening of possibility for stories to take place. As the maker of possibility for the holding of place—the place-taking of events in their telling—the *chora* itself exists only as something that incessantly gives itself up.

This concept of *chora* as a maker of place which allows the place-holding that is figuration is central to my critique of Kristeva's political agenda. More specifically, the *chora* raises questions about Kristeva's utopian claims for revolutionary mother-effects that emerge in the rhythms unleashed by avant-garde artistic practice. This focus on the ethical and political dimensions of Kristeva's maternal theory is not unwarranted. In fact, in the Greek context from which it is drawn, the *chora* denotes not space as an abstraction, but a notion of place as political space, the territory over which wars are waged and empires are built, the ground for the construction of the republic. As Derrida puts it, *chora* always implies "the sense of political place or more generally *invested* place, in opposition to abstract space. *Khôra* 'means': place occupied by someone, country, inhabited place, named seat, rank, post, assigned position, territory or region" (*Khôra*, 58). Derrida goes on to point out that *chora* will always be space that is occupied; in fact, that is exactly how the *chora* distinguishes itself from that which it allows to come into being, the figures and forms that take their place within space.

Further, in the *Timaeus* the logic that makes it possible to conceptualize the *chora* as a matrix of being is the mimetic structure of model and copy already articulated through the *hustera*. That logic constructs the *chora* as a third term that is neither model nor copy but constitutes the necessity of the relation between them. In his description of the formation of the universe, Timaeus discusses the invisible ideal of an everlasting God as the pattern after which the heavens and all of creation are modeled. That imitation of the divine governs the logic of representation through which reason structures the fashioning of ideal being. Further, as we have seen, it is a logic based on visual perception: "God discovered and bestowed sight upon us in order that we might observe the orbits of reason which are in heaven and make use of them for the revolutions of thought in our own souls, which are akin to them, the troubled to the serene; and that learning them and acquiring natural truth of reasoning we might imitate the divine movements that are ever unerring" (*Timaeus*, 165). There exists, however, a more originary, previsual structure that constitutes the conditions of possibility of that mimetic system of divine imitation based on reason. That structure is "errant," based not on visual perception guided by reason, but on a more originary and necessary cause. To the forces of reason, says Timaeus, "we must add also the nature of the Errant Cause, and its moving power" (167). Like Orpheus turning around a second time, Timaeus makes a supplementary turn toward "a second fitting cause," beginning over again "from the beginning" in order to "examine what came before the creation of the heavens" (169).

It is here, in that secondary movement of return to a more originary origin, that the *Timaeus* introduces the *chora*. Again, Plato rearticulates the logic of model and copy that structured the *hustera* to frame the *chora* within the story of the creation of being: "Then we distinguished two forms, but now a third kind must be disclosed. The two were indeed enough for our former discussion, when we laid down one form as the pattern, intelligible and changeless, the second as a copy of the pattern, which comes into being and is visible" (171). Now, however, the move toward a moment before representation and reason, into the necessary and invisible conditions of possibility of representation, produces the gap of the relation between the "pattern" and its "copy," between visible form (copy) and the being (ideal model) after which that form is fashioned. The gap of that relation, what Plato calls the "third kind," is the *chora*, the space of becoming that receives all form, "the receptacle, and as it were the nurse, of all becoming" (171). As "the nature which receives into it all material things" (177), the *chora* is a function rather than a thing, "for it never departs from its own function at all," which is to "receive all things into it." As a function of receiving, the *chora* is itself without form, "being stirred and informed by the entering shapes; and owing to them it appears different from time to time" (177).[15]

Plato then repeats the triadic structure of model, copy, and the relation between them in order to explicate the *chora*'s function of receiving form; it is through that receiving function that the *chora* constitutes the passage between becoming and being. The shapes that pass in and out of the *chora* are copies fashioned after the ideal model; thus the *chora* becomes the extra term within a previously binary logic of mimesis, the extending of space through giving itself up, the making of space for the place-holding of figures. In this way Plato's dual system of imitation is triangulated to include "three kinds," thereby moving beyond the articulation of a static structure (model and copy) toward the hovering movement that is the relation between them: "For the present however we must conceive three kinds: first that which comes to be, secondly that wherein it comes to be, third that from which the becoming is copied when it is created" (177).

The triangulation of a previously binary mimetic structure results, paradoxically, in the simultaneous positing and rupture of the logic of imitation that the shift from the *hustera* to the *chora* presupposes. The ontological space of becoming that is the *chora* is the space of mediation "most bewildering and hard to comprehend" (179) that both founds and disrupts the analogical system by which any knowing or comprehension is ever possible. As part of an ontology, the *chora* is the space of becoming constituting the conditions of possibility of being upon which representation is founded. However, as we have seen, that being is predicated on an epistemological logic of imitation where form is posited as the visible manifestation, or copy, of the transcendent and invisible truth after which that form is modeled. That logic can only function within a structure of direct correspondence between copy and model, form and idea; in other words, for the system to work, there can be no gap of undecidability between them. In *The Republic*, that structure produces the analogical reductions through which the concave space or gap of the *hustera* is flattened into a two-dimensional mirror or icy lake of reflection. The introduction of the *chora* in fact undermines the mimetic system of identity on which its very articulation is founded, since the *chora* becomes that gap. In other words, by positing the *chora*, the *Timaeus* points to the fissure that breaks open the entire Platonic system of naming and knowing, the structure upon which the ideal republic is founded. By returning to an origin before the origin, the *Timaeus* uncovers the space that is also like an empty hole, "a viewless nature and formless, all-receiving," that constitutes the conditions of possibility of a structure of truth and denies the possibility of ever knowing that truth. Indeed, although Plato's system suggests that we can perceive nothing which is not a relational movement taking place in space, that place-holding in space, or figuration, means at the same time losing our ground or being lost in space.

What is the relationship between that triangulation of a two-part model into "three kinds" and Kristeva's theory of aesthetic subversion? Further, what role does the mother play in that theory? Here again, the link between Kristeva, Irigaray, and the more general problem of the feminine in language is crucial. Reading Kristeva through Irigaray allows us to compare the *chora* with the *hustera*, and to develop that comparison in order to ask political questions about the maternally coded instability which both founds and threatens signification in language. The *chora* and the *hustera* constitute moments of undecidability in Plato's philosophical system. Not surprisingly, then, Kristeva and Irigaray seize on those moments in order to theorize about the instability of the feminine, either in ontological (Kristeva) or epistemological (Irigaray) terms. The implications of that parallel are integral to a reading of the disappearing maternal figure. Crucially, while Irigaray uses the *hustera* to talk about the mother as an illusory ground of philosophical truth, Kristeva uses the *chora* as a maternal element of negativity that threatens the possibility of being itself.

Indeed, the Platonic text provides Kristeva with the vocabulary to posit negativity as maternal; as we have seen, Timaeus describes the *chora* as a "receptacle, and as it were the nurse, of all becoming," and later he will describe that space as a "mother" (177). Further, because the *chora* fits into a logic of imitation to explain the formation of the universe, it can also be related to the paternal structure of discursive authority revealed by Irigaray's reading of the parable of the cave. In that structure, the logic of mimesis hinges a metaphorical economy to the production of sameness masked as sexual difference, and in that way both privileges invisible paternal truth and denies the possibility of true alterity. However, whereas *The Republic* is about the rational mechanisms guiding the construction of the ideal state around the principle of truth, the *Timaeus* is about the conditions of possibility for that truth. The difference between them then becomes crucial in regard to the question of sexual difference. Whereas the maternal origin as *hustera* grounds paternal meaning through a reduction of difference to the same, the origin as *chora* is the undifferentiated precondition without which meaning would have no ground. In Kristeva's theory of the semiotic that space is the *chora*, the formless matrix that makes figuration possible, the preorigin of language itself. In that sense, Kristeva's ontological essentialism becomes clear: while Irigaray's theory never escapes the cinematic realm where the meaning of beings always presupposes their construction through representation, Kristeva tries to leave the cave, along with the other philosopher-kings, in order to find a prelinguistic, originary source of being.

From Maternal Rhythm to the Maternal Body

In fact, Kristeva never leaves the cave, any more than Socrates, who, in the *Timaeus*, tries but fails to escape the *hustera* for a more originary origin. Both Kristeva and Socrates hide the necessary epistemological apparatus of specular reason, exposed in *Speculum*, by evoking an origin which would precede that reason. So once again, the dialogue between Luce and Julia, the *hustera* and the *chora*, reveals the foundation upon which Kristeva builds her theory of the maternal semiotic. It is precisely because she remains in the epistemological cave of representation that Kristeva is able to transform an essential but formless ontological matrix into the recognizable form of a maternal body. True, already in Plato's text, as well as in Kristeva's appropriation of it, the *chora* marks yet another logic of a disappearing origin that is feminized as a maternal space. Plato himself describes his three-part structure in terms of a family model: "And we may liken the recipient to a mother, the model to a father, and that which is between them to a child" (177). For Plato, the structure of copy and model builds itself as a relationship between son and father mediated by a maternal matrix. But in the *Timaeus* the making of space is the groundless movement of a referential relation whose referent, the maternal body, is already the imprinting of form onto something that can never be seen or figured. The mother for Plato remains a referential ground that can only exist as a metaphorical relation inserted within a linguistic structure.

So although Plato deploys a vocabulary based on the family triangle, the Kristevan psychoanalytic grid through which the *chora* is interpreted produces a concept that differs significantly from the Platonic source. Kristeva's deployment of the concept of space must be conceived as part of the Freudian construct of the psyche. To put it simply, Kristeva always regards space itself as a fundamentally narcissistic *psychic* space, and, consequently, the *chora* exists within a self-reflective psychic structure. That self-reflective structure is the discursive space upon which Plato's *hustera* was already constructed. Kristeva's psychoanalytic overlay gives that epistemological structure the contours of the modern individual psyche. As Kristeva puts it in her musings on the alienation of modern subjects who are condemned to love in a perpetual state of exile: "Today Narcissus is an exile, deprived of his psychic space, an extra-terrestrial with a prehistory bearing, wanting for love. . . . The ET's are more and more numerous. We are all ET's.[16] So while in the Platonic text the *chora* is still ultimately a self-reflective space, it is also, more specifically, a *political* space that lacks the individualistic elements of Kristeva's psychoanalytic subject. For Kristeva, then, any thinking about space—about exile or belonging, acquisition or privation—is ultimately a self-referential thinking about the psychic territories and the borders of the imaginary of an individual subject.

Kristeva's anachronistic imposition of a psychoanalytic grid over the Platonic text is paralleled by another misreading of Plato: her insistence on the *chora* as a figure which, as we saw earlier, marks the impossibility of its own representation as figure. While Plato wants to keep the *chora* in constant motion (in that sense, it cannot be thought), Kristeva can only build her theory of the semiotic on the back of the *chora* by repeatedly freezing it in representation. Although she first presents the *chora* in *Revolution* as movement—"the drives . . . articulate what we call a *chora*" (25)—her subsequent presentation of the *chora* arrests that movement within the limits which will allow her to give it a figural form. Whereas in her first introduction of the concept, Kristeva asserts that the drives articulate the *chora*, she subsequently states that the *chora* articulates the drives, adding further that the only way the drives (premeaning, nonsensical) can be articulated is in their stasis.[17] The pivot between those two seemingly contradictory affirmations is the figure of the maternal body. Without the *chora*, there can be no figure—no mother, no nurse, no body-as-receptacle—but in order for the concept itself to be articulated, the maternal body/nurse/receptacle must already be in place. Joining the reproductive logic of the psychoanalytic construction of sexual difference with the essentializing logic of Plato's ontology, Kristeva articulates a maternal *chora* that, although a formless matrix of space itself, must already have a place—form and figure—in order to exist as space.

That contradictory articulation of the *chora* as both a precondition and a product of the process of figuration forms the crux of my argument about Kristeva's political claims for the feminine instability of language. On the one hand, Kristeva describes woman as an element of heterogeneity that, as such, cannot be assimilated into the social structure except in her homologization as a *semblant*[18]—as wife, mother, or the other roles into which the feminine is codified. On the other hand, and at the same time, Kristeva also talks about those very figures of the *semblant*—in particular those of mother and nurse—as the elements of heterogeneity that reorganize the *chora*. Thus Kristeva describes the *chora* as the "mobile-receptacle place of the process"[19] that can be *figured* by a matrix or nurse. To return to the vocabulary of space in Plato, Kristeva puts the brakes on and, so doing, transforms the *chora* (space in its extension) into a *topos* (a restricted space).

The reasons for that shift from movement to freezing, *chora* to *topos*, formless matrix to maternal form, are epistemological, rhetorical, and political. Kristeva wants the reader to know the *chora*, but the *chora*, by definition, is unknowable. The only reasoning by which that unknowable movement can be explicated is circular: we know the unseeable *chora* because it is articulated by drives which, in their stasis, allow us to see it. However, that very logic by which the *chora* is made accessible to cognition also keeps us from ever seeing and knowing it except as that which it is not: drives in their stasis, or feminine heterogeneity in its homologization as *semblant*. But Kristeva needs us to see the *chora*, because she will ultimately use it as a basis for political claims anchored by the figure of the maternal body. In rhetorical terms, the Platonic *chora* is the nonsensical rhythm of iterability, nothing but movement itself. That rhythm can only be appropriated for theory through the catachrestic transformation of a nonfigural blank that means nothing—"facilitations and stases that mean nothing" (*Revolution*, 81)—into the *topos* of the receptacle, or the maternal body. The verb—*chora* as function—which would be constitutive of a potentially liberatory movement, is arrested as the noun—*chora* as maternal thing—around which an ideology of subversive, self-perpetuating individuality is constructed.[20]

The Poet as Imperialist

It was pointed out earlier that Kristeva uses the semiotic to make political claims about the revolutionary force of poetic language, and further, that her claim is grounded by a shift from epistemology to ontology. Indeed, Kristeva acknowledges that ontological frame in the opening pages of *Revolution in Poetic Language*. In the broadest terms, one could say that her entire project has an aim to undermine the philosophy of being that constitutes the construction of the unified subject. As Kristeva puts it in *Revolution*, modern conceptions of subjectivity in language (she cites Benveniste and Chomsky) all share a metaphysical foundation: "consciousness as a synthesizing unity and the sole guarantee of Being" (*Revolution*, 237n3). Her project is to shatter the presubjective foundations upon which the synthetic unity of consciousness is built. Not surprisingly, then, in introducing the *chora* as the key to her understanding of the semiotic/symbolic opposition, Kristeva immediately extracts it from the ontological apparatus of the Platonic system: "Neither model nor copy, the *chora* precedes and underlies figuration and thus specularization, and is analogous only to vocal or kinetic rhythm. We must restore this motility's gestural and vocal play . . . on the level of the socialized body in order to remove motility from ontology and amorphousness where Plato confines it" (*Revolution*, 26). By purportedly extracting the *chora* from ontology, Kristeva ostensibly frees her own theory from the metaphysical assumptions of being that underlie the unified subject.

However, Kristeva in fact depends on and assumes both ontological essence and a notion of the unified subject, all in the name of professing a theory that appears to fragment or subvert that subject. Although her political claims revolve around images of shattering, pulverization, multiplicity, and heterogeneity, those claims are grounded by a mix of ontological and psychoanalytic essentialism that ends up privileging the individual as the basis for all forms of aesthetic and political liberatory practice.[21] So although Kristeva claims to subvert the totalizing view of the subject at the heart of ontology and the individualist tradition, the very terms through which her theory is articulated reinforce what Levinas describes as the imperialism of ontology, "the usurpation of spaces belonging to the other."[22]

Kristeva's theory of poetic language presupposes, therefore, a fundamentally conservative, totalizing view of human agency in which the individual subject in isolation becomes the final repository of revolutionary change. In Kristeva's texts, that view of human agency is translated in the aesthetic terms inherited from Romanticism, wherein the individual artist becomes the heroic agent of political transformation. Kristeva is not concerned, however, with any concept of justice or ethics which would govern that transformative praxis. Rather, her thinking is framed by the privileging of individual freedom that, symptomatically, is expressed as an asocial force: "the artist introduces into the symbolic order an asocial drive" (*Revolution*, 70–71).[23] Kristeva's system therefore not only marks the apotheosis of the revolutionary artistic subject; that subject is abstracted, for reason in its freedom, from any thinking about sociality, justice, and the ethical relation.[24]

Those limitations of her theory stem from the psychoanalytic model (which she openly embraces) and from the ontological context (which she attempts to jettison) that form the basis of her conceptual rubric. As has already been noted, Kristeva alters the Platonic model through her reliance on psychoanalysis as a conceptual grid, thereby transforming a political concept into a psychic one. Indeed, as Kelly Oliver and others have noted, through the course of her writings Kristeva has increasingly proclaimed the virtues of psychoanalysis to the exclusion of other approaches or methodologies.[25] So what are the political implications of her approach? What happens conceptually when a political concept is overlaid by a psychic one and then reified as a maternal body?

For the Kristevan exile of psychic space, the only project imaginable is the nostalgic movement of return. That movement of return reinforces a self-reflective structure of identity wherein the self—like Narcissus before the pool—keeps going back to itself in an endless repetition. Further, that structure denies the possibility of a movement toward a non-maternal other—Echo, perhaps?—which would open toward alterity. In that sense, the mother becomes the anchor of an unchanging structure founded on a nostalgic model of loss and return. The self-repeating return of nostalgic movement requires a maternal body as its origin and end; as Beauvoir puts it, the mother "is the chaos whence all have come and whither all must one day return."[26] Further, the only way such a return can occur is through a movement of displacement whereby space that has been lost becomes reoccupied. That reoccupied space is figured by Kristeva as the maternal body. To use some political metaphors, Kristeva's project involves the reacquisition of a maternal lost space, the occupation of woman as territory or land, the grasping of the feminized other for the self: the movement of imperialism par excellence. In its most extreme, narcissistic articulation, that grasping act of acquisition stretches to the limits of outer space. In his quest to occupy and subdue the ultimate feminine dark hole that is the universe itself, the artist moves to Hollywood and becomes E.T.

In the imaginary conversation that opens this chapter, Luce says to Julia: "You, a feminist?" Like Luce, I want to speak explicitly about Kristeva's political agenda. Indeed, Kristeva's comments about imperialism, to say nothing of her explicit antifeminism, are by now well known.[27] Sometimes these comments are seen as aberrations, sometimes as representative of the imperialism of Eurocentric theory in general, or of the limitations of a kind of feminism that denies the possibility of differences within the category of woman. Not only would I argue that, for Kristeva, these positions are *not* aberrations, but I would claim that Kristeva's antifeminism is symptomatic of the conservative ideology that frames all of her thinking about sexual difference, oppression, and freedom.[28]

In fact, Kristeva's "revolutionary" model contains the basic components of an ideological structure bent on the effacement of alterity or difference. But what does this mean in concrete terms? To be sure, both literature and psychoanalysis have the potential of opening the space of ethical address that I have found to be so lacking in Kristeva's theory of revolutionary language. Indeed, one could argue that both literature and psychoanalysis involve an address to the other; so why does Kristeva's psychoanalytically based, literary model necessarily efface the difference of the other? I contend that despite those possibilities of ethical address which potentially exist in both literature and psychoanalysis, Kristeva's picture of revolutionary language *requires* the effacement of the other who would hear such an address, put it into question, draw it up short. Despite Kristeva's precise historical placement of her revolutionary subject in a postindustrial, modern world, one ultimately has the impression that the Kristevan artist performs his pulverizing work in a social vacuum. Kristeva fails to consider the subjectivity and voice of the one by whom such work is received. As Toril Moi puts it, "Kristeva is unable to account for the relations between the subject and society" (171). And this failure is not simply a matter of an oversight on Kristeva's part, one that could be easily remedied by bringing ethics into her model. We cannot simply "add the other" and stir, thereby creating an enhanced Kristevan theory that would account for ethical questions.

Rather, Kristeva's entire theoretical edifice for articulating the semiotic is built around a metaphorical system whose aim is the displacement and annihilation of the other for the occupation of space. In ethical terms, that space is the opening movement or becoming of the other.

It is precisely that ontological appropriation of space which grounds the avant-garde artistic practice that Kristeva places on the front lines of her poetic revolution. To return to Richard Klein's provocative formulation; indeed, Kristeva's world is "a dream in the body of the mother": a postindustrial, advanced capitalist, imperialist world driven by an acquisitive dream of power. That dream, in its self-articulation as art, appropriates and consumes the *chora*, transforming it from an opening space into a *topos*, a maternal body to be appropriated into the self. That body then functions as a figure which masks the movement of displacement, aestheticizing an underlying violence. Thus silenced and obliterated as the lost space without which, according to Kristeva, no truly avant-garde artistic practice can occur, the mother is frozen as that space, becomes a figure in the process of giving itself up, ceding itself to the rule of an aesthetic ideology, the apotheosis of individualism that is the avant-garde. In her passivity as that which gives—gives herself up and over to those who would conquer her—the mother becomes the aesthetic figure that both marks and hides an always prior violence whose *telos* is death: the effacing of difference in the name of civilization through the appropriative gestures of conquerors, capitalists, narcissistic poets, and philosopher-kings.

Kristeva's Freedom

Thus Kristeva's nostalgic return to the maternal *chora*—the more originary Platonic origin—reveals her to be trapped in a self-reflective cavernous space where being itself is structured according to a mimetic logic of the same. Despite her attempts to extract herself from Platonic ontology, Husserlian phenomenology, or the various epistemologies that posit the synthesizing unity of the thinking subject, Kristeva's theoretical edifice follows just such a philosophical tradition. Kristeva's thought models itself on a philosophy that, as Levinas observes, refuses to put ethics first, where the dialectic of reason moves toward a horizon of transcendent being through the subsumption of alterity into the grasping understanding of a universal subject. Indeed, Kristeva remains a would-be philosopher-king, and the culmination of her theory of the semiotic as a paean to individual freedom most clearly exposes her philosophical and political conservatism. Her privileging of a concept of freedom that calls for "free time" and "leisure"—a freedom *to*—both reinforces the notion of the subject of being at the foundation of ontological and epistemological systems, and upholds the individualism that grounds both modern psychoanalysis and the American political tradition that she so often celebrates. Ultimately, the masculine individual in *his* freedom becomes, over and over again, the revolutionary Kristevan hero.

Kristeva's apotheosis of individual freedom brings her full circle back to the Platonic origins of her theory of the maternal semiotic. Moreover, the freedom that Kristeva invokes has little to do with the struggle of marginalized groups who, in resisting their oppression, work collectively for themselves and others in the name of justice. Instead, Kristeva celebrates marginalization by romanticizing the violence that fragments those who are marginalized. She does this *not* by talking about those groups which are truly marginalized in modern society by racial, sexual, and economic injustice; rather, she invokes the figures of individual poets like Lautréamont and Mallarmé. Kristevan freedom is thereby ushered in with aesthetic works produced, almost without exception, by canonical male European writers. According to Kristeva, through the signifying practice of their "marginalized" texts society will be transformed.

It is important to point out here that Kristeva's underlying assumption about the transformative potential of artistic works is not, in itself, problematic. Indeed, the complex relationship between texts and politics constitutes one of the crucial questions of contemporary scholarship, occupying theorists not just in the traditional disciplines of literary studies, history, anthropology, political theory, and philosophy but also in more recent interdisciplinary fields such as gender studies, queer theory, critical race theory, and cultural studies. In light of that work, Kristeva's formulation of the question appears surprisingly vague and inadequate, precisely because it fails to articulate the exact nature of the links between textual practice and sociopolitical structures. And yet, despite that failure, the "revolutionary" claim of her entire argument rests on our acceptance of her assumption that those links are simple, direct, and unmediated by other social, economic, and political forces. In fact, in generating her vision of social change, Kristeva places all of her eggs in one aesthetic basket. Citing a fragment from Marx that suits her purposes—namely, a celebration of "leisure" (*Revolution*, 106), which, for her, marks the end of old-style capitalism's reign of necessity—Kristeva privileges a concept of freedom as "free time" and "free works" such as "musical composition" (106). Thus she ultimately claims that *only* through artistic practice can we bring forth an era of true liberation.

What are we to make of a theory of liberation that lacks the conceptual vocabulary to talk about justice, work, and social responsibility? And in the context of those questions, how are we to interpret Kristeva's celebration of individual freedom? Beyond the conceptual inadequacy of Kristeva's delineation of the links between texts and politics, there are deeper philosophical issues at stake here, problems that are illuminated by Levinas's critique of ontology. It is no accident that the ontological basis of Kristeva's theory is coupled with a disregard for ethical questions. Indeed, in his articulation of ethics as a "first philosophy," Levinas declares ontology to be murderous in its subsumption of alterity into itself, its annihilation of the other. As Levinas argues in his critique of Heidegger, a philosophy wherein the thinking of the Being of beings becomes the *telos* of understanding denies the possibility of an ethical relation. To affirm the priority of Being (*être*) over beings (*étants*) is to subordinate the relation with someone who is a being (*étant*), or the ethical relation, to a relation with the Being of being (*l'être de l'étant*), or a relation of knowing.[29] That movement, described by Levinas in his critique of ontology, is the philosophical movement of self-reflection, the nostalgic movement of return in which thought, like Narcissus, can only think itself. In that impersonal relation of self-reflective thought, the ethical relation is subordinated to knowing, and the particularity of beings in their ethical relation is neutralized for universal understanding.

Levinas explains that in this way the ethical relation of a concept of justice is subordinated to the concept of freedom upon which the possibility of knowing truth through reason is built. While a concept of justice demands a responsibility to the other, a concept of reason in its freedom means knowing beings through a reduction of the Other to the Same.[30] Levinas further argues that ontology should thus rightly be described as a philosophy of force or power that affirms the destiny of sedentary peoples, the possessors and builders of the earth. Ontology is therefore fundamentally a philosophy of nature as the matrix of particularity upon which the grasping of understanding can proclaim itself as freedom. As Levinas says: "Ontology becomes ontology of nature, impersonal fecundity, faceless generous mother, matrix of particular beings, inexhaustible matter for things" (*Totality*, 46).

Levinas helps us to clarify what is wrong with Kristeva's picture of a freedom without ethics.[31] Never completely free, the ethical self is responsible for the other: "Responsibility for the other, this way of answering without a prior commitment, is human fraternity itself, and it is prior to freedom."[32] That always prior responsibility undoes the nostalgic structure that posits a maternal origin as an equally inaccessible origin and end of thought and being. Thus, as Levinas puts it, "subjectivity is hostage. This notion reverses the position where the presence of the ego to itself appears as the beginning or as the conclusion of philosophy. This coinciding in the same, where I would be an origin, or, through memory, a covering over of the origin, this presence, is, from the start, undone by the other" ("Substitution," 116).

For Kristeva, there is no other except in the form of a mother who is produced only to be consumed by the machinery of self-reflective thought. Both ontology and psychoanalysis allow Kristeva to posit a theory of liberation within a conservative philosophical essentialism and an equally conservative reproductive model of sexual difference. Nonetheless, Kristeva's theory has been hinged by many of her interpreters to a feminist political discourse. But that appropriation of Kristeva's theory of the semiotic in the guise of feminism only hides the political conservatism of her approach to thinking about social change. As we have seen, for Kristeva "freedom" has meaning only for individual artists who are already privileged in a postindustrial but completely capitalist system of production. Further, the metaphor of the *chora* as space extends that advanced capitalist frame to include an imperialist structure wherein the space of the other is annexed, appropriated, and subsumed into the self. But because she draws on a vocabulary of sexual difference and, more specifically, a discourse that links freedom, feminine alterity, and nostalgia for the mother, Kristeva has been celebrated in the name of feminist liberation.[33]

As this chapter shows in its analysis of the philosophical presuppositions behind Kristeva's claims, and as Kristeva herself has stated again and again, Kristeva and feminism have nothing to do with each other. Nor should they.[34] Indeed, not only is Kristeva's work antithetical to feminism, her theoretical project is antithetical to any politics of liberation grounded by ethical commitments. Kristeva does not appear to be interested in justice or a notion of responsibility that would lie "outside of any place . . . , on the hither side of the autonomy of auto-affection and identity resting on itself" (Levinas, "Substitution," 107). Rather, she is interested in individual genius, the aesthetic pleasures of the bourgeoisie, and the smooth functioning of an economic and social structure which allows that system to continue.

In the end, Kristeva remains deep in the cave, dazzled by the light of avant-garde truth. In that rarified space of wealth and privilege the mother is a body to be appropriated and consumed, an echo always disappearing offstage so that Narcissus can celebrate his own death—like the postmodern death of man—in a hall of mirrors. Kristeva, like man, continues to celebrate that illusion of death at the expense of a concept of social responsibility, claiming as her own that ontologically grounded special place in the sun, that place in the *hustera* which closes off the possibility of the other. Kristeva tells the story of the imperialist subject, losing himself only to find himself again, in an endless process of self-reflection, laying claim to space itself as it spreads open before him, all in the name of his "freedom."

Luce 'et veritas':
Toward an Ethics of Performance

How can I say it? . . . Our all will come.
— L U C E   I R I G A R A Y , "When Our Lips Speak Together"

How can we talk about the way things are? How can we know what to do? Though dauntingly broad and hardly original, these basic philosophical questions define the parameters of what I offer here: a challenge to contemporary articulations of the relationship between language and politics. In making that challenge, I move away from the mother and the problem of nostalgia, and focus more closely on the question of ethics raised in the previous chapter. In that chapter's opening conversation, Kristeva and Irigaray touched on a nexus of issues, including feminism, ethics, mimicry, the development of theory in the United States, and the institutional power of the philosophical tradition. Those issues provide me with a springboard for approaching the problems I want to address here. More specifically, they point to the relationship between ethics and the somewhat amorphous body of thought known as performative theory.

In many ways, this shift in direction away from the mother can be read, paradoxically, as a return to Irigaray, particularly since Irigaray's influence on contemporary theory includes both ethical and performative questions. The paradox, of course, is that such a gesture of return appears suspiciously nostalgic; however, I maintain (stubbornly, perhaps) that this is decidedly not the case. As this chapter makes clear, there are no wombs here . . . just lips which, as I argued in the Introduction and Chapter 2, are fundamentally antinostalgic. Further, undergirding the arguments I make in this chapter lies the corollary of that assertion: namely, like the mimetic lips on which it draws, performative theory rejects the nostalgic structure of lost origins. As Barbara Johnson argues, "the performative refers only to itself" and, therefore, "does not refer to any exterior or prior origin."[1] However, just as the Kristevan *chora* closes off the possibility of alterity, so performativity fails to provide a concept of ethics that would address the question of the other. Although I'm no longer mapping the mother here, this chapter explores the blank spaces in the powerful alternative model provided by performative theory. Like the maternal maps analyzed in previous chapters, the performative map is inadequate for tracing and understanding the connections between language, identity, and the social bonds that constitute the political and ethical sphere.

Generally, in the pages that follow I challenge recent developments in performative theory by asserting the necessity of an ethical call for justice. Now, more than ever, many of us don't quite know what we're saying, much less what we're doing to make things better. How do we define the terms of our politics, when we're not even sure who *we* are? What does it mean to be a political agent? a feminist? queer? What is identity anyway, if it's always already the jargonized, spectacularized, institutionalized construction of an infinitely mobile subject position? What happens to politics if everything is a performance?[2]

The question of performance marks a starting point for this inquiry into the broader questions about language, politics, and identity. Again using Irigaray as a guide, this chapter examines the work of Judith Butler and J. L. Austin in order to assess performative theory in relation to feminist and queer strategies of resistance. Those performative strategies involve a contestation of identity categories with an aim to bring about political change. And while the intended liberatory aims of feminist and queer performativity are laudable, performative theory tends to be flawed by its disregard for ethical questions, a problem that looms large in Butler's work.[3] Unlike Butler, Irigaray places ethical concerns at

the center of her consideration of the epistemological problems of identity and truth.[4] And while that philosophical stance is made clear in her
Ethics of Sexual Difference, most readers of Irigaray have not recognized
the extent to which she already engages with ethics in *Speculum* and
This Sex Which Is Not One. More specifically, in the closing essay of
This Sex Which Is Not One, "When Our Lips Speak Together," Irigaray
inscribes an ethical model of speech that would contest Butler's performative act, despite the apparent affinities between performativity
and Irigaray's concept of mimesis.[5] In the lips essay Irigaray both theorizes and performs a relational model of subjectivity that would allow
for the irreducible difference of the other. As theory and performance,
Irigaray's lips speak the instability of either a pure truth-telling or an
absolute performative concept of language. So doing, they perform an
ethical model of social and discursive relation in which the specular
performative subject is put into question by the other's narrative truth.[6]

Why do we need ethics? Because without it the play of representation is unleashed into a field of power that can harness, abuse, and
distort it for the accomplishment of its own ends. Without ethics,
"freeplay"[7] can be murderous and illusion can be literalized into the
real oppression of persons perceived to be threats. Without ethics as
a *foundation*,[8] the force of a performance can become anything at all,
commanded by the desire of anyone at all: a democratic president, a
fascist dictator, or a progressive academic superstar.[9] As Shoshana Felman has shown, the performative subject plays the role of Don Juan;
the political effect of any performance is determined by its success as a
seduction. If our performance fails to ask the ethical question, the seduction goes unchecked in its own potential for violence, despite the
avowed intention of its agent to contest that very violence.

So where do we find ethics, this thing that is missing? Not a simple
question, since in the moment of finding we face the recognition that
there is still, and always, something missing. Armed with a belief in
transcendent reason which rests on the universalizing claims of an epistemological a priori, but faced with the destabilizing crises of the "postmodern" condition, we still look to theory in order to know what is
missing. So doing, we have learned to reject as illusory the totalizing
truth of the knowledge to be found there. We have learned that the

"true" is contingent, formed and articulated according to particular histories and specific regimes of power. We have learned, *ad nauseam*, that there is no truth. But who is this *we*? What have we been saying, and to whom? And in dismissing Truth, whose truths have we not been hearing?[10]

Act I: Judy

In terms of feminist thought, particularly in the humanities, the loss of Truth and a "we" who would speak it has led to the theorization of gender as performance. According to Butler, gender identity, like any identity, is founded and regulated through the repetition of signifying practices that appear to naturalize those identities. Consequently, "the feminist 'we' is always and only a phantasmatic construction" (Butler, *Gender Trouble*, 142), and "'identity' as a point of departure can never hold as the solidifying ground of a feminist political movement" ("Contingent Foundations," 15). It follows, then, according to performative theory, that a similar process of repetition might subvert those very identities. Butler writes: "it is only *within* the practices of repetitive signifying that a subversion of identity becomes possible" (*Gender Trouble*, 145). Gender is exposed as an "act" through practices of parody such as drag; the bodies performing that act "become the site of a dissonant and denaturalized performance that reveals the performative status of the natural itself" (146). Hence, performance reveals the naturalized "truth" of gender "as an inevitable fabrication," and exposes "every claim to the origin, the inner, *the true*, and the real as *nothing other* than the effects of *drag*" ("Imitation," 29; my emphasis). The exposure of the instability of that truth has the effect of "proliferating gender configurations, destabilizing substantive identity, and depriving the naturalizing narratives of compulsory heterosexuality of their central protagonists: 'man' and 'woman'" (*Gender Trouble*, 146).

The loss of "man" and "woman" does not mean, according to Butler, that we've lost the possibility of feminist politics, but, rather, puts the very terms of that politics into question. For Butler, one of those questionable terms is the concept of narrative. Butler replaces narrative, the possibility of telling stories within discursively coherent frames, with a more disruptive performance.[11] This move from narrative to performance corresponds to the epistemological shift of postmodernism, in which the "hegemonical claims of any group or organization to 'represent' the forces of history"[12] are subverted by the locally contextualized speech acts of situated subject positions within specific structures of power. More specifically, American feminists in the early 1970's named women's oppression and, so doing, produced a "quasi-metanarrative"[13] of their own to counter the grand narratives of History and Man.[14] However, that feminist narrative about Woman tended to elide the ethnic, racial, economic, sexual, and national differences between particular women. In that context, performance "brings into question the foundationalist frame in which feminism as an identity politics has been articulated" (Gender Trouble, 148), exposing as a ruse the "transhistorical commonality" of a feminist "we" constructed through "standards of narrative coherence" ("Gender," 339).

Butler asserts that "performance may preempt narrative as the scene of gender production" ("Gender," 339). Further, not only does she use performance to explain the construction of gendered identities; she also affirms its capacity to subvert the status quo by repeating the very fictions through which those gendered identities were constructed in the first place. Butler implies that the telling "of a unique life-story, of a meaningful tale" (Benhabib, 217–18) is not a viable model for resisting or contesting gender oppression. Rather, we lose narrative along with Man, Woman, History, and Truth, by putting it all inside quotation marks. Having done away with narrative and its purportedly oppressive corollaries, Butler then claims performance as a model for a different form of political practice that would avoid the totalizing tendencies of narrative truth-telling. Indeed, according to Butler, the quotation marks expose the truth as illusory. By mocking that truth, the performative "we" begins to build a "new" politics. "Cultural configurations of sex and gender might then proliferate," and "a new configuration of politics would surely emerge from the ruins of the old" (Gender Trouble, 149).

Not surprisingly, Butler's exposure of the trouble with gender has revealed other troubled waters as well. The performative disruption of gender identity seems to work equally well with other categories of difference, be they racial, ethnic, national, sexual, or other. Performativity has been most widely deployed in recent theories about the multiple identities marked by the term "queer." Indeed, Andrew Parker and Eve Kosofsky Sedgwick claim that "the performative has . . . been from its inception already infected with queerness."[15] The term "queer" itself is, in Sedgwick's words, "recurrent, eddying, *troublant*" (*Tendencies*, xii), dramatically celebrating the explosion of identity and the proliferation of excess and loss set into play by the performative subversion of gender. Thus "queer" can mean "the open mesh of possibilities, gaps, overlaps, dissonances and resonances, lapses and excesses of meaning when the constituent elements of anyone's gender, of anyone's sexuality aren't made (or *can't be* made) to signify monolithically" (8). Indeed, "queer" isn't limited to thinking about gender and sexuality alone; for example, Sedgwick argues that "intellectuals and artists of color whose sexual self-definition includes 'queer' . . . are using the leverage of 'queer' to do a new kind of justice to the fractal intricacies of language, skin, migration, state" (9). In fact, "[a] word so fraught as 'queer' is . . . never can only denote; nor even can it only connote" (9). Rather, "part of [the] experimental force [of queer] as a speech act is the way in which it dramatizes locutionary position itself" (9). Paradoxically, while both Butler and Sedgwick use "queer" to disrupt the foundations of coherent identity, that disruption does not seem to include the authority—theirs perhaps?—of the performative "I." "Queer," Sedgwick suggests, "can signify only *when attached to the first person*" (9).

My argument with "queer" is *not* that Sedgwick or Butler's recurrent, troubling, and eddying first-person "queer" doesn't matter, particularly when that person has been marginalized by a society bent on her or his annihilation. Rather, I think the effect of theorizing a "queer I" as "a person's undertaking particular, performative acts of experimental self-perception and filiation" (*Tendencies*, 9) has led, inadvertently, to a key omission—namely, an omission of *ethical* questions about (1) the possibility of conversation between two people with different stories to tell and (2) the potential for negative, even violent effects of a performative act.[16] In regard to the first point, the following questions can be asked: To whom does a performance speak? Can the performer hear the response of the one to whom she would speak? Does the concept of response, and thus responsibility, even matter in theories of performativity? Another set of issues is raised by the second point, namely: How might a performance be read? What might cause the performance to fail, to make it work in ways that veer dangerously off course, away from the liberatory intentions of its agents?

More pointedly, ethical discourse would have us ask: how does the first-person queer speak to the other? How does that first person account for and think the second person who would hear it, draw it up short, put it into question? How does the experimental force of a queer speech act *do more* than simply "dramatize locutionary position itself"? How does it speak its relation to a "Thou,"[17] its ethical relation to an other?

Why do these questions matter? Most urgently, they matter because people continue to suffer, and they suffer as constructed identities.[18] No performance can parodically resignify the harm that is inflicted on a "woman" who is abused, a "fag" who is killed, a "dyke" who commits suicide, a "black" who is beaten by the "white" police.[19] The quotation marks don't perform away the pain, despite the claim that placing terms like "violence" and "sex" in quotation marks reveals them to be "under contest, up for grabs" (Butler, "Contingent Foundations," 19). What might inadvertently be performed away by parodic quotation is the possibility of a narrative that would speak the truth of that pain. Precisely because of the empirical fact that our identities still get us abused, beaten, and killed, we *still* need to elaborate a discourse and a politics about rights and justice,[20] about the relation between "I" and "you." We need to imagine an ethical politics in which, as Levinas puts it, murder becomes impossible.[21] What happens to blacks, women, fags, and dykes? We still need to tell our stories, to narrate the harms that befall us. We still need to speak the truth, a truth that *is more* than "the effects of *drag*" (Butler, "Imitation," 29). Tell the truth. Truth matters.

Act II: John

Philosophy traditionally separates truth from error, statements of fact from the nonserious play of fiction. At least since Plato, that division between fact and fiction has allowed philosophy to exclude itself from the representational realm of illusion, thereby focusing on the more serious project of finding the truth.[22] J. L. Austin's speech act theory marks an intervention into the exclusion of truth from representation by asking about the link between the way things are said and what those things do. In the first lecture of *How to Do Things with Words*, Austin posits his famous distinction between performative and constative utterances, only to problematize the binarism of his own opposition in the subsequent eleven lectures.[23] A performative utterance is a statement in which to say something "is to do it"; "the issuing of the utterance is the performing of an action" (Austin, 6). Austin opposes performatives to constative utterances, the kinds of statements that have traditionally occupied philosophers. "It was far too long the assumption of philosophers," Austin complains, "that the business of a 'statement' can only be to 'describe' some state of affairs, or to 'state some fact,' which it must do *either truly or falsely*" (1; my emphasis).

The emphasis on performatives makes Austin something of a rebel in his own British philosophical tradition. However, despite what many of his interpreters claim, Austin doesn't do away with the value of truth; rather, he complicates what Timothy Gould calls "philosophy's fantasy of an all-purpose, hypertheatrical Constative."[24] So doing, Austin "points to the region of swampiness that the performatives share with constatives" (Gould, 26) and reveals the constative to be "a condensed fantasy of a certain philosophical form of tyranny" (Gould, 40). In critiquing the philosophers who celebrate Truth but who fail to acknowledge the structures of authority that make their claims possible, Austin also lays bare the structures of authority that govern nonphilosophical discourse, what Stanley Cavell calls "the voice of the everyday or the ordinary" ("Counter-Philosophy," 62). By extension, one can legitimately argue, as Gould does, that Austin exposes "the uncanny ability of social power to cloak itself as the natural language of the world" (41). *How to Do Things with Words* thus opens the way to contemporary theories of representation in which speaking is acknowledged to be a constructed, context-bound signifying event. Austin's theory of performatives reveals speech acts to be acts of force which, rather than simply providing a means for reaching Truth, constitute the very terms through which truths are articulated and received.

Austin's speech act theory undoubtedly provides a key philosophical base for contemporary articulations of performativity. Significantly, the logic of example through which Austin lays out that theory has had important implications for queer theory as well. As Butler and others have noted, Austin's favorite example of the "performative utterance" is the statement "I do" in the context of the marriage ceremony. To say "I do" is to make the marriage real: to say it is to do it. Austin's reliance on the marriage ceremony to theorize performativity suggests, as Butler points out, "that the heterosexualization of the social bond is the paradigmatic form for those speech acts which bring about what they name" (*Bodies*, 224). Indeed, in repeating the exemplary words "I do" throughout *How to Do Things with Words*, Austin himself is making "it" so, the "it" being theory qua heterosexuality. Performativity therefore is inscribed within a model of heterosexuality as norm that serves to legitimate the power of the performative utterance. Performatives not only perform an action but also "confer a binding power on the action performed" (Butler, *Bodies*, 225); it follows, then, according to Butler, that "the performative is one domain where discourse acts *as* power" (225).

It is Butler who also introduces the term "queer" as a destabilizing intervention into the Austinian construct of a heterosexualized performativity. She asks: "To what extent . . . has the performative 'queer' operated alongside, as a deformation of, the 'I pronounce you ... ' of the marriage ceremony?" (*Bodies*, 226). Butler thus uses the term "queer" to mark a performative practice that would both destabilize and contest heterosexuality as norm. In this way, "the subject who is 'queered' into public discourse through homophobic interpellations of various kinds *takes up* or *cites* that very term as the discursive basis for an opposition. This kind of citation will emerge as *theatrical* to the extent that it *mimes and renders hyperbolic* the discursive convention that it also *reverses*" (*Bodies*, 232).

But how can we know the difference between Austin's heterosexual theater and the spectacular performances to which Butler refers? The die-ins by ACT-UP, the kiss-ins by Queer Nation, and the other varieties of "theatrical rage" (*Bodies*, 233) cited by Butler as examples of a queer-positive opposition to the status quo, undoubtedly are intended to contest the "heterosexualization of the social bond" inscribed in Austin's theory of performativity and played out in the oppressive practices of contemporary society.[25] Further, those contestatory political acts occur within a particular context in which AIDS discrimination, homophobia, racism, and other forms of oppression are being targeted. Austin himself asserts that in order to interpret the force or meaning of an utterance (like "I'm queer," for example), the "occasion" or "context" of that utterance "matters seriously" (*How to Do Things with Words*, 100). Without context, neither the interpretation nor the reception of the utterance can be theorized.

However, a difficulty arises with the following paradox: context sets limits on the possible meanings of an utterance; at the same time, context itself is *without* limits. The particular context of an utterance must be empirically evaluated and understood in any reading of the historical force of that utterance; but, in theory, the possible contexts of that utterance are potentially boundless, because utterances are repeatable. Indeed, as Derrida points out, an utterance has meaning *because* it is repeatable; its force, therefore, cannot be controlled or fixed in place and time. As a result, its contexts are both particular and generalizable, both the irreducible event of a particular performance, and the infinite future of all possible repetitions of that performance. Both that particularity and that generality constitute the "occasions" of the utterance. Further, it is the act of moving from the particular scene of an utterance to the conceptual generality which attempts to think about its other possible occasions that constitutes the act of theorization. Particular scenes of performance by, say, ACT-UP, are subsumed by a discourse that attempts to talk about "queer" performance in an evaluative and universalizing way. That theory, in turn, is taken up as a formula for preparing, enacting, and understanding particular scenes of performative practice.

The problem with contemporary theories of queer performativity is that they fail to account for the possibility, or even the inevitability, of their own failure. Indeed, the possibility of failure is built into Austin's definition of a performative, since a performative has force only in a context, and contexts are necessarily ever-changing. To use, once again, Austin's favorite example, marriage is paradigmatic as a cornerstone of his theory and yet, as his "doctrine of *Infelicities*" suggests, in marrying there will always be a case in which "something *goes wrong*" (*How to Do*

Things with Words, 14). The performative will fail "if we, say, utter the formula incorrectly, or if, say, we are not in a position to do the act because we are, say, married already" (15–16). Another example might be a case in which the person performing the ceremony lacks the authority to "make it so," thus turning the performance into "a mockery, like a marriage with a monkey" (24). In fact, as Cavell reads him, what Austin is saying is that to fail is human: "if utterances *could* not fail they would not be the human actions under consideration, indeed not the actions of humans at all" ("Counter-Philosophy," 85). Failure, therefore, "is not for Austin an *accident* of the performative" (Felman, *The Literary Speech Act*, 66); rather, its possibility is "inherent in it, essential to it. In other words, like Don Juan, Austin conceives of failure not as external but as internal to the promise, as what actually constitutes it" (Felman, 66).

So what if a queer performance proves itself to be human: goes astray, wanders off its intended path, produces *error* rather than contesting it? That possibility of error and errancy is linked to the question of identity and the violence of totalization. Butler admits, of course, that a "queer" self-naming, like any identity, can never be total or "fully owned"; as a word that "carries the pain of social injury," "queer" can never be a term created "from nothing" that would come to "represent our 'freedom.'" Rather, she argues, "queer" marks both "the *limits* of agency and its most *enabling conditions*" (*Bodies*, 228–29). In that sense, we can certainly imagine the utterance "I'm queer," like "I do," in situations where "something goes wrong" (Austin, 14). It is precisely because those words cannot be pinned down that they can be harnessed and repeated with vastly differing intentions and effects.

The question becomes: who is doing the naming? As Sedgwick points out, there is a difference between the shaming utterance, "You queer," and the "I'm queer" that expresses pride. But can we control an effect of shame or pride when, as Sartre famously put it, history deprives us of our intentions? Butler implies that we *do* have that control when she asserts the necessity of a fixed, self-identical notion of "queer," however provisional that fixing may be: "the temporary totalization performed by identity categories is a necessary error." Although we can never be fully constituted as subjects, "queer" or otherwise—"the subject as self-identical is no more" (*Bodies*, 230)—we must, according to

Butler, pretend that *as* queers we can speak and, like Austin's man and wife, make our identities real. To perform is to act, to "make it so" (Austin, 6); to say "I'm queer" is "to do it."

The problem, of course, is that we can never be sure what the "it" might be, precisely because "it" will be repeated. However, that uncertainty should not be a reason for giving up on contestatory politics altogether. Rather, "it" forces us to think about the *potential* for violence in our own failure to fully know what we think we're doing.[26] And that possibility of violence is linked, however obliquely, to the "necessary error" of identity on which queer performativity depends. A theory that relies on the "necessary error" of self-identity has the potential for violence because, philosophically, it repeats the mimetic logic that reduces difference to a repetition of the same.[27] As we saw in the previous chapter on Kristeva, identity itself becomes totalized, however provisionally, as an ontological force that would subsume the other into its self-identity. In other words, the self-knowing logic of that identity is potentially murderous, as Levinas has shown, because it lacks an ethical *foundation* that would demand a response to an irreducible other.[28]

Without ethics, a performance can be anything it wants to be within a context where conventionalized authority continually reauthorizes itself. "Behind the fiction of the subject," Barbara Johnson writes, "stands the fiction of society" (60). Thus performative subjects become "identities that are alternately instituted and relinquished according to the purposes at hand" (*Gender Trouble*, 16). The politics of a performance are therefore, by definition, radically "contingent" (16), and its value of *force*—as opposed to the *truth* value of a constative utterance—gives it a power of seduction that remains unchecked by truth.[29] Indeed, as Butler herself points out, "one is, as it were, in power even as one opposes it," and the "effects of performatives" are "incalculable" (*Bodies*, 241). The theatrical rage of an ACT-UP demonstration, or the spectacular desire of butch-femme lesbian performance, cannot know its effects. All the more reason to ask questions about a saying that is also a doing and that, in the moment of that doing, refuses to contest its own identity. Such self-contestation in saying can only happen in a form that articulates the horizon of an ethical relation, one that cannot tolerate self-identity but, rather, produces an opening toward the other.[30]

Intermission: Behind the Curtain

> In ancient Persia . . . to consecrate the marriage, the boy
> makes his agreement heard loudly and clearly; the fiancée, the
> girl, is put in the next room amid other women, near the door
> over which a curtain falls. In order to make the necessary yes
> audible, the women hit the young girl's head against the door,
> causing her to moan.   —DJEBAR, *Women of Algiers*

As the paradigmatic model of performativity, marriage requires a "necessary yes," an utterance of acquiescence to the bond of matrimony that transforms boy and girl into man and wife. I want to use Austin's heteronormative example of marriage in order to ask some pointed questions about the relationship between performativity and violence. Does Austin's "I do" mask a moan of pain, as in Assia Djebar's account of the curtained "yes" that falls between the Persian girl and the boy she is forced to wed? Is there in the structure of marriage a potential violence that undergirds the "necessary yes"? If so, what might that threat of marital violence suggest about the possible violence of performativity itself?

Not only does Austin's performative rest on an assumption of the unquestioned legitimacy of all heterosexual marriage, its intrinsic possibility for failure is illustrated by marriage ceremonies in which the implicit "rightness" of the marital bond is put at risk by occasions where "something goes wrong." But why is marriage necessarily right and its failure "wrong"? Austin appears never to have asked himself that question, despite his attention to the rights and wrongs of "accuracy and morality," or his concern for the "solid moralist" who surveys "the invisible depths of ethical space" (Austin, 10).[31] In fact, for an unwilling bride in a forced marriage where a moan of pain is taken as "yes," the failure of that "necessary yes" might be welcome. Similarly, a hypothetical victim of spousal abuse might argue, in the context of a marriage ceremony where something went wrong and the performance was "unhappy," that finally something "right" and "happy" had happened. In other words, by focusing only on the ceremonial trappings of an utterance, Austin fails to account for the sociopolitical institutions that ground the utterance within systems of power. So while Austin is right to question philosophy's concern with Truth to the exclusion of the force behind speech acts, the target of his critique is primarily philosophy itself, rather than the broader structure within which philosophy exists. To return to the admittedly loaded example of marriage, I find that there is nothing in Austin's theory that would provide the means for critiquing the sociopolitical setting within which the utterances of the ceremony occur. And yet, those utterances make the marriage binding and link it to a larger context—a third party, namely, the state. In patriarchy, that context privileges one of the participants in the marriage while it disadvantages the other. To put it more bluntly, in the case of "I do," the institutional context for the utterance is a system of power that perpetuates a gendered structure of domination and subordination. Not only does Austin take the privilege of the "he" ("a solid moralist"?) within that structure for granted, he unwittingly exposes the hidden violence through which the binding power of his "moral" act is imposed and reinforced.

To be sure, in Austin's "doctrine of 'illocutionary forces,'" the "act performed," or "illocution," acquires its force through a particular "context" (Austin, 100). In taking seriously the notion that "the occasion of an utterance matters seriously," Austin shows how mere meaning—a locution—is necessarily contextualized and thus becomes an "illocutionary act" (Austin, 100, 101). To illustrate this point he comes up with an example that, like marriage, is loaded:

Act (A) or Locution

He said to me [Austin? the solid moralist?] 'Shoot her!' meaning by 'shoot' shoot and referring by 'her' to *her*. (Austin, 101)

When I read this example, I can't help asking: just who is this italicized feminine pronoun and why is she going to be shot? Might she be the solid moralist's wife or wife-to-be? Austin leaves out that part of the story, but the least we can surmise is that, as in all of Austin's examples, the agent of the speech act is a "he" with a considerable stock of authority. As Austin's tale continues, we read about illocution and perlocution finishing up the job: "He urged (or advised, ordered, &c.) me to shoot her"; "He persuaded me to shoot her"; "He got me to (or made me, &c.) shoot her" (Austin, 102). By the time we get to what might be dubbed a counterlocution ("He said to me, 'You can't do that'" [Austin, 102]), Austin's attempt at resurrection appears somewhat feeble, since by that time *she* is already dead. The performance is over, and she is just a statistic like, say, the four American women killed every day in incidents of domestic violence. This is not to suggest that Austin promotes spousal abuse or wants women to be killed. Indeed, most would read his "trivial if amusing examples" (Cavell, "Counter-Philosophy," 59) as tongue in cheek and consistent with Austin's general tone of poking fun. Such a reading is certainly justified, but it fails to address the structural limitations of Austin's speech act theory. Although Austin continually insists on the importance of context, his own implicit understanding of context is actually quite narrow. To put it somewhat provocatively, if a paradigmatic performative is a marriage in which "he" weds a "she," its wider "occasion" (Austin, 100), to use Austin's term, is a system of violence that perpetuates "his" power, as well as that of the dominant group of which he is a member. No matter how "it" is performed, "she" ends up getting shot.

How would Butler's performatives avoid the error of that possibility of violence? I know that Butler does not want women to be shot, any more than she wants them to be married. But her theory, like Austin's, fails to articulate the terms through which that murder would become impossible. In ethical terms, the force of performance cannot be thought without the response of she who would be bound by its terms. We need to hear the story of the one who gets shot, beaten, raped, or abused, and survives to narrate its truth. We need to hear so that she, with another, can perform a different economy of speech, resistance, pleasure, and love. That's what Irigaray's lips are saying. Listen.

Act III: Luce

Darkness. A murmur of voices. The curtain rises.[32]

Luce 1 (backstage): So did it work? Did he seduce you?
Luce 2 (in the audience): Who? Don Juan?
Luce 1: Yeah. You know, Don John Austin. Was it a felicitous scene? He has a reputation, you know. So did it work?[33]

Luce 2: Are you kidding? His failure to seduce me may have been infelicitous for him, but I assure you that, for my part, it was a happy bungle. I'd rather not end up being shot to prove a point, thank you very much. Besides, I don't know about you, but I prefer girls.

Luce 1: Yeah, I know. I do too. So what about the girl? Did she seduce you?

Luce 2: Who? Judy? Well, I was tempted. But it didn't quite work. You see, I've heard it all before. Take this stuff on hysteria, for example. Not so very different from what Judy says. (*Reading*) "And anyway why would she not be 'hysterical'? Since hysteria holds in reserve, in suspension/suffering, something in common with the mime that is a sine qua non of sexual pleasure." I've learned to interpret that language: the hysteric repeats and exaggerates the gendered fictions that construct her as "woman." But you know, I don't think it necessarily gets her anywhere. The phallus always stops her, and his play keeps on going: "The problem is that the ludic mimicry, the fiction, the 'make believe,' the 'let's pretend'—which, as we know, made the hysteric subject to all kinds of disbelief, oppression, and ridicule—are stopped short, impeded, *controlled by a master-signifier*, the Phallus, and by its representative(s)." Or take the chapter in *Speculum* on Plotinus as another example. Nothing but quotes. Quite audacious, if I do say so myself. But what do we have to show for all that work?

Luce 1: So you no longer believe in mimicry? We put a lot of stock in it for a while, to say nothing of all the others.[34] (*Reading*) "To play with mimesis is thus, for a woman, to try to recover the place of her exploitation by discourse, without allowing herself to be simply reduced to it . . . to make 'visible,' by an effect of playful repetition, what was supposed to remain invisible. . . . If women are such good mimics, it is because they are not simply resorbed in this function. *They also remain elsewhere*." That's what we're famous for, you know.

Luce 2: I suppose. But to tell you the truth, I think it's a stop-gap measure, to keep us from disappearing altogether. And as I said before, it's hard work. (*Reading*) "And hysterical miming will be the little girl's or the woman's work to save her sexuality from total repression, disappearance." You know, our real story never quite gets going—"let us say that *in the beginning was the end of her story.*"

Luce 1: Which is why I thought: OK, let's stop being stagehands and put ourselves in the spotlight, just like Charcot's hysterics every Tuesday at the Salpêtrière. Quite a show, you know. If we can't have a story, let's perform. (*Pause*) Luce, you look tired.

Luce 2: I am tired. Or rather, we're tired. The performance is still on his stage, the props and the story are his. (*Reading*) "You imitate whatever comes close. You become whatever touches you. . . . Taking one model after another, passing from master to master, changing face, form, and language with each new power that dominates you" (210). As Audre says, the master's tools, the master's house... it just seems like there's no way out.[35] And there's no telling how they'll read us. Look what happened to those poor hysterics. So we perform, become the symptom of an aetiology, and then we simply disappear. And either way, the abuse continues.[36]

Pause. Faint light on the audience, then backstage. The stage remains dark.

Luce 2: What about the lips? Are they still hiding among us, here in the audience, backstage?

Luce 1: Ah yes, the lips. They're still here. But they're not just about pleasure, you know.

Luce 2: Sounds pretty pleasurable to me. All those wonderful, funny combinations: mouth to mouth, mouth to labia, labia to mouth, labia to labia, inner labia to outer labia, outer labia to mouth, outer to outer, inner to inner, outer to inner, to mouth, to labia... (*Reading*) "Doesn't that make you laugh?"[37]

Luce 1: Sure, it makes me laugh, and it's pleasurable too. But there's pain here as well.

Luce 2: Wait. Listen. The lips are speaking. From behind the scenes, moving across the stage, toward the other listening lips: we're here to hear them. Hear them, to speak our story, here, hear, to laugh with pleasure. That's what I call making love. Between us, the lips make love.

Luce 1: But in all that speaking and all that loving, the stage is still there. Even in darkness, the actors are set and ready to go, waiting to trap us as we start to move. And it's all there for his satisfaction, his happiness, his felicitous doctrine. His pleasure keeps us quiet, frozen. His blank, the "*semblant*," white blood.

Luce 2: Yes, I know. (*Reading*) "*Env(i)olées* into proper names." Violated by his words but, still, with words, taking flight toward something else, moving over and through and under the stage. Oh, how can I say it? Trapped in his "proper skins" to keep the meaning up, to keep those "dead skins" from drooping. His meaning is our blood, his *sens* is our *sang*, the blood of our lips for his show, his story. Our story? Gagged and raped. Our lips parted, "*écartées*," for him "they would have to stay apart." The word is our bond and our bondage: "the gag upon our lips."[38]

Luce 1: (*Sigh*) I know. But I still think there's hope. Remember catachresis? Like the "face" of a mountain or a "head" of cabbage. That's what our lips are. Impossible. What those eggheads call "an abuse of trope."[39] No way to say it, except as something it's not. Nonexistent on his stage, except in his image, as his "face" or his "head." So how can we say it? And yet we say it, our lips, together...

Luce 2: We're doing it now...

Luce 1: Well, you can never be certain. But, yeah, something's happening, some sort of shift. Backstage, and in the audience, speaking together. And look, the stage is still dark. Why should we continue to keep Man's play going? Avid spectators, devoted stagehands, mesmerized, working, doing anything for him.[40] For what? For his world, his stage, his knowledge, his pleasure? No. Let's get going, move our lips in another direction. No more lighting up his Truth on his stage. A different truth, listen...

Luce 2: OK, it sounds great. Let's move our lips. But how can we say it? I know, you're talking about love... funny, lesbian, outrageous love.[41] An ethics of lips, making love. (*Reading*) "entre nous: toute(s)... between us: all." "How can I say it?" "Entre nous: toute(s)." How can I say it? (*Reading*) "I love you." (*Pause*) But really: "I love you"? Have you ever heard such a trite cliché?[42]

Doesn't "I love you" just prop up his play? Give a face to his mountain? Turn a stupid vegetable into a talking head?

Luce 1: I know. It's inescapable. All those cabbage heads. But we can still say it, our lips, and hear them, differently, and then ask again about how to say it, and hear them, our lips, another way. Speaking, making love, with our lips. This is what happens when we get aroused: our lips fill with blood, turn red. (*Reading*) "While our lips are growing red again. They're stirring, moving, they want to speak" (212). It's the truth about us, together. That's what happens when we get excited. As lesbians, we're their blank, but when we speak together, we speak the truth about another pleasure and another love. And we break the silence of our violation. And their blank, white blood, becomes red. How can I say it, this impossible blank, like the blank of a mountain or a cabbage blank? Don Juan Austin would call it nonsense, the refusal to be blank, to be seduced by his promise. The refusal to hide the truth of our pain behind the curtain of his felicitous play.

Luce 2: But all the world's a stage... Listen, his play is starting again.

Luce 1: Yes, there they go. (*Loudly*) You may kiss the bride! (*Laughing*) But look, it's just a curtain, drooping and rising, the one that marks *his* stage.[43] *Read my lips*: another opening, another woman, red lips filling with blood, with other stories, with other lips to open...

Luce 2: Kiss me.

Luce 1: I thought you'd never ask. I love you.

Luce 2: (*Reading from This Sex*) "Two lips kissing two lips: openness is ours again. Our 'world.'"

Toward Another Model

From Lesbos to Montreal:
Brossard's Urban Fictions

Every journey conceals another journey within its lines: the
path not taken and the forgotten angle. These are the journeys I
wish to record. Not the ones I made, but the ones I might have
made or perhaps did make in some other place or time. I could
tell you the truth as you will find it in diaries and maps and
log-books. I could faithfully describe all that I saw and heard
and give you a travel book. You could follow it then, tracing
those travels with your finger, putting red flags where I went.

For the Greeks, the hidden life demanded invisible ink.
They wrote an ordinary letter and in between the lines set out
another letter, written in milk. The document looked innocent
enough until one who knew better sprinkled coal-dust over it.
What the letter had been no longer mattered; what mattered
was the life flaring up undetected . . .

till now.

—JEANETTE WINTERSON, *Sexing the Cherry*

Helen, my grandmother, lived to be 103 years old. Never remarrying
since her husband died more than 35 years before her death, she dined
and played bridge with the other elderly residents of the group facility
where she lived in Toledo, Ohio. It's funny how women endure. Like a
lesbian enclave, the place was virtually without men. I always thought

of this as some strange connection between us, a certain similarity between her home and mine, but one that would never be spoken. My grandmother never knew about me, nor will she ever read these lines. She never knew about the woman, my mother, who married her son, and who later came out as a lesbian, long before I did, when the going was rough and the stakes were high. Now, among the aunts and uncles and distant cousins, some know about us and whisper discreetly. Others, to be fair, are sympathetic. A few embrace us. But when you become a lesbian, you automatically get written out of someone's history. There is no branch there, for mother and daughter and the women we love, on the precious family tree.

Sometimes details, like trees and cousins, can bring you through detours to the heart of a matter. In one branch of the family we recently discovered the captain of a ship: a distant cousin, I believe. Not long ago my uncle found this cousin's logbook in my grandmother's safe. The travel log, dated 1811, recorded his movements, his thoughts, the food he ate, the weather he encountered, as he crossed the Atlantic. When my uncle sat down and plotted the ship's course from Dublin to New York he found, not surprisingly, that sailing ships never travel in straight lines. Although journeying from east to west, most days the boat traveled northeast to southwest or southeast to northwest. Some days it sailed backwards or scarcely changed its position at all. It moved erratically, like the lightning flare of a heart, pumping, flashing across an EKG monitor.

After more than a century of life, my grandmother's heart finally stopped beating. But I would like her rhythm to be recorded, just as the zigzagging motion of a ship was given pulse and flare again through my uncle's diligent tracings. And there are other journeys within those lines: the hidden lives that will not be recorded on my uncle's map or the family tree. These are the journeys I want to record.

Maps

We can conceive of a life lived, like we can a journey, as a game of connect the dots. Moments in experience, like points on a map, can be linked to reveal a pattern. The result is a network of beginnings, destinations, and bridges that only make sense when they are plotted against other visible cultural patterns. So if meanings assemble like flags on a map or letters on a page, how might a cartographer of the invisible proceed? In particular, how might a cartographer of lesbian history and culture plot the unrecorded movements of lesbian lives?

Let's look again at Winterson's parable about the Greek letter. She gives us a recipe for writing and reading the hidden life: one part milk, one part coal dust sprinkled, of course, by someone who knows what she's doing. Reading Winterson's description of the coded letter, I want the "life flaring up" to be subversive, lesbian, refusing invisibility and silence. But is it? Is lesbian writing like a secret message written in milk and made visible by those who know better? I can see it now:

Lesbian #1: Ah hah! Look what I found! An ancient letter!
Lesbian #2: Yeah, and it's sticky! I think I'll sprinkle it with coal dust! What do you think?
Lesbian #1: Go for it, babe. I have a good feeling about this one...
Lesbian #2: Hmmm, let's see... Yep, just as I suspected! A message from Sappho...
Lesbian #1: It takes one to know one...

Is secret communication the way of liberation? It's true that oppression forces people to be creative in finding alternative forms of expression.[1] But, *pace* Cixous,[2] I cringe at the thought of snapping a cartridge filled with milk into my fountain pen. I'd rather work at changing the conditions of our lives: we all deserve a pen, lots of paper, and a lifetime supply of ink. Besides, these days coal dust is hard to come by.

Still, I'm attracted to cultural myths, like the Sapphic one, about hushed secrets finding voice. Some days, for example, I dream of sailing away, like a good lesbian, to Lesbos. I'd bring my mother along, and together we'd plot our course back through some other history, some other time, to an alternative family origin. Gathering like sibyls to read the crumpled leaves strewn beneath the family tree, we'd map shapes and scenes of passion from the censored thoughts and silent scribblings lying there like unmailed letters. Casting off, we'd say goodbye to patriarchy and oppression: "farewell black continent of misery and suffering farewell ancient cities we are embarking for the shining radiant isles for the green Cytheras for the dark and gilded Lesbos."[3]

Of course, this kind of escapist vision in which I sometimes indulge is hardly new, as a whole lesbian separatist tradition can attest, to say nothing of a long line of lesbian and nonlesbian writers who celebrate some version of a Sapphic heritage.[4] Leaving the continent for the island is a frequently plotted route for those who find in Lesbos a symbol of political and cultural origins. As Judy Grahn puts it: "Sappho wrote to us from (this) island . . . to those of us holding Sappho in our mind's eye as *the* historic example both of Lesbianism and of Lesbian poetry, everything she represents lives on an island."[5]

If, for Grahn and others, Sappho is *the* historic example of lesbian life and lesbian writing, the move from the continent to the island is hardly surprising. However, isn't this pilgrimage to a Greek island another version of the secret milk-writing described by Winterson? Isn't this just a lesbian form of nostalgia?[6] Finding a lost island is like finding the lost lines of a letter: both function to constitute an exclusive community around the revelation of a secret. Again, we can ask this question: is this hidden, insular, coded communication the way of liberation? Do lesbians just need to get back to the island, to the source of our desire, to the milky place of our Sapphic mother?

If we answer, "No! That's not it!" and "No, again, that's still not it!" the problem becomes: so now what? If we agree that "every journey conceals another journey within its lines" (Winterson, 2), how do we trace that other journey without falling into the nostalgic trap of coded letters and secret islands? How do we map invisibility and silence? What is revealed, and what disappears in that mapping? The question is complex, as Adrienne Rich reminds us in her poem "Cartographies of Silence":

> Silence can be a plan
> rigorously executed
> the blueprint to a life
>
> It is a presence
> it has a history a form
>
> Do not confuse it
> with any kind of absence[7]

History and form go together: a game of connect the dots. Like bits of family history brought to light as a branch on a verdant tree, a certain version of lesbian history can assemble itself into a deceptively singular shape—a Greek letter, an island—that gives it cultural meaning. To ignore the island and the sticky letter would be to do what Rich warns us not to do: to erase the blueprint, to confuse silence with absence. But to remain stuck there isn't the answer either. Crucially, many lesbians will never find their way with that milky map. What do Sappho, Lesbos, and Greek culture represent, for example, for a lesbian of African descent? For the native people of North America? Indeed, the plotting of that journey back to ancient Greece not only fails to acknowledge other histories and other maps, but it has effaced the paths and cultural symbols through which those stories can be traced. Liberation means more than making maps from silence and giving shape to the invisible. What flares up as a flag on the map, and what is erased by that marker?

Rich's poem suggests that lesbian writing, like silence, has a history and a form, but its shape is dynamic, multilayered, and changing. Here I'm reminded of my uncle's discovery: sailing ships never travel in straight lines. Recording "the unrecorded"[8] can only be an erratic and complex undertaking; like history itself, lesbian lives might be seen as layers of journeys superimposed on a map thick with time. Lesbian writing cannot be a straight shot home to some Sapphic paradise: check the turn of the compass needle and watch the change of sails as the ship shifts direction to find the wind. There it is: another "path not taken," another "forgotten angle" (Winterson, 2).

My Map: Urban Fairies and Nicole Brossard

"Every journey conceals another journey within its lines": grandmothers hide logbooks and ships and sailors; lesbian daughters hide lesbian mothers; continents hide islands; silence hides the blueprint to a life, someone writing. Like every journey, every writing conceals another writing: behind Homer hides Sappho; behind Proust hides Colette; behind France and its literary canon hide Sénégal and Senghor, Martinique and Césaire, Guadeloupe and Condé, Québec and Hébert. Conversely, writ-

L'AMÈR
OU
LE CHAPITRE EFFRITÉ

Pour Lynne Huffer.
Au coeur de l'écriture
pour faire pencher la
réalité du côté de la
lumière.
Avec le bon souvenir
de notre rencontre

Nicole Brossard

30 octobre 1993
Montréal

Inscription on the title page of *L'Amèr,* from Nicole
Brossard to Lynne Huffer:

> For Lynne Huffer
>   At the heart of writing
>   to make reality bend
>   toward the side of light.
>   With the happy memory
>   of our meeting
>   Nicole Brossard

ing, flaring up, can make other writings disappear, just as new cities can violently efface old ones, as the conquest of continents makes abundantly clear. The flight of sailors into the uncharted azure may be the stuff of poems as well as family lore, but those expansive journeys are hardly innocent: poof! there goes a city, a civilization, an island.

I remember the light through the window, splashing the table, taking shape at the heart of writing:

Me: In *Aerial Letter* you talk about urbanity, and more precisely, of "urban radicals," urban women who write and publish. Do you feel that there is still a *Québecois* specificity to this radical urbanity?

Nicole Brossard: It is strange, but I have always felt that speaking and writing about Montreal is making a statement about being a North American of French descent. . . . I am from the city; I've always lived there; and I love the city and the freedom it allows even if it is dangerous for women. So I'm an urban radical. It's also a metaphor for me to say: I am a girl in combat in the city of men.[9]

After my conversation with Nicole Brossard, I met up with my friend Serene. We were there in Montreal, and we loved the image of girls in the city, with diaphanous wings and combat boots: "an urban radical," "a *fairy* in combat in the city of men." This translation of Brossard's metaphor was a mistake on my part, I was later to learn. She had said "*fille* en combat," not "*fée* en combat." Oh well, I thought, French is a language that is never mastered. I was embarrassed at my linguistic ineptitude; but to be honest, I was also... disappointed. I have to admit, I still want them to be fairies: urban fairies, in combat, in the city of men, "in this dark adored adorned gehenna" (Wittig, 15).

So I've been looking for a place for my fairy to live, and I think I've found it, right here in the city, in the pages of Brossard's *French Kiss*. As in kissing, so in speaking: it's never certain where those lips and swirling tongues will take you. Her lips pronounced *fille* and I heard *fée*, a fairy in "a forest smelling pungently of brick, cool green forest painted on a wall of brick."[10] I remember Brossard saying: "if each woman could project the best that she senses in herself onto other women, we would already have accomplished a lot" (Huffer, "Interview," 115–21). So that's how I became an urban fairy, projected by her, coming out into a forest painted cool and green. I was still myself, but I was also just a bit more than myself: braver, slightly larger, more expansive.

She was a sight to behold, this urban fairy I became, unfolding beyond the mirror Brossard was holding. She belonged to another dimension: magnified and armed to the hilt, not with milk and parchment, but with spray paint, a wand, and wings to take her spiraling up and down those walls. What a dyke! I perceived her clearly, moving "under the surface with wing-like texture to confront reality" (*French Kiss*, 92), writing her aerial letter for all to see.[11]

Graffiti-writing fairies may seem a long way off from secret letters and sailing ships, to say nothing of my grandmother from Toledo, Ohio. I can't help seeing the connections, though: family trees become urban forests, coal-sprinkled letters become graffiti-marked walls. How do we remember and record what is lost? Who is writing, and who is reading?

I'm still moving through the glass that Brossard holds before me: there, beneath the surface, where wings and wand turn to arc and spiral, people stand on platforms waiting for the trains to come. Their daily travels across the city reveal the writing on the walls, the places beneath the surface where meanings appear, like fairies coming out into an urban forest.

Which realities do we remember and choose to record? Brossard has written: "I am an urban woman on the graffiti side of the wall, on the sleepless side of night, on the free side of speech, on the side of writing where the skin is a fervent collector of dawns." And she continues: "I guess it is difficult for me to stay on the island because I am a woman of the written word" (quoted in Huffer, "Interview," 120). I keep imagining her, like my urban fairy, finding her home among the paint-scribbled walls of the city.

Brossard's Map: Lesbians in Montreal

> The mythic island is in me, in books, in the women with
> whom I surround myself. —NICOLE BROSSARD

In leaving the island behind, Brossard's urban radical also leaves behind the milk-writers and coal-dust-readers whose privilege allows them to construct for themselves an exclusionary world difficult to access, one that begins and ends with Greek culture. Unlike that private world of coded letters, Brossard's work should be imagined as "publicly fiction,"[12] kaleidoscopic layers of graffiti that illuminate an opening space of lesbian writing. Further, this contrast between Brossard's public urban fictions and a private Sapphic island represents more than just a difference in decor or geographical predilections. Unlike Brossard's Montreal, Lesbos functions symbolically both as a utopian escape and as a space of origins. In that sense, Brossard's oeuvre distinguishes itself from an entire Sapphic tradition of lesbian writing by demystifying nostalgia rather than celebrating it. In fact, most of Brossard's writing, in one way or another, uncovers and subverts the nostalgic structures through which a concept of origins is produced.

Focusing on the workings of nostalgia allows me to map Brossard's journey as a lesbian writer in relation to the concept of an originary blank space and, ultimately, to ask political questions about the subversive potential of her writing. From her earliest days as a poet, Brossard has rejected the nostalgic thinking that constructs an empty origin as the lost object of the poet's desire. As Karen Gould points out, for Brossard and others at the avant-garde journal *La Barre du jour* during the late 1960's, "to be modern meant to 'look lucidly into the hole'[13] and to refuse to fill it, rejecting the lure of myth, ideology, and nostalgia" (Gould, 58). Brossard's early work explores the space of that unfilled hole by inscribing, within literature, literature's own dissolution. Confronted with a blank origin that refuses to hold a content, the poetic subject disappears into the movement of the work itself; both subject and object disappear, and all that remains is the pure desire that brings the work into being.

By the mid-1980's, Brossard's critique of nostalgic thinking had moved from fundamentally aesthetic questions to more explicitly political concerns related to her identity as a woman and as a feminist. Commenting on the influence of Blanchot, his concept of neutrality,[14] and the notion of literature as a subjectless space of dissolution, Brossard explains this shift in her thinking:

Blanchot was very important to me. What was involved in the question of neutrality was the white space, which was linked to the question of ecstacy, to the present, the place where the "I" is dispersed to make room for the science of being, its contemplation. Neutrality also meant putting a halt to lyricism and to romanticism, to inspiration, in the ways in which I of course understood these words. Needless to say, neutrality was undoubtedly a fine displacement allowing me to forget that I was a woman, that is to say that I belonged to that category of non-thinkers. Feminist consciousness would de-neutralize me.[15]

Just as Brossard found she could no longer forget she was a woman, so the identity politics of writing as a lesbian became increasingly important. That recognition gives birth to the "girl in combat in the city," the "urban radical,"[16] and the "fabular subject."[17] Brossard rejects the structure of origins that produces "woman" and, in so doing, also questions the nostalgic thinking that produces Lesbos as home of the True Lesbian. As Brossard puts it in reference to the girl in combat in the city:

She is the product of a choice that I make which is to stay in the *polis* in order to confront patriarchal meaning instead of retiring to the mythic island of the Amazons, whose subtext to me is peace and harmony, while the subject for *la cité* is the law (not harmony), the written word (not the song), and constant change. The mythic island is in me, in books, and in the women with whom I surround myself. ("Interview," 120)

So while Brossard's "urban radical" doesn't explicitly reject Lesbos and Sappho as empowering cultural symbols, she isn't about to catch the next boat to lesbian paradise either. "I am a woman of the here and now," she says. Brossard begins where she finds herself: in Montreal, on the North American continent, in the material world. That world is plagued with misery and pain, "*the silence of bodies elongated by hunger, fire, dogs, the bite of densities of torture*" (*Lovhers*, 99); but, that same world also offers hope, possibility, and the creative desire that brings an affirmation of life, "like the ultimate vitality and wisdom" (106).

Brossard not only anchors herself in a city, on a continent, and in a world heavy with the baggage of history and tradition; through her writing she continually creates another city, another continent, and another world as well. Grounded in the reality of the everyday, Brossard's project is also visionary, virtual, aerial. "I am a woman of the here and now, fascinated with the virtual that exists in the species" ("Interview,"

120). Thus, while she grounds herself in her own identity—"I am still Nicole Brossard, born in Montreal, with a sense of the history of Quebec and of belonging in that French part of the North American continent" ("Interview," 115)—she also creates the virtual figure of *"MA continent"* (*Amantes*, 105), an intuitive dream of a lesbian body as light, lucidity, and transformation. But even in that projection of an opening lesbian space—"(mâ) it's a space/an hypothesis" (*Lovhers*, 105)[18]—the lesbian continent is still grounded in the gravity and the weight of the everyday world:

> *my continent woman* of all the spaces
> cortex and flood: a sense of gravity
> *bringing me into the world.*
> (*Lovhers*, 106)

Similarly, in *French Kiss*, the protagonists are anchored in Montreal and, to a large extent, are part of an infinitely layered, virtual Montreal, "glowing volatile in darkness" (*French Kiss*, 11) among the "illuminated cities issued from the method of writing."[19] Like the characteristically Brossardian hologram, the surface of the city contains other pictures, exposes deeper three-dimensional realities within itself. The city contains the multiplicity of the memories of its inhabitants: "Memory makes itself plural, essential like the vertigo precursor of an aerial vision. . . . So I come to imagine myself hologram, real, virtual, three-dimensional in the necessity of a coherent light (*Lettre*, 43, 83; my translation). Just as a three-dimensional image allows multiple surfaces to appear, so memory can become plural, synchronic, holographic. One reality doesn't replace the other; rather, they coexist: Homer and Sappho; the French and British empires and the province of Québec; the lives of Montreal and those of Caughnawaga.[20]

"What's left for our story is to break up and be lost. Caughnawaga's underbrush. *Expenditure* for a sign" (*French Kiss*, 122). Holographic writing reveals not only the virtual possibilities of future stories and future paths, but also uncovers the breakup and loss of stories that form the fabric of past identities and past histories. In the holographic image, both memory and possible futures are pluralized. This Brossardian logic of the hologram exposes a political aspect of nostalgic origin myths.

The nostalgic gesture—to create an empty originary place and give it a content—falsely and imperialistically starts from the premise that the space for that content was in fact empty to begin with.

On the surface, the hologram may seem similar to the nostalgic myth. When the holographic picture comes into focus, something flares up but something else slips out of sight, just as the identity of the nostalgic son makes the mother disappear. However, unlike the complementary parts—subject and object, son and mother—of a nostalgic structure, every part of a holographic plate also contains an image of the whole; thus each fragment contains what is real, already there, or in the background, as well as what is virtual, possible, and waiting to be seen. When something flares up and something else disappears, that shift occurs because of a change in focus. So unlike the binary logic of presence and absence underlying the nostalgic gesture, the hologram allows for a synthesis of the multiple layers of realities and fictions contained within it.

Let's take the urban radical again as an example. Grounded in the city, she is a potential victim of rape, injustice, discrimination, and violence. But she is also, simultaneously, projected toward the realm of invented possibilities: another mythic figure, she is the lucid lesbian, "ma continent femme" (*Amantes*, 106) coming into expression. Similarly, the city she inhabits and reconfigures is not just the reality of modern-day Montreal. The urban landscape that appears is a present-day Montreal thick with histories to be uncovered and, simultaneously, a virtual Montreal to be imagined and created. Brossard's metaphor of holographic writing points to the layered meanings, like the textured surfaces of graffiti on city walls, inscribed in the trace of pen on paper: that trace is the mark that says "someone was here" and the opening path toward an "unrecorded thought" (*Lovhers*, 17) waiting to be imagined, waiting to be written.

How can the grounding mark and the virtual path coexist *in writing*? Comparing writing to holograms, Brossard imagines that "sentences," like holographic fragments, "might also contain the whole of what is at stake in a novel" ("Interview," 117). So what *is* at stake in Brossard's writing? Again, to begin with, what is at stake for *me* (I want to say *us*, but my friend Carla won't let me) is the undoing of nostalgic structures. This core of Brossard's work can be examined not just conceptually, but also, more fundamentally, in the particular textured surfaces of the writing itself. In nostalgic writing, when something flares up something else is covered over; when the Greek letter is sprinkled with coal dust, the blank of its milky origin disappears. In contrast, Brossard's holographic metaphor suggests that a single sentence of her writing would contain: first, the visible lines of the original letter; second, the lines in between, in their manifestation both as milk and coal; and third, a plurality of other lines tracing other lives lived and other potential lives. It would open up multiple origins and multiple futures. It would invite inclusive communities of readers and writers instead of shutting out all but an educated, Eurocentric elite. So the question remains: does she pull it off? And if so, what does this have to do with lesbian writing?

To begin answering these questions, let's take Montreal in *French Kiss* as an example: "What's left for our story is to break up and be lost. Caughnawaga's underbrush. *Expenditure* for a sign." The final page of *French Kiss* suggests that writing requires an "expenditure": "*expenditure* for a sign." That expenditure of writing uncovers a reality by naming what is there and at the same time creates a layered vision of a past and future city. But in addition to naming and creating a fictional reality called Montreal, the expenditure of writing also produces a reserve, an excess called Caughnawaga that the name "Montreal" cannot contain: "Leaving the city, now, by Route 2, heading for the Mercier Bridge. Its rusty old steel and worn white lines. Out of line. The blackness of the blue. The river and the Caughnawaga *Reserve*" (*French Kiss*, 110).

So how does Caughnawaga function as the excess and reserve of the writing of Montreal in *French Kiss*? On a historical level, when Brossard alludes to Caughnawaga, she exposes the "reserve" of native peoples on which a "North American of French descent" identity depends. When that identity was "founded" in 1535 with Jacques Cartier's arrival at the Saint Lawrence River, the blank space on which that founding was inscribed, in fact, wasn't blank at all. Someone was already there: "Montreal surface and totems: 'And in the middest of those fieldes is the sayd citie of Hochelaga, placed neere, and as it were ioyed to a great mountaine that is tilled round about, very fertill, on the toppe of which you may see very farre'" (*French Kiss*, 122).[21]

Brossard's citation of Cartier's journal exposes a deeper reality beneath the surface of Montreal. Hochelaga was the city Cartier "discovered" when he traveled up the river in search of a mythical land of gold and jewels called the Kingdom of Saguenay. Standing at the site of modern-day Montreal, Hochelaga was home to more than a thousand people who were part of an extensive group of tribes known as the Saint Lawrence Iroquoians. What we know of the Hochelagans comes from Cartier's notebooks and the speculations of scholars who have gathered evidence and unearthed artifacts, thereby mapping their own versions of the history of the Saint Lawrence Valley. Most agree that Hochelaga was probably a walled city, that its inhabitants lived and worked in longhouses, and that they subsisted primarily on the planting and harvesting of corn. The arrival of the French most likely drew them into the economy of the fur trade, as it did other native tribes like the Algonquin, the Montagnais, the Mahican, the Abenaki, the Sokoki, and the Iroquois. Exactly what happened to Hochelaga after the beginning of the European invasion in the sixteenth century will probably never be known with certainty. By the turn of the seventeenth century, however, the Hochelagans had disappeared.[22]

So "what's left . . . for our story," for history? What's left is Montreal and Caughnawaga: a French-founded city, and a space outside it designated for the descendants of the native people who survived that founding. What's left for the writing of reality and fiction is the breakup, loss, and symbolic reconstruction of lives lived, of "villages scrambled in the ink of history" (*French Kiss*, 110). In the nostalgic model, the map of French history and culture needs the blank page of its writing: Hochelaga "disappears" and French history moves on. Nostalgic memory would therefore found Montreal on an originary blank, an empty space to be conquered and inscribed with a French identity. In contrast, Brossard's holographic, graffiti memory exposes the real and symbolic violence that produces the illusion of that originary blank. Reading *French Kiss* is like deciphering the many coats of scrawl that collect as graffiti on subway walls. That graffiti becomes holographic: layers of paint simultaneously come into focus as the many faces of

Montreal-Hochelaga. To ignore those layers is to repeat the violence that both replaced Hochelaga with Montreal and produced the "reserve" called Caughnawaga. "For your whole life," Brossard writes, "you will remember the graffiti in the subway, my only daughter."[23] That uniquely Brossardian graffiti contains the "frescoes, multiple in the prism" (*These Our Mothers*, 29) that trace the invisible: mapping, as Rich puts it, "the blueprint to a life" (*Dream*, 17).

More Maps

Does Brossard succeed in dismantling the logic of presence and absence at the heart of nostalgia and writing? I would like to think of her work as another kind of lesbian writing that is not just *by* a lesbian or *about* lesbians, but explores the very processes through which people and their stories are made invisible. Such a writing would think about Hochelagans as well as lesbians; and it would tell a story, as in *French Kiss*, not just of woman-loving tongues swirling in mouths but also of the genocidal "kiss" of death that is the legacy of the mapmakers, fur-trappers, conquerors, and colonizers of this planet. In addition, such a writing would not just replace one story with another, but would re-structure the very logic of replacement, reconfiguring the relation between the writing subject and the reserve on which the writing depends. In that sense, this other kind of "lesbian" writing might come to name a thick, holographic, urban poetry in which reality, fiction, and utopia would coexist.

But what would it look like, exactly? Ah, there she would be: "The generic body would become the expression of woman and woman would have wings above all, she'd make (a) sign" (*Picture Theory*, 154). Yes, she might disappear for a while, but then I would see her, my urban fairy, tracing spirals of graffiti up and down the walls. A holographic projection—"woman and woman would have wings above all"—there she (and I) would be "plunged into the centre of the city, I would dream of raising my eyes. FEMME SKIN TRAJECTOIRE. *Donna lesbiana* dome of knowledge and helix, already I'd have entered into a spiral and my being of air aerial urban would reproduce itself in the glass city like an origin" (*Picture Theory*, 154). There she, and I, would be. We would find each other through the words in their reading, and there we would be: a "being of air aerial urban," reproducing ourselves "*like* an origin," but already changing, spiraling elsewhere.

This reading can only happen, at least for me, in the form of a conditional: it would tell a story... and it would look like this... and there, can't you see?, we (or perhaps just I) would be... That conditional reading, like the hologram, is always there, waiting to be read, waiting to flare up like a flag on a map. But beyond that conditional, more explicitly political questions remain.

What does Brossard's writing say or do for lesbian politics? How does her urban radical work for feminism? Where is the link between the memory of Hochelaga and the contemporary struggles of native people in North America? Does the writing itself function as the kind of public fiction that the theory proclaims? Indeed, one of the most commonly heard complaints about Brossard's writing is that it is opaque and inaccessible, that it speaks to an audience of educated elites who have in common a practice and a way of thinking. Who is reading her, and to whom is she writing? Do her complex urban fictions really speak like graffiti on a subway wall?

What *is* at stake in her writing? Perhaps that question, more than any other, contains the seeds of my impatience at the difficulty of Brossard's writing. We all live in one world, but privilege allows some of us to choose a room of our own from among many possible worlds. Brossard lives in an urban room filled with fractals, holograms, and virtual realities. And I know that she from her room, as I from mine, wants the world to heal. But who among us can hear her? Some of us need narrative and the prose of preachers, not translucent letters in a metaphorical cyberspace. To be sure, I deeply respect and admire Brossard's holographic writings. But I long for stories that my mother might hear.

"And now," says Winterson, stepping out from the wings backstage, "swarming over the earth with our tiny insect bodies and putting up flags and building houses, it seems that all the journeys are done" (88). Alas, we long for stories, but it seems that there are no more earthly places to travel. The world is mapped: there are no more journeys and no more stories to tell. "Not so," I hear, and it's Winterson speaking again (88). But it could just as easily be Brossard, saying, "Not so! Not so! See, here's another layer of graffiti, another aerial letter!" OK, I think, so let's look again.

Something's happening beneath the surface waiting to be noted and marked. It could be my mother, proud, with her lover, on a wide leafy branch of the family tree. It could be my grandmother's century-old heart, beating again to the rhythm of my cousin's ship, or measuring time across my uncle's chart. It could be other rhythms and other lives uncovered, stories whose lines on my particular map might only be obvious to me. Who knows what patterns I'll end up tracing? Who knows what I'll end up saying?

More important, who knows what *we'll* choose to say and do? As Brossard puts it, "*I* speak to an *I* to ensure the permanence of the *we*. If I don't take on that which says *we* in *me*, the essence of what I am will have no longevity but the time of one life, mine, and that's too short for us" (*Lettre*, 97; my translation). I think Brossard is one of those cartographers of an invisible *I* who speaks from the heart of an invisible *we*. The line of that *we* runs parallel with mine, for a moment, perhaps, but it also stretches away behind and before me. Of course, we have to constantly ask the question: who are *we*? For Brossard that asking is part of the struggle. Nothing is given from the start, especially not the origin of an identity. The *we* can only find itself in the effort and the struggle of the searching.

In that sense Brossard is a mapmaker, working for liberation, who can help us pull ourselves together and find our way when we're lost in the forest or adrift at sea. And if it's true that all the journeys aren't done, perhaps it's also true that new maps and new discoveries don't have to efface old ones. "Round and flat," Winterson says, "only a very little has been discovered" (88). So perhaps Brossard can help us to make different maps and different journeys "toward the idea of a future, another shore" ("Interview," 121). And perhaps that future will bring healing to the places erased in violence, uncovering sedimented histories and shifting forms in the spaces on the map where there was never absence, just a "rigorously executed" silence.

Feminist Futures

Maternal pasts, feminist futures: where do we go from here? This book has examined the relations between nostalgia, gender, and foundational systems of meaning through a critique of the notion of the lost mother as a ground for thinking about sexual difference. But if we jettison the lost mother as ground, with what can we replace her? That question indicates a threshold between the critical, deconstructive impulse of much of contemporary feminist theory and the more difficult, constructive work that is absolutely vital for a truly transformative feminism. As Irigaray, Butler, and many others have shown, gender can indeed be ungrounded from its traditional epistemological and ontological moorings: in that ungrounding, "man" and "woman" are revealed to be fictions, performative repetitions determined by a binary, heteronormative system of gender identities. But how do we move from that moment of ungrounding toward a constructive feminist vision and practice?

To begin with, we can move in the direction of ethics, which I define as moral reflection on the quality of our social interactions. I have made a plea throughout these pages for a serious reconsideration of ethical concerns, questions that, in my view, have not been adequately addressed by feminist theoretical projects involved in the ungrounding of gender. To be sure, there is a large body of theory that examines issues of morality, justice, and ethics in relation to gender, feminism, and the politics of difference.[1] Carol Gilligan's empirical investigations of female moral development mark the beginning of a growing, transdisciplinary field of feminist work on the "ethics of care," where a female-oriented ethical model of connectedness, interdependency, and maternal caregiving replaces the paradigmatic masculine ideal of autonomy and independence. Following Gilligan, Seyla Benhabib's work on the relations between gender, postmodernism, and contemporary moral theory constitutes an exemplary model for the systematic elaboration of a feminist ethical system. Benhabib draws on a number of traditional sources, including Aristotle, Kant, Rawls, and Habermas, as well as Gilligan's ethics of care, in order to theorize a normative ethical system that also takes seriously the particular differences of historically situated subjects.

Benhabib criticizes the extreme forms of relativism that characterize contemporary feminist theories in which meaning is destabilized and selves are fragmented, because those theories elide any possibility of making normative claims about justice and ethics. Drawing on Habermas's theory of communicative action, Benhabib contends that in a truly participatory democracy we must all take part in generating the norms which govern our moral and ethical life. Benhabib further argues that two universal constraints must always be in place to allow a conversation around the table to occur: (1) respect for others, or universal respect, and (2) a willingness to listen, or egalitarian reciprocity. To be sure, Benhabib recognizes that the very process of getting to the table and having a voice at all can be difficult and complicated for those who have been delegitimized by an oppressive system. In that context, Benhabib calls for a moral theory that recognizes both a "generalized" and a "concrete" other, the former expressing the right of every human being to universal respect, and the latter recognizing the intimate, particularistic aspects of human relationships traditionally associated with the female sphere, relationships that feminists have theorized as an ethics of care. Benhabib argues that both concepts—the generalized other and the concrete other, a concept of justice and a concept of care—must exist if there is to be a viable and inclusive system of ethical norms.

Although Benhabib locates herself within the discipline of political philosophy, her theory of a generalized and concrete other is extremely useful for thinking more expansively about the relationship between the ungrounding of gender and a constructive feminist vision for the future. Indeed, Benhabib's recognition of the importance of universal ethical ideals *and* the claims of the particular provides a normative frame for thinking about difference across the trajectory mapped by this book: from nostalgia to ethics, from the mother to a nonmaternal other.

So what exactly is the relationship between the critique of nostalgia at the center of this project and Benhabib's ethical model? First, there is a nostalgic component to most formulations of a feminist ethics of care, and Benhabib's model is no exception. The "different voice" that emerges in an ethics of care is usually some version of a maternal voice. For example, Benhabib asserts that "women in their capacities as primary caregivers have had to exercise insight into the claims of the particular" (14). Like other theorists of an ethics of care, Benhabib complements traditional moral theories with the "different" morality of maternally coded behaviors and values, associating her concept of the concrete other with the "private sphere" (14) where children are mothered.

Not surprisingly, this association of the particular with a maternal sphere has the potential of repeating the problems of a nostalgic structure: the critique of nostalgia with which this book begins is also, philosophically speaking, a critique of any originary system of meaning that is purportedly "neutral," generalizable, or universal. If we accept that critique, the maternalization of the concrete other has a similarly reductive and neutralizing potential, threatening the very particularity that Benhabib claims is essential for a truly inclusive ethical theory. In other words, the gesture of identifying the concrete other of an ethics of care with a maternal origin runs the risk of leading us right back into the same old trap of nostalgic thinking. In that trap, the specificity of difference, figured as the mother, is that system's excluded other. It matters little whether the philosophical system in which that analogical reduction occurs is epistemological, ontological, aesthetic, or ethical. In every case, the maternal other denies the possibility of true alterity, collapsing copy into model and bringing us, as Irigaray has shown, to a repetition of the hegemonic masculine "same."

This recognition of the problems inherent in maternal thinking does not mean that we should give up altogether on the insights of a feminist ethics of care. Rather, the trajectory traced here between nostalgia and ethics points to the need for a fuller articulation of the concept of an ethical other. Indeed, there is much work to be done. How do we take seriously the claims of antifoundationalism, of which Butler is the paradigmatic feminist example, and also take seriously Benhabib's concerns about moral constraints and ethical norms?[2]

That question brings me to the ethical horizon that marks the end of this book and a beginning from which to construct different feminist futures. One of Benhabib's crucial insights into feminist ethics is the connection she establishes between the concrete other and the narratives that articulate the claims of the particular. Benhabib argues that while postmodernism destabilizes the "grand narratives" of the Western tradition, this does not necessitate doing away with narrative altogether. Rather, the concrete other demands the recognition of what Jean-François Lyotard calls the "petits récits," the "small narratives" that speak the truths of particular people traditionally relegated to the domestic sphere or to history's unknowable margins.[3] Benhabib also draws on Hannah Arendt's association of the moral capacity to judge with the retrospective faculty of culling meaning from the past, thereby highlighting the importance of narrative for ethical life.[4] Our capacity for memory, Arendt contends, is essential to the art of storytelling, and our ability both to hear and tell stories is central to our existence as moral beings.

Benhabib's reading of Lyotard and Arendt suggests that there is a profound connection between storytelling and judgment, narrative and ethics. Further, this connection between narrative and ethics contrasts dramatically with Butler's assertion that "performance may preempt narrative as the scene of gender production."[5] To give due credit to Butler, her implicit rejection of narrative is based on the psychoanalytic insights into the illusory nature of narrative coherence as a foundation for an equally illusory coherent identity. Those insights, along with the more general postmodern critique of the rational Enlightenment subject, must continue to be taken seriously. However, Butler's outright dismissal of narrative is both politically and theoretically problematic. Without performance, Butler implies, there are no "men" and there are no "women." Although that may be true in a limited, ahistorical sense,

I would argue that Butler misses a crucial point about the ways in which identities are constructed in history. Without narrative, there is no possibility of culling meaning from the past, much less of constructing narratives to guide us toward the future. While performativity rejects the illusory trap of nostalgia, it enters into the equally illusory trap of an eternal present without narrative, without memory, without a past, without a future. And as Arendt convincingly argues, without access to a past from which we draw meaning, we can never live as ethical, future-oriented beings.

So the question becomes: how can we theorize an ethical other without naïvely recreating the illusion of narrative coherence so effectively debunked by the postmodern critique of the Enlightenment? This is precisely where work in literary theory can productively ally itself with philosophy and political theory. Indeed, although Benhabib's concept of the concrete other is crucial for feminist ethical theory, she remains wedded to the illusion of narrative unity that Butler and others have critiqued. For Benhabib, the coherence of a self's identity is revealed through the unity of her life story: "The self is both the teller of tales and that about whom tales are told. The individual with a coherent sense of self-identity is the one who succeeds in integrating these tales and perspectives into a meaningful life history" (198).

But how do we approach life histories in which this successful integration of self and story fails to occur? How do we account for gaps in communication, the sphere of the irrational, or the violent obliteration of subjectivity if we work within the frame of Benhabib's model? More broadly, how do we theorize narrative incoherence and subjective fragmentation within an ethical frame? Because of her reliance on the rational discourse model provided by Habermas, Benhabib does not attend to these questions.[6] Benhabib envisions a table where everyone wants to and is able to talk, and where all of the voices will be rational and coherent. A student in my graduate seminar on feminist theory illustrated the blind spots of this vision by describing the relationship between the former generals of a murderous dictatorship and the families of the disappeared in her home country of Argentina. In the context of such a table, the image of a rational, coherent, consensus-building conversation among equals becomes ludicrous. As a rational conversation among coherent selves, Benhabib's ethical ideal fails to attend to questions of power and the realities of oppression, silence, marginalization, and violence.

The future of feminist ethics, then, lies in the elaboration of a bridge between the moral commitments represented by Benhabib and the fractured realities of our past and present lives. The narratives we generate to speak those realities may be far from coherent, rational, or unified. As Cathy Caruth has demonstrated in her work on trauma and narrative, the traumatic events which we are ethically called to remember are often the events that remain inaccessible to memory and therefore resistant to narrativization.[7] Yet this hardly means we should stop speaking our stories, however fragmented, indirect, and displaced they might be. Nor should we stop listening, even if what we are hearing is silence.[8] As narratives are woven around those unspoken places shattered by violence and we learn to speak in many different voices, we also must learn how to hear differently, to open ourselves to what remains in those spaces locked in silence.

Our ethical challenge is to hear both the voice and the silence of the other. If we meet that challenge, our narratives of the past will grow deeper and more complex. Our collective memory will become, in Nicole Brossard's terms, plural, multilayered, holographic. If nostalgia gave us a model of memory and relation based on annihilation and replacement, ethics will give us a model of mutual reciprocity and coexistence. Further, the narrative threads that link us to a past whose meanings are crucial to our ethical life will also empower us to articulate a future, to move toward what Drucilla Cornell calls a collective responsibility "to re-imagine our forms of life" (*Feminist Contentions*, 79). So if nostalgia gave us the static *blueprint* of a future by pulling us back into a lost paradise, ethics will provide us with the *constraints* of a future whose contours remain unknowable. If nostalgia was closed, unidimensional, and homogeneous, ethics will be open, dialogic, heterogeneous. Finally, if nostalgia gave us the flattening of differences into sameness, ethics will give us the irreducible difference of another woman: sister... lover... lesbian mother... who knows what our feminist futures might call her?

Reference Matter

Mom

1. Luce Irigaray, "And the One Doesn't Stir Without the Other," trans. Hélène Vivienne Wenzel, *Signs: Journal of Women in Culture and Society* 7/1 (1981): 67.

2. Nicole Brossard, *These Our Mothers, Or: The Disintegrating Chapter*, trans. Barbara Godard (Toronto: Coach House Press, 1983), 13.

3. See Monique Wittig and Sande Zeig, *Lesbian Peoples: Material for a Dictionary*, trans. Wittig and Zeig (New York: Avon Books, 1979).

Introduction

1. Simone de Beauvoir, *The Second Sex*, trans. Howard Madison Parshley (New York: Random House, 1952), 166.

2. "The linguistic entity is not accurately defined until it is *delimited*, i.e. separated from everything that surrounds it on the phonic chain. These delimited entities or units stand in opposition to each other in the mechanism of language" (103). Along the same lines, Saussure speaks of the value of the word as never "fixed": "one must also compare it [the value] with similar values, with other words that stand in opposition to it. Its content is really fixed only by the concurrence of everything that exists outside it" (115). See Ferdinand de Saussure, *Course in General Linguistics*, trans. Wade Baskin (New York: Philosophical Library, 1959).

3. "In actuality the relation of the two sexes is not quite like that of two electrical poles, for the man represents both the positive and the neutral, as is indicated by the common use of *man* to designate human beings in general; whereas woman represents only the negative, defined by limiting criteria, without reciprocity" (Beauvoir, *The Second Sex*, xviii).

4. For an influential work that attempts to recuperate the maternal sphere in order to highlight its positive cultural and political value, see Sara Ruddick's *Maternal Thinking: Toward a Politics of Peace* (Boston: Beacon Press, 1989). While I recognize the political and psychological reasons for this reversal of the dom-

inant patriarchal script, my argument in this book points to the limitations of such an approach. For a more nuanced consideration of motherhood, see Adrienne Rich, *Of Woman Born: Motherhood as Experience and Institution* (New York: Norton, 1976).

5. Richard Klein, "In the Body of the Mother," *Enclitic* 7/1 (1983): 68.

6. Jeanette Winterson, *Sexing the Cherry* (New York: Random House, 1989), 88.

7. As Elizabeth Abel puts it in a useful summary of this trend: "The excavation of buried plots in women's texts has revealed an enduring, if recessive, narrative concern with the story of mothers and daughters—with the 'lost tradition,' as the title of one anthology names it, or, in psychoanalytic terminology, with the 'pre-Oedipal' relationship, the early symbiotic female bond that both predates and coexists with the heterosexual orientation toward the father and his substitutes" (163). See Elizabeth Abel, "Narrative Structure(s) and Female Development," in *The Voyage In: Fictions of Female Development*, ed. Abel, Marianne Hirsch, and Elizabeth Langland (Hanover, N.H.: University Press of New England, 1983), 161–85. Prominent examples of the feminist articulation of a female-authored literary tradition to counter a paternal genealogy include Cathy N. Davidson and E. M. Broner, eds., *The Lost Tradition: Mothers and Daughters in Literature* (New York: Frederick Ungar, 1980); Mary Ellman, *Thinking About Women* (New York: Harcourt, Brace and World, 1968); Sandra Gilbert and Susan Gubar, *The Madwoman in the Attic: The Woman Writer and the Nineteenth-Century Literary Imagination* (New Haven, Conn.: Yale University Press, 1984); Ellen Moers, *Literary Women* (New York: Anchor Books, 1977); Elaine Showalter, *A Literature of Their Own* (Princeton, N.J.: Princeton University Press, 1977); and Patricia Meyer Spacks, *The Female Imagination* (New York: Avon Books, 1972). For a bibliographical essay covering this feminist celebration of the mother through 1981, see Marianne Hirsch, "Mothers and Daughters," *Signs: Journal of Women in Culture and Society* 7/1 (1981): 200–222. Also see Marianne Hirsch, *The Mother/Daughter Plot: Narrative, Psychoanalysis, Feminism* (Bloomington: Indiana University Press, 1989). For an example of the ongoing influence of this approach, see Maryline Lukacher, *Maternal Fictions: Stendhal, Sand, Rachilde, and Bataille* (Durham, N.C.: Duke University Press, 1994).

8. For an important early essay, see Peggy Kamuf, "Writing Like a Woman," in *Women and Language in Literature and Society*, ed. Sally McConnell-Ginet, Ruth Borker, and Nelly Furman (New York: Praeger, 1980), 284–99. For a canonical articulation of the differences between deconstructive and non-deconstructive approaches to gender, see the debate between Peggy Kamuf

("Replacing Feminist Criticism," 42–47) and Nancy K. Miller ("The Text's Heroine: A Feminist Critic and Her Fictions," 48–53) in *Diacritics* 12 (1982). Also see the reprise of this debate: Peggy Kamuf and Nancy K. Miller, "Parisian Letters: Between Feminism and Deconstruction," in *Conflicts in Feminism*, ed. Marianne Hirsch and Evelyn Fox Keller (New York: Routledge, 1990), 121–33.

9. See especially Janice Doane and Devon Hodges, *Nostalgia and Sexual Difference: The Resistance to Contemporary Feminism* (New York: Methuen, 1987). Doane and Hodges examine nostalgia as "a frightening antifeminist impulse" (xiii) in the works of male writers who "construct their visions of a golden past to authenticate woman's traditional place and to challenge the outspoken feminist criticisms of it" (3). Although Doane and Hodges acknowledge the danger of nostalgic models in feminist works as well (they cite, for example, Gilbert and Gubar's appropriation of Harold Bloom's paradigm of continuity and influence as "a nostalgic search for origins" [92]), their analysis differs significantly from mine in its focus on male, antifeminist reactions to feminist writing. One of the most incisive critiques of feminist nostalgia remains Mary Jacobus's "Freud's Mnemonic: Women, Screen Memories, and Feminist Nostalgia," in *Women and Memory*, ed. Margaret A. Lourie, Domna C. Stanton, and Martha Vicinus, a special issue of *Michigan Quarterly Review* 26 (1987): 117–39; reprinted in Mary Jacobus, *First Things: Reading the Maternal Imaginary* (New York: Routledge, 1995), 1–22. Also see Donna Jeanne Haraway's postmodern, antinostalgic dream of a cyborg world "without genesis, . . . without end" (174–75), in "A Manifesto for Cyborgs: Science, Technology, and Socialist Feminism in the 1980's," in *Coming to Terms: Feminism, Theory, and Politics*, ed. Elizabeth Weed (New York: Routledge, 1989), 173–204. Also see Mary Ann Doane's response to Haraway's antinostalgic argument, "Cyborgs, Origins, and Subjectivity," in *Coming to Terms*, 209–14. For other examples of critiques of feminist nostalgia, see Lynne Huffer, "Inscribing a Gendered *Auctoritas*: Colette's Maternal Model," in *Another Colette: The Question of Gendered Writing* (Ann Arbor: University of Michigan Press, 1992), 15–44; Carla Kaplan, "Reading Feminist Readings: Recuperative Reading and the Silent Heroine of Feminist Criticism," in *Listening to Silences: New Essays in Feminist Criticism*, ed. Elaine Hedges and Shelley Fisher Fishkin (New York: Oxford University Press, 1994), 168–94; and Susan S. Lanser, "Feminist Criticism, 'The Yellow Wallpaper,' and the Politics of Color in America," *Feminist Studies* 15/3 (1989): 415–41.

10. See especially Jane Gallop, *The Daughter's Seduction: Feminism and Psychoanalysis* (Ithaca, N.Y.: Cornell University Press, 1982) and *Thinking Through the Body* (New York: Columbia University Press, 1988); Hirsch, *The Mother/Daughter*

Plot; Alice Jardine, *Gynesis: Configurations of Woman and Modernity* (Ithaca, N.Y.: Cornell University Press, 1985); Barbara Johnson, *A World of Difference* (Baltimore: Johns Hopkins University Press, 1987); Ann Rosalind Jones, "Writing the Body: Toward an Understanding of *l'écriture féminine*," in *Feminist Criticism: Essays on Women, Literature, and Theory*, ed. Elaine Showalter (New York: Pantheon, 1985), 361–77; Peggy Kamuf, *Signature Pieces: On the Institution of Authorship* (Ithaca, N.Y.: Cornell University Press, 1988); Toril Moi, *Sexual/Textual Politics: Feminist Literary Theory* (London: Routledge, 1985); Nancy K. Miller, *Subject to Change: Reading Feminist Writing* (New York: Columbia University Press, 1988); Naomi Schor, *Breaking the Chain: Women, Theory, and French Realist Fiction* (New York: Columbia University Press, 1985) and *Reading in Detail: Aesthetics and the Feminine* (New York: Methuen, 1987); and Domna C. Stanton, "Language and Revolution: The Franco-American Dis-Connection," in *The Future of Difference*, ed. Hester Eisenstein and Alice Jardine (Boston: G. K. Hall, 1980), 73–87. Also see the articles in *Feminist Readings: French Texts / American Contexts*, ed. Colette Gaudin, Mary Jean Green, Lynn Anthony Higgins, Marianne Hirsch, Vivian Kogan, Claudia Reeder, and Nancy Vickers, an issue of *Yale French Studies* 62 (1981).

11. John Brenkman, *Straight Male Modern: A Cultural Critique of Psycho-analysis* (New York: Routledge, 1993), 225–26.

12. To be sure, this binary gendered structure of patriarchy is complicated by issues of race and class.

13. Of course, as Brenkman points out, Freud's elaboration of the Oedipus narrative as a story of normal masculine psychic development is ultimately paradoxical: "The simple positive Oedipus complex marks out the path of normal maturation, and yet is so rare as to be a theoretical fiction" (*Straight Male Modern*, 16).

14. As Jim Swan explains: "The adult man maintains his independent freedom by keeping up a constant, defensive preparedness, mostly unconscious, against the incessant demands of primitive instinctual impulses" (51). More specifically, Swan cites Freud's description in *Inhibitions, Symptoms, and Anxiety* (1926) of heterosexual intercourse as "'a phantasy of returning into his mother's womb'" (54). See Jim Swan, "*Mater* and Nannie: Freud's Two Mothers and the Discovery of the Oedipus Complex," *American Imago: A Psychoanalytic Journal for Culture, Science, and the Arts* 31/1 (1974): 1–64.

15. Again, Brenkman's analysis is important here. First, psychoanalysis constructs the relationship between the boy and an oceanic, consuming mother as pre-Oedipal; however, as Brenkman demonstrates, the boy's perception of a maternal threat of engulfment is the result of a *post*-Oedipal repudiation of the mother and femininity (*Straight Male Modern*, 180). Second, although the Oedi-

pus complex is, like the myth from which it draws its name, imbued with purportedly universal meanings, it in fact is the result of specific cultural forms and social institutions. "The Oedipus complex," Brenkman writes, "is integral to a process of socialization-individuation whose goal is for young men to adapt to the symbolic-institutional configuration made up of male-dominated monogamy, the restricted family, capitalist social relations, and patriarchal culture" (29).

16. For arguments promoting Afrocentricity in a North American context, see especially Molefi Kete Asante, *The Afrocentric Idea* (Philadelphia: Temple University Press, 1987); *Afrocentricity* (Trenton: Africa World Press, 1988); and *Kemet, Afrocentricity, and Knowledge* (Trenton: Africa World Press, 1990). On black nationalism and the nostalgia for the Muslim origins of the Nation of Islam, see Essieu Udosen Essieu-Udom, *Black Nationalism: A Search for Identity in America* (Chicago: University of Chicago Press, 1962). In the Afro-Caribbean context, see especially Aimé Césaire, *Notebook of a Return to My Native Land*, trans. Mireille Rosello with Anne Pritchard (Newcastle upon Tyne: Bloodaxe Books, 1995). For an important source of Afrocentric thought, see Marcus Garvey, *Philosophy and Opinions of Marcus Garvey*, ed. Amy Jacques-Garvey, 2 vols. (New York: Universal Publishing, 1923–25). For an example of nostalgia in black feminist criticism, see Abena P. A. Busia, "What Is Your Nation? Reconnecting Africa and Her Diaspora Through Paule Marshall's *Praisesong for the Widow*," in *Changing Our Own Words: Essays on Criticism, Theory, and Writing by Black Women*, ed. Cheryl A. Wall (New Brunswick, N.J.: Rutgers University Press, 1989), 196–211; in black feminist theory, see Patricia Hill Collins, "Toward an Afrocentric Feminist Epistemology," in *Black Feminist Thought: Knowledge, Consciousness, and the Politics of Empowerment* (New York: Routledge, 1991), 201–20.

17. For example, see Judy Grahn, *The Highest Apple: Sappho and the Lesbian Poetic Tradition* (San Francisco: Spinsters Ink, 1985); and Bonnie Zimmerman, "*An Island of Women*: The Lesbian Community," in *The Safe Sea of Women: Lesbian Fiction, 1969–1989* (Boston: Beacon Press, 1990), 119–63.

18. For feminist revisions of the Oedipus narrative, see especially Jessica Benjamin, *The Bonds of Love: Psychoanalysis, Feminism, and the Problem of Domination* (New York: Pantheon, 1988); Nancy Chodorow, *The Reproduction of Mothering: Psychoanalysis and the Sociology of Gender* (Berkeley: University of California Press, 1978); and Carol Gilligan, *In a Different Voice: Psychological Theory and Women's Development* (Cambridge, Mass.: Harvard University Press, 1982). Chodorow's work has been particularly influential among feminist literary critics and theorists in providing an alternative model of female development that nonetheless retains the basic structure of the Freudian paradigm.

19. As told in one of the earliest of the Homeric hymns, the story of Demeter (in Latin, Ceres), the great Earth goddess, focuses on the loss of her daughter, Persephone (Proserpina), the maiden of spring. Demeter lost Persephone after Zeus, her brother and Persephone's father, placed a narcissus in a shady part of a meadow to tempt her. Hades, the lord of the Underworld, had reached an agreement with Zeus that Persephone become his bride. Upon picking the narcissus, Persephone was captured by Hades and taken to the land of the dead. Demeter, in her grief, withheld her gifts of fertility and growth. To appease her, Zeus agreed to restore Persephone to her mother, under the condition that she eat nothing while still with Hades. However, upon leaving the Underworld, Persephone succumbed to the temptation to eat a pomegranate that Hades held out to her. As punishment, Zeus decreed that Persephone must spend a third of each year in Hades' kingdom as his wife. Thus, during the summer months, daughter and mother are together and the earth is glad; during the winter months, the barrenness of the earth symbolizes Demeter's grief at the loss of her daughter. For a rewriting of the story as an empowering countermyth about the pre-Oedipal bond, see Hélène Cixous, *Illa* (Paris: Editions des femmes, 1980).

20. This structure of forgetting is inscribed in the constitution of psychoanalysis itself. As Shoshana Felman points out, the science of psychoanalysis is based on the forgetting of the fictive, generative moment of the Oedipus myth: "Insofar as it embodies *its own forgetting* . . . the Oedipus myth is constitutive of the *science* of psychoanalysis" (1050). See Shoshana Felman, "Beyond Oedipus: The Specimen Story of Psychoanalysis," *Modern Language Notes* 95 (1983): 1021–53.

21. Jacobus's argument about memory here parallels Brenkman's insights into the psychoanalytic construction of the "pre-Oedipal" mother: "Much of what psychoanalytic theorists consider 'pre-Oedipal' about the maternal relation—oceanic body, semiotic *chora*, precommunicative flux—are images of dubious origin which come to designate the mother retrospectively, retroactively" (*Straight Male Modern*, 184).

22. On the liberatory potential of conflicts in feminism, see especially Carla Kaplan, *The Erotics of Talk* (Oxford: Oxford University Press, 1996). Kaplan points out that feminism has always been characterized by disagreement, conflict, and internal differences, and suggests that the present perception of "crisis" within feminism is the result of "a current of nostalgia for an imagined utopian moment of sisterhood and mutual recognition" (295). Also see Hirsch and Fox Keller, *Conflicts in Feminism*; and Seyla Benhabib, Judith Butler, Drucilla Cor-

nell, and Nancy Fraser, eds., *Feminist Contentions: A Philosophical Exchange* (New York: Routledge, 1995).

23. Regarding recent examples of feminist nostalgia, Kaplan also asks: "At the heart of this feminist nostalgia is there resistance to the kinds of challenges posed by women of color and lesbians who found feminism's putative sisterhood a cultural conversation that did not include them and whose rules and norms did not provide a base for adequate intervention?" (*Erotics*, 295).

24. Teresa de Lauretis's work in lesbian theory is important here. Specifically, in "The Seductions of Lesbianism," de Lauretis responds to both Jacobus and Madelon Sprengnether in their nostalgic readings of the Rich poem, "Transcendental Etude." Like Jacobus, Sprengnether reads the poem as a universal expression of wonder at the "carnal enigma" of being born from maternal flesh, concluding: "What we need is a whole new metaphysics beginning here" (246). However, de Lauretis points out that "Transcendental Etude" is a "lesbian love poem" (169), and is about not "feminist politics or myth, but lesbian desire" (171). While I agree with de Lauretis's critique of the homophobic blindness in feminist theory exemplified by Jacobus's and Sprengnether's readings of the Rich poem, her critique does not constitute a *structural* intervention into the heteronormative workings of desire. De Lauretis's argument differs from my own in its insistence on maintaining the centrality of the maternal metaphor in lesbian desire. As she puts it: "The fantasmatic relation to the mother and the maternal/female body is central to lesbian subjectivity and desire, as Rich's poem exemplifies" (171). I argue, on the contrary, that Rich explicitly rejects the analogy between "woman" and "mother" (what de Lauretis calls the "maternal/female body") by invoking a desire freed from the patriarchal ideology exemplified by such a collapse in meaning. See Teresa de Lauretis, "The Seductions of Lesbianism: Feminist Psychoanalytic Theory and the Maternal Imaginary," in *The Practice of Love: Lesbian Sexuality and Perverse Desire* (Bloomington: Indiana University Press, 1994), 149–202. Also see Madelon Sprengnether, *The Spectral Mother: Freud, Feminism, and Psychoanalysis* (Ithaca, N.Y.: Cornell University Press, 1990).

25. Adrienne Rich, "Transcendental Etude," in *The Dream of a Common Language: Poems 1974–1977* (New York: Norton, 1978), 76.

26. The first anthology to introduce the term "French feminism" to an English-speaking public was *New French Feminisms: An Anthology*, ed. Elaine Marks and Isabelle de Courtivron (New York: Schocken Books, 1981). Recent anthologies that reread "French feminism" include *Revaluing French Feminism: Critical Essays on Difference, Agency, and Culture*, ed. Nancy Fraser and Sandra

Lee Bartky (Bloomington: Indiana University Press, 1992), and *Another Look, Another Woman*, ed. Huffer, an issue of *Yale French Studies* 87 (1995).

27. Christine Delphy, "The Invention of French Feminism: An Essential Move," *Yale French Studies* 87 (1995): 196.

28. See Toril Moi's *Sexual/Textual Politics* for a classic example of an anti-essentialist critique. Also see *The Essential Difference: Another Look at Essentialism*, a special issue of *Differences: A Journal of Feminist Cultural Studies* 1/2 (1989); Diana Fuss, *Essentially Speaking: Feminism, Nature, and Difference* (New York: Routledge, 1989); and Tina Chanter, "Tracking Essentialism with the Help of a Sex/Gender Map," in *Ethics of Eros: Irigaray's Rewriting of the Philosophers* (New York: Routledge, 1995), 21–46.

29. See especially A. R. Jones, "Writing the Body."

30. The term *écriture féminine* is most closely associated with the work of Hélène Cixous, who first used it in her well-known essay, "The Laugh of the Medusa" (*Signs: Journal of Women in Culture and Society* 1/4 [1976]: 875–93). In her excellent introduction to the English translation of Cixous's *Manna*, Catherine MacGillivray points out that *écriture féminine* was not coined by Cixous, as some have erroneously suggested. See Cixous, *Manna: For the Mandelstams, For the Mandelas*, trans. MacGillivray (Minneapolis: University of Minnesota Press, 1994). *Ecriture féminine*, or "feminine writing," has become a term loosely used to describe the writing of authors such as Chantal Chawaf, Hélène Cixous, Assia Djebar, Marguerite Duras, Madeleine Gagnon, Jeanne Hyvrard, Luce Irigaray, Annie Leclerc, and Christiane Rochefort. For a discussion of this term by Cixous, see her exchange with Verena Andermatt Conley in *Hélène Cixous: Writing the Feminine* (Lincoln: University of Nebraska Press, 1984), 129–61.

31. To be sure, there are other key sources of the current interest in the body, one of the most important of which is cultural studies.

32. In drawing a distinction here that separates Irigaray from both Cixous and Kristeva, I also want to argue, like Naomi Schor and others, that Irigaray, of the three, has the most to offer feminist theory. As Schor puts it: "Whereas in the early stages of the development of French feminisms Irigaray's writings were almost always invidiously compared to those of Kristeva and Cixous, to-day, although Kristeva remains a major intellectual presence (especially in the field of psychoanalysis) and Cixous continues to exert her influence through her seminar, her fiction and playwriting, it is becoming apparent that, as the major French theoretician, Irigaray is actually Simone de Beauvoir's chief successor" (4). See Naomi Schor, "Previous Engagements: The Receptions of Irigaray," in *Engaging with Irigaray*, ed. Carolyn Burke, Schor, and Margaret Whitford (New York: Columbia University Press, 1994), 3–14.

33. Domna C. Stanton, "Difference on Trial: A Critique of the Maternal Metaphor in Cixous, Irigaray, and Kristeva," in *The Poetics of Gender*, ed. Nancy K. Miller (New York: Columbia University Press, 1986), 157–82.

34. See Jane Gallop, "Lip Service," in *Thinking Through the Body*, 92–99; and Maggie Berg, "Luce Irigaray's 'Contradictions': Poststructuralism and Feminism," *Signs: Journal of Women in Culture and Society* 17/1 (1991): 50–70.

35. Christine Holmlund, "The Lesbian, the Mother, the Heterosexual Lover: Irigaray's Recodings of Difference," *Feminist Studies* 17/2 (1991): 283–308. As Holmlund points out, in the trajectory of Irigaray's thought, she has moved away from a focus on the lesbian relation, first toward the mother and, most recently, toward a preoccupation with heterosexual lovers. However, Holmlund writes, "Irigaray's current preference for the heterosexual female lover and corresponding neglect of the lesbian . . . does not mean she has repudiated the one for the other. But given the force of heterosexual assumptions and privileges in today's world, we may well need to insist that the lesbian is *not* a stage to be outgrown en route to mature heterosexuality" (304).

36. Irigaray herself, when asked in an interview if the lips could be interpreted as "the entrance to the mother's body," replied that "it's a mistake" to think of them in that way. See Kiki Amsberg and Aafke Steenhuis, "Interview with Luce Irigaray," *Hecate: A Women's Interdisciplinary Journal* 9/1–2 (1983): 196.

37. For an excellent analysis of Irigaray's shift in focus in the early 1980's, see Carolyn Burke, "Romancing the Philosophers: Luce Irigaray," in *Seduction and Theory: Readings of Gender, Representation, and Rhetoric*, ed. Dianne Hunter (Urbana: University of Illinois Press, 1989), 226–40. Burke describes *Speculum* as "a massive dismantling of the 'phallogocentric' mechanisms of Western metaphysical tradition" and *This Sex* as "a kind of postface to *Speculum*" (226). As early as 1979 the maternal presence takes center stage in "Et l'une ne bouge pas sans l'autre" and again, in 1981, with *Le Corps-à-corps avec la mère* (Montreal: Editions de la pleine lune, 1981). With *Amante marine, de Friedrich Nietzsche* (Paris: Minuit, 1980), Irigaray begins a new strategy of "romancing the philosophers," including most importantly Nietzsche, Derrida, Heidegger, and Levinas. Irigaray's own account of this shift in direction reveals the frame of heterosexual seduction: *Amante marine*, she says, "is not a book *on* Nietzsche but *with* Nietzsche who is for me an amorous partner" (*Corps-à-corps*, 44).

38. See Judith Butler, *Gender Trouble: Feminism and the Subversion of Identity* (New York: Routledge, 1990) and *Bodies That Matter: On the Discursive Limits of "Sex"* (New York: Routledge, 1993).

39. Since the publication of *Ethique de la différence sexuelle* (Paris: Minuit,

1984) (*An Ethics of Sexual Difference*, trans. Carolyn Burke and Gillian Gill [Ithaca, N.Y.: Cornell University Press, 1993]), Irigaray herself has increasingly put ethical questions at the forefront of her reflections on sexual difference. For a recent example of these ethical concerns, see Luce Irigaray, "The Question of the Other," *Yale French Studies* 87 (1995): 7–19. Also see Seyla Benhabib, *Situating the Self: Gender, Community and Postmodernism in Contemporary Ethics* (New York: Routledge, 1992); Chanter, *Ethics of Eros*; Drucilla Cornell, *Beyond Accommodation: Ethical Feminism, Deconstruction, and the Law* (New York: Routledge, 1991); and Gayatri Chakravorty Spivak, "French Feminism Revisited: Ethics and Politics," in *Feminists Theorize the Political*, ed. Judith Butler and Joan W. Scott (New York: Routledge, 1992), 54–85.

40. Luce Irigaray, *This Sex Which Is Not One*, trans. Catherine Porter with Carolyn Burke (Ithaca: Cornell University Press, 1985), 76 (emphasis added).

41. See, for example, Emma Pérez, "Irigaray's Female Symbolic in the Making of Chicana Lesbian *Sitios y Lenguas* (*Sites and Discourses*)," in *The Lesbian Postmodern*, ed. Laura Doan (New York: Columbia University Press, 1994), 104–17.

Chapter 1

1. Maurice Blanchot, *The Space of Literature*, trans. Ann Smock (Lincoln: University of Nebraska Press, 1982), 172.

2. Michel Foucault, "Maurice Blanchot: The Thought from the Outside," trans. Brian Massumi, in *Foucault/Blanchot* (New York: Zone Books, 1987), 15.

3. See Roland Barthes, "The Death of the Author," in *Image/Music/Text*, trans. Stephen Heath (New York: Noonday Press, 1977), 142–48. Also see Michel Foucault, "What Is an Author?" in *Textual Strategies*, ed. Josué Harari (Ithaca, N.Y.: Cornell University Press, 1979), 141–60.

4. For example, see the early debate (1982) between Peggy Kamuf and Nancy K. Miller and its more recent epistolary sequel (1990) on the question of killing the female author: Kamuf, "Replacing Feminist Criticism"; Miller, "The Text's Heroine"; and Kamuf and Miller, "Parisian Letters." Also see Naomi Schor, "Dreaming Dissymmetry: Barthes, Foucault, and Sexual Difference," in *Men in Feminism*, ed. Alice Jardine and Paul Smith (New York: Methuen, 1987), 98–110.

5. The work of Luce Irigaray remains, in my opinion, the most clear and rigorous articulation of this phenomenon. See especially *Speculum of the Other Woman*, trans. Gillian C. Gill (Ithaca, N.Y.: Cornell University Press, 1985). For an early feminist overview of the celebration of the feminine in French

modernity, see Jardine, *Gynesis*. See also Linda Nicholson's introduction to *Feminism/Postmodernism* (New York: Routledge, 1990), 1–16.

6. P. Adams Sitney, "Afterword," in Maurice Blanchot, *The Gaze of Orpheus and Other Literary Essays*, trans. Lydia Davis, ed. Sitney (Barrytown, N.Y.: Station Hill Press, 1981), 166. Geoffrey Hartman, "Preface," in Blanchot, *The Gaze of Orpheus*, xi. Timothy Clark, *Derrida, Heidegger, Blanchot: Sources of Derrida's Notion and Practice of Literature* (Cambridge: Cambridge University Press, 1992), 78.

7. That said, I am indebted to the work that has been done on Blanchot from a feminist perspective. See Ann Smock, " 'Où est la loi?': Law and Sovereignty in *Aminadab* and *Le Très-haut*," *Sub-stance* 14 (1976): 99–116; Larysa Mykata, "Vanishing Point: The Question of the Woman in the Works of Maurice Blanchot" (Ph.D. diss., State University of New York at Buffalo, 1980); and Jane Gallop, "Friends/Corpses/Turds/Whores: Blanchot on Sade," in *Intersections: A Reading of Sade with Bataille, Blanchot, and Klossowski* (Lincoln: University of Nebraska Press, 1981), 35–66. The work of Mykata, although it focuses on Blanchot's fiction, resonates with my own, as is evidenced by her incisive remark: "Even if women cannot be treated as subjects or themes because they represent the void, if they are nonetheless pervasive in Blanchot's fiction and necessary for the elaboration of his theoretical positions, why has no effort been made to relate their negative identity to the fundamental questions?" (8).

8. Of course, Blanchot is not alone in theorizing the specificity of literary discourse. See the work of the Prague Structuralists, especially Roman Jakobson, "Linguistics and Poetics," in *Style in Language*, ed. Thomas A. Sebeok (Cambridge, Mass.: MIT Press, 1960), 350–58. Also see Roman Ingarden, *The Literary Work of Art: An Investigation on the Borderlines of Ontology, Logic and Theory of Literature*, trans. George Grabowicz (Evanston, Ill.: Northwestern University Press, 1973); Karl Bühler, *Theory of Language: The Representational Function of Language*, trans. Donald Fraser Goodwin (Philadelphia: J. Benjamins, 1990); and René Wellek and Austin Warren, *Theory of Literature* (New York: Harcourt Brace Jovanovich, 1977).

9. See Jean-François Lyotard, *The Postmodern Condition: A Report on Knowledge*, trans. Geoff Bennington and Brian Massumi (Minneapolis: University of Minnesota Press, 1984).

10. See especially Jacques Derrida, "White Mythology," *New Literary History* 6 (1974): 5–74; and "The Law of Genre," *Glyph* 7 (1980): 202–32. Significantly, "The Law of Genre" is built around a reading of Blanchot's *La folie du jour* (Montpellier: Fata Morgana, 1973). For a critique of this slippage in Der-

rida, see especially Jürgen Habermas, "Excursus on Leveling the Genre Distinction Between Philosophy and Literature," in *The Philosophical Discourses of Modernity*, trans. Frederick G. Lawrence (Cambridge, Mass.: MIT Press, 1987), 185–210.

11. For a more explicit engagement with the Oedipus myth, see the third section of "The Most Profound Question" in Blanchot's *The Infinite Conversation*, trans. Susan Hanson (Minneapolis: University of Minnesota Press, 1993), 17–24.

12. Maurice Blanchot, *L'espace littéraire* (Paris: Gallimard, 1955), 225.

13. Derrida, for example, describes the Blanchotian "death sentence" as "death *and* survival" (208; my translation). See Jacques Derrida, *Parages* (Paris: Galilée, 1986). Similarly, Geoffrey Hartman describes Blanchot's characters as "despairing men [who] are sick unto death yet deprived of the ability to die" (107). See Geoffrey Hartman, *Beyond Formalism: Literary Essays 1958–1970* (New Haven, Conn.: Yale University Press, 1970), 93–110. Blanchot's *Death Sentence* exemplifies the contradictory imperative of figuration and disappearance that characterizes the literary work: "When someone who has disappeared completely is suddenly there, in front of you, behind a pane of glass, that person becomes the most powerful sort of figure [*une figure souveraine*]" (43). See Maurice Blanchot, *Death Sentence*, trans. Lydia Davis (Barrytown, N.Y.: Station Hill Press, 1978).

14. Here Blanchot follows the Prague Structuralists, and in particular Roman Jakobson, who distinguished between the poetic function and the functions of everyday speech. As Habermas puts it in his critique of Derrida's denial of this distinction: "When language fulfills a poetic function, it does so in virtue of a reflexive relation of the linguistic expression to itself. Consequently, reference to an object, informational content, and truth-value—conditions of validity in general—are extrinsic to poetic speech" ("Excursus," 200).

15. Mary Jacobus's reading of Freud's "Childhood Memories and Screen Memories" in *The Psychopathology of Everyday Life* (1901) is pertinent here. Jacobus demonstrates that with Freud's concept of screen memories "the status of memory is put in question. Instead of being a recovery of the past in the present, it always involves a revision, reinscription, or representation of an ultimately irretrievable past" (118). See Jacobus, "Freud's Mnemonic."

16. See Lacan on the structure of the look and the deception of philosophical contemplation: "Ce en quoi la conscience peut se retourner sur elle-même—se saisir, telle la Jeune Parque de Valéry, comme *se voyant se voir*—représente un escamotage. Un évitement s'y opère de la fonction du regard" (71). Jacques Lacan, *Le séminaire XI: Les quatre concepts fondamentaux de la psych-*

analyse (Paris: Seuil, 1973). Also see Jacqueline Rose, *Sexuality in the Field of Vision* (London:Verso, 1986).

17. For a similar formulation, see Jacques Derrida, *Spurs: Nietzsche's Styles / Eperons: Les Styles de Nietzsche*, trans. Barbara Harlow (Chicago: University of Chicago Press, 1987).

18. See Andrzej Warminski, *Readings in Interpretation: Hölderlin, Hegel, Heidegger* (Minneapolis: University of Minnesota Press, 1987), xlix.

19. This idea of the "mother" as a "place-holder" assumes a context in which language is understood as pure iterability, and where the word "mother" is the "differential, nonsignifying, syntactical marker put in the place of that which was *not there* in the first place" (Warminski, *Readings in Interpretation*, xxxiv).

20. Jacques Derrida, "Otobiographies: The Teaching of Nietzsche and the Politics of the Proper Name," trans. Avital Ronell, in *The Ear of the Other: Otobiography, Transference, Translation*, ed. Christie McDonald (Lincoln: University of Nebraska Press, 1985), 38.

21. See Paul de Man's reading of Rilke's *Sonnets to Orpheus* in "Tropes (Rilke)," *Allegories of Reading: Figural Language in Rousseau, Nietzsche, Rilke, and Proust* (New Haven, Conn.:Yale University Press, 1979), 48.

22. Characteristically, the biographical blurb for *L'espace littéraire* describes Blanchot as "silent": "Maurice Blanchot, novelist and critic, was born in 1907. His life is entirely devoted to literature and to the silence that is particular to him/it [*qui lui est propre*]" (my translation). Along the same lines, French journalist Jean-Marc Parisis gives Blanchot "a perfect score [*noté vingt sur vingt*] for the effectiveness of his self-effacement" (cited in Ungar, 5). Of course, many have wondered about specific silences during Blanchot's career as a writer and, in particular, his silence regarding the articles he published during the 1930's for the collaborationist newspapers *Combat* and *L'Insurgé*. As Blanchot himself puts it in regard to Heidegger's notorious refusal to address *his* wartime ties to the Nazi party: "Allow me after what I have to say next to leave you, as a means to emphasize that Heidegger's irreparable fault lies in his *silence* concerning the Final Solution" (cited in Ungar, 63; my emphasis). See especially Steven Ungar, *Scandal and Aftereffect: Blanchot and France Since 1930* (Minneapolis: University of Minnesota Press, 1995). Also see Jeffrey Mehlman, "Blanchot at *Combat*: Of Literature and Terror," in *Legacies of Anti-Semitism in France* (Minneapolis: University of Minnesota Press, 1983), 6–22.

23. Statement made by Hélène Cixous in her seminar at the Université de Paris VIII on December 1, 1979; cited by MacGillivray in the introduction to her translation of Cixous's *Manna*, xxxvii.

Chapter 2

1. See especially Benhabib, *Situating the Self*; Collins, *Black Feminist Thought*; Irigaray, *Speculum*; Irigaray, *This Sex*; and Audre Lorde, *Sister Outsider: Essays and Speeches* (Freedom, Calif.: The Crossing Press, 1984).

2. However, as I point out in the Introduction, Irigaray moves from an overtly contestatory position vis-à-vis philosophy (in *Speculum* and *This Sex*) to a strategy of seduction. See Burke, "Romancing the Philosophers."

3. As this chapter will show, Irigaray's concept of the same comes from her reading of the parable of the cave in books 6 and 7 of Plato's *Republic*. Her interpretation of Plato asserts that the self-identical logic of model and copy on which the republic and its truth is founded does not allow for alterity, difference, or deviation from the form of the Ideal, the paternal model. See Irigaray, *Speculum*, 243–364. For a lucid and helpful explanation of Irigaray's reading of Plato, see Margaret Whitford, *Luce Irigaray: Philosophy in the Feminine* (London: Routledge, 1991), esp. 101–22.

4. See note 8 in this chapter for recent examples of this ongoing interest. In addition, see Burke, Schor, and Whitford, *Engaging with Irigaray*; Chanter, *Ethics of Eros*; Serene Jones, "This God Which Is Not One: Irigaray and Barth on the Divine," in *Transfigurations: Theology and the French Feminists*, ed. C. W. Maggie Kim, Susan M. St. Ville, and Susan M. Simonaitis (Minneapolis: Fortress Press, 1993), 109–41; and Serene Jones, "Divining Women: Irigaray and Feminist Theologies," *Yale French Studies* 87 (1995): 42–67.

5. Simone de Beauvoir begins *The Second Sex* by asking and repeating precisely the same question: "What is a woman?" (11); "What is a woman?" (13).

6. For a close analysis of what Irigaray calls Freud's *devenir femme*, his construction of the journey toward adult femininity, see Irigaray, *Speculum*, 13–129.

7. Irigaray, *Speculum*, 243.

8. On Irigaray and mimicry, see especially Rosi Braidotti, *Patterns of Dissonance: A Study of Women in Contemporary Philosophy*, trans. Elizabeth Guild (New York: Routledge, 1991); Dianne Chisholm, "Irigaray's Hysteria," in *Engaging with Irigaray*, 263–84; Cornell, *Beyond Accommodation*; Gallop, *Thinking Through the Body*; Elizabeth Grosz, *Sexual Subversions: Three French Feminists* (Sydney: Allen and Unwin, 1989); Moi, *Sexual/Textual Politics*; Naomi Schor, "This Essentialism Which Is Not One: Coming to Grips with Irigaray," *Differences* 1/2 (1989): 38–58; and Whitford, *Irigaray: Philosophy in the Feminine*.

9. Derrida, *Spurs*.

10. For an excellent summary and explanation of this process, see Whitford, *Irigaray: Philosophy in the Feminine*, 105–13.

11. "Behaviour of the *elementary* sexual organisms is indeed a model for the conduct of sexual individuals during intercourse" (Freud, cited in Irigaray, *Speculum*, 15).

12. In her reading of *The Republic*, Irigaray replaces Plato's term for cave or den, *spelaion* (σπήλαιον), with the Greek word meaning uterus or womb, *hustera* (ὑστέρα).

13. Irigaray's terminology here plays on the double meaning of *enceinte* as both a noun, meaning "enclosure," and as an adjective, meaning "pregnant."

14. The verb, "to trope," which means to embellish with a figure of speech, comes from the Greek *tropos* (τρόποζ), "a turn."

15. "*copula in effigy only*" (*Speculum*, 252). Irigaray's wordplay here hints at two meanings. First, the "*copula in effigy only*" could refer to the rigid syntactical ordering of language in the predicative copula, the part of a proposition that connects subject to predicate through the verb "to be." Second, "*the copula in effigy only*" could refer to the rigidly ordered coupling, or copulation, of man and woman who, in the false difference of their heterosexual relation, function like cardboard effigies of the same.

16. "*modeled* on a male representation of female desire" (*Speculum,* 30n8; my emphasis).

17. "But how can I put 'I love you' differently?" (*This Sex*, 207); "How can I tell you?" (211); "How can I say it?" (214); "How can I say 'you'?" (214).

18. The extension of metaphorical meaning beyond the figural is what classical rhetoric calls an abuse of trope, or catachresis, a figure that lacks an original or proper meaning (a *head* of cabbage, the *face* of a mountain, etc.). As markers of a feminine libido that lacks a proper meaning, Irigaray's lips and clitoris are catachrestic: the extension of anatomical metaphors of femininity that cannot be reduced into the equations of a metaphorical economy. For a reading of the lips as ironic, see Maggie Berg, "Irigaray's 'Contradictions.'"

19. "A few lips remain that may open, like a cave, revealing a slit that has been covered up with an art that will be attributed to nature" (*Speculum*, 288).

20. Irigaray articulates the relationship between sexual difference and *eidos* in her defense of her doctoral thesis: "I am a woman. . . . The motive of my work lies in the impossibility of articulating such a statement. . . . In other words, the articulation of the reality of my sex is impossible in discourse, and for a structural, eidetic reason" (*This Sex*, 1448–49).

21. The proleptic possibilities of a posthysterical saying set into movement are as intriguing as they are impossible to formulate. One can begin, however, to think about a different "third term" that is not a milieu, beyond the opposition between the "obsessional" (enumeration) and the "hysterical" (metaphori-

cal conversion) (see *Speculum*, 61). For a rhetorical reading of this opposition, see Paul de Man, "Anthropomorphism and Trope in the Lyric," in *The Rhetoric of Romanticism* (New York: Columbia University Press, 1984), 239–62. De Man's conclusion about the nontropological "sheer blind violence" of history might be linked to Sarah Kofman's rejection of the complicitous hysteric for the more radical, nonfigural woman-as-criminal. See Sarah Kofman, *L'énigme de la femme: La femme dans les textes de Freud* (Paris: Galilée, 1980).

22. Irigaray uses the term "specula(risa)tion" throughout *Speculum* to designate simultaneously: (1) philosophical speculation; (2) observation of the heavens; (3) enterprise in goods or land; (4) to speculate, observe, or view mentally; (5) to talk over, conjecture; (6) to look at or gaze at something. The term also draws attention to Irigaray's title, *Speculum* (from the Latin, *specere*, "to look [at] or observe"), which means: (1) a surgical instrument used for dilating orifices of the body; (2) a mirror or reflector and, by extension, a telescope; (3) a diagram or drawing, especially of the planets (from the *Oxford English Dictionary*, 2d ed.). The parenthetical intrusion of (risa) into "speculation" also draws attention to the notion of specularity, thereby highlighting the visual, self-reflective economy through which the various forms of speculation justify themselves. My thanks to Micol Seigel for suggesting that the Spanish term for laughter, *risa*, might also be read into Irigaray's wordplay.

23. As Nietzsche puts it: "Neither the house, nor the stride, nor the clothing, nor the clay jug betray the fact that need invented them; they seem intended to express an exalted happiness and an Olympian serenity and, as it were, a playing with serious matters" (256). See Friedrich Nietzsche, "On Truth and Lying in an Extra-Moral Sense," in *Friedrich Nietzsche on Rhetoric and Language*, ed. and trans. Sander L. Gilman, Carole Blair, and David J. Parent (New York: Oxford University Press, 1989), 246–57.

24. See Gallop, *The Daughter's Seduction*, for an early reading of Irigaray's strategy of asking im-pertinent questions of her discursive fathers.

25. Irigaray uses the word *semblant*, or "resemblance," to describe the logic of identity that reduces women to a repetition of the same. The structure of the *semblant* is like its homophone, *sang blanc*, or "white blood," which freezes difference into a homogenous blank. "And what about your life? You must *pretend* to receive it from them [Tu dois faire *semblant* (*sang blanc*): la recevoir d'eux]" (*Ce sexe*, 207; my emphasis).

26. Jacques Derrida, "La mythologie blanche: La métaphore dans le texte philosophique," in *Marges de la philosophie* (Paris: Minuit, 1972), 253.

27. See Derrida, "La Structure, le signe et le jeu dans le discours des sciences humaines," in *L'écriture et la différence* (Paris: Seuil, 1967), 409–28. Re-

garding the temptation to privilege pleasure in the struggle for sexual liberation, the comments of Sheila Jeffreys (as cited in Jenny Kitzinger and Celia
Kitzinger, "'Doing it': Representations of Lesbian Sex," in *Outwrite: Lesbianism
and Popular Culture*, ed. Gabriele Griffin [London: Pluto Press, 1993]) are apt:
"An issue on housing would not be expected to focus on interior decoration at
the expense of looking at homelessness. An issue on women's work would
probably not just focus on individual fulfilment but on the issue of exploitation. It is inconceivable that an oppositional group of socialists would set themselves up to say that there has been altogether too much gloom and doom
about oppression, now was the time to talk about fashion, interior decoration,
eating out and so on. . . . It is only in the area of sexuality that individual pleasure has taken precedence over the ending of oppression" (23).

28. Irigaray significantly alters Plato's version of the story here. In book 7 of
The Republic, it is the freed prisoner who is put to death: "and if one tried to
loose another and lead him up to the light, let them only catch the offender,
and they would be put to death." See Plato, *The Republic: The Complete and
Unabridged Jowett Translation* (New York: Random House, 1991), 257.

29. Irigaray, *Corps-à-corps*, 15–16. All translations of this text are mine.

30. Clytemnestra, the wife of Agamemnon, king of Mycenae, was killed by
Orestes, her son, to avenge her plotting of her husband's death at the hands of
Aegisthus. After killing his mother with the help of his sister, Electra, Orestes
was punished for his crime by the Furies, who visited him with madness.

31. Irigaray, *Corps-à-corps*, 33 (my emphasis).

Chapter 3

1. Irigaray, *Speculum*, 243.

2. Julia is alluding here to two of her most well-known celebrations of the
mother. See Julia Kristeva, "Motherhood According to Giovanni Bellini," in
Desire in Language: A Semiotic Approach to Literature and Art, ed. Leon S.
Roudiez, trans. Thomas Gora, Alice Jardine, and Roudiez (New York: Columbia University Press, 1980), 237–70; and "Stabat Mater," in *Tales of Love*, trans.
Roudiez (New York: Columbia University Press, 1987), 234–63. For an analy-
sis of Kristeva's Bellini essay as a subversion of Freud's Oedipal family romance,
see Mary Bittner Wiseman, "Renaissance Paintings and Psychoanalysis: Julia
Kristeva and the Function of the Mother," in *Ethics, Politics, and Difference in Ju-
lia Kristeva's Writing*, ed. Kelly Oliver (New York: Routledge, 1993), 92–115.
Also see Mary Jacobus, "Madonna: Like a Virgin; or, Freud, Kristeva, and the
Case of the Missing Mother," *Oxford Literary Review* 8 (1986): 35–50.

3. *Speculum*, 42; translation modified.

4. *Speculum*, 43.

5. Maurice Blanchot, *The Writing of the Disaster*, trans. Ann Smock (Lincoln: University of Nebraska Press, 1986), 196.

6. Claire Nouvet, "An Impossible Response: The Disaster of Narcissus," *Yale French Studies* 79 (1991): 127.

7. See Plato, *The Republic*; and *The Timaeus of Plato*, ed. and trans. R. D. Archer-Hind (New York: Arno Press, 1973).

8. For comparisons of Kristeva and Irigaray, see Butler, *Gender Trouble*; Cornell, *Beyond Accommodation*; Delphy, "The Invention of French Feminism"; Nancy Fraser, "Introduction" and "The Uses and Abuses of French Discourse Theories for Feminist Politics," in *Revaluing French Feminism*, 1–24, 177–94; Gallop, *The Daughter's Seduction*; Jane Gallop and Carolyn Burke, "Psychoanalysis and Feminism in France," in *The Future of Difference*, ed. Eisenstein and Jardine, 105–21; Jardine, *Gynesis*; A. R. Jones, "Writing the Body," 247–63; Ann Rosalind Jones, "Inscribing Femininity: French Theories of the Feminine," in *Making a Difference: Feminist Literary Criticism*, ed. Gayle Greene and Coppélia Kahn (London: Methuen, 1985) 80–112; Ann Rosalind Jones, "Imaginary Gardens with Real Frogs in Them: Feminist Euphoria and the Franco-American Divide, 1976–88," in *Changing Subjects*, ed. Greene and Kahn; Moi, *Sexual/Textual Politics*; Kelly Oliver, *Reading Kristeva: Unraveling the Double-Bind* (Bloomington: Indiana University Press, 1993); Stanton, "Language and Revolution"; Domna C. Stanton, "Difference on Trial: A Critique of the Maternal Metaphor in Cixous, Irigaray, and Kristeva," in *The Poetics of Gender*, ed. Miller, 157–82; Rosemary Tong, *Feminist Thought: A Comprehensive Introduction* (Boulder, Colo.: Westview Press, 1989).

9. Julia Kristeva, *Revolution in Poetic Language*, trans. Margaret Waller (New York: Columbia University Press, 1984).

10. As Timaeus explains, the matrix of becoming precedes syllables themselves: "Now we must examine what came before the creation of the heavens, the very origin of fire and water and air and earth, and the conditions that were before them. For now no one has declared the manner of their generation; but we speak as if men knew what is fire and each of the others, and we treat them as beginnings, as elements of the whole; whereas by one who has ever so little intelligence they could not plausibly be represented as belonging even to the class of syllables" (*Timaeus of Plato*, 169).

11. See, for example, Toril Moi, who states that for Kristeva "the endless flow of pulsions is gathered up in the *chora*," which she defines incorrectly: "from the Greek word for enclosed space, womb." See Toril Moi, introduction

to Kristeva, *The Kristeva Reader*, ed. Moi (New York: Columbia University Press, 1986), 12–13. Moi also describes Kristeva's "struggle against the 'phallic sign'" as "a hysterical obsession with the neutralizing cave" (*Kristeva Reader*, 11). Similarly, in her analysis of Irigaray in *Sexual/Textual Politics* she translates *hustera* as cave (129). In both instances, not only does Moi mistranslate the Greek idiom from which those concepts are drawn, but she also, through that mistranslation, reduces both the *hustera* and the *chora* to one of many interchangeable metaphors privileged by "essentialist" thinkers to describe a concept on which femininity might be grounded. For a critique of Moi, see especially Shari Benstock, *Textualizing the Feminine: On the Limits of Genre* (Norman: University of Oklahoma Press, 1991), 206; and Kaja Silverman, *The Acoustic Mirror: The Female Voice in Psychoanalysis and Cinema* (Lincoln: University of Nebraska Press, 1983), esp. 99–132.

12. Jacques Derrida, *Khôra* (Paris: Galilée, 1993), 63. All translations of this text are mine.

13. As Derrida puts it: "Without a real referent, that which in effect resembles a proper name is therefore an *X* whose property or, as the text puts it, its *physis* and its *dynamis*, is that nothing is proper to it and that it thus remains formless (*amorphon*). This quite singular impropriety, which in fact is nothing, this is precisely what *khôra* must, if you will, *hold on to*. . . . In that sense, we must not confuse it with a generality in attributing to it precisely the properties of a determinate being [*un étant déterminé*], one of the beings that it 'receives' or from which it receives an image: for example a being of the feminine gender— which is why the femininity of the mother or the nurse will never be properly attributed to it" (*Khôra*, 33, my translation).

14. See Martin Heidegger, *An Introduction to Metaphysics*, trans. Ralph Mannheim (New Haven, Conn.: Yale University Press, 1959).

15. Derrida points out that *khôra* thus defies the logic of noncontradiction: "neither 'sensible' nor 'intelligible,' it belongs to a 'third genre' (*triton genos*)" (*Khôra*, 16, my translation).

16. Kristeva, "Extraterrestrials Suffering for Want of Love," in *Tales of Love*, 382–83.

17. "The semiotic *chora*, converting drive discharges into stases" (*Revolution*, 241n23).

18. Here I use the word *semblant*, or "resemblance," as Irigaray does in *Ce sexe qui n'en est pas un*, to describe woman as a repetition of the same. See Chapter 2, note 25.

19. Kristeva, "Le sujet en procès," *Polylogue* (Paris: Seuil, 1977), 57 (my translation).

20. In a more positive reading of the Kristevan *chora*, Michael Payne defends the contradictions I have criticized. He connects Plato's *chora* (χώρα) to the *chorion* (χοριον), a term used by Aristotle in *Historia Animalium* to signify the membrane around the fetus in the womb. Payne sees the *chorion* as "an apt Kristevan metaphor" because of its "double structure of tissue, . . . a place where simultaneously the structure of the mother's body ends and that of the fetus begins," thus constituting "the space within which the otherness of the fetus is distinguishable" (168). While Payne's point is compelling, his focus on the physicality of the maternal *chorion* simply reinforces my argument about the nostalgic and essentializing logic behind Kristeva's theory. See Michael Payne, *Reading Theory: An Introduction to Lacan, Derrida, and Kristeva* (Oxford: Blackwell, 1993).

21. In an interview with Rosalind Coward, Kristeva makes this position quite clear: "My reproach to some political discourses with which I am disillusioned is that they don't consider the individual as a value. . . . That's why I say that, of course, political struggles for people that are exploited will continue, but they will continue maybe better if the main concern remains the individuality and particularity of the person" (27). See Kristeva, "Julia Kristeva in Conversation with Rosalind Coward," *Desire* [ICA Documents, 1984].

22. Emmanuel Levinas, "Ethics as First Philosophy," in *The Levinas Reader*, ed. Seán Hand (Oxford: Blackwell, 1989), 82. Also see Levinas, *Totality and Infinity: An Essay on Exteriority*, trans. Alphonso Lingis (Pittsburgh: Duquesne University Press, 1979), esp. 42–48.

23. Kristeva is not alone in her celebration of the revolutionary promise of this "asocial drive." See, for example, Leo Bersani's *Homos*, which makes a similar argument in the name of homosexuality: "*homo-ness itself*," Bersani writes, "*necessitates a massive redefining of relationality*. More fundamental than a resistance to normalizing methodologies is a potentially revolutionary inaptitude—perhaps inherent in gay desire—for sociality as it is known" (76). See *Homos* (Cambridge, Mass.: Harvard University Press, 1995).

24. In *Revolution in Poetic Language*, Kristeva addresses ethics in a discussion of "the *ethical function* of the text" (232). Kristeva defines ethics as "the negativizing of narcissism within a *practice*; in other words, a practice is ethical when it dissolves those narcissistic fixations (ones that are narrowly confined to the subject) to which the signifying process succumbs in its socio-symbolic realization. . . . The text fulfills its ethical function only when it pluralizes, pulverizes, 'musicates' these truths, which is to say, on the condition that it develop them to the point of laughter" (233). In many respects, Kristeva's concept of ethics recalls the liquefaction of Narcissus in the pool; for her, ethics is defined

with regard to the pulverization of the subject in and through art. This concept of ethics fails to consider sociality or the question of the other in the social relation. For an overview of Kristeva and ethics, see Kelly Oliver, "Introduction: Julia Kristeva's Outlaw Ethics," in *Ethics, Politics, and Difference in Julia Kristeva's Writing*, 1–22.

25. See Oliver, *Reading Kristeva*. Also see John Lechte, *Julia Kristeva* (London: Routledge, 1990).

26. Beauvoir, *The Second Sex*, 166.

27. For example, see Gayatri Chakravorty Spivak, "French Feminism in an International Frame," *Yale French Studies* 62 (1981): 154–84, for a critique of imperialism in Kristeva's *About Chinese Women*, trans. Anita Barrows (London: Marion Boyars, 1977). Also see Lisa Lowe, "*Des Chinoises*: Orientalism, Psychoanalysis, and Feminine Writing," in *Ethics, Politics, and Difference in Julia Kristeva's Writing*, 150–63. Lowe's analysis of Kristeva's "orientalism" is particularly germane to my concerns about maternal nostalgia; regarding Kristeva's fantasy description of Chinese matriarchy, Lowe writes: "Kristeva does more than idealize this Mother; she 'orientalizes' her" (154). Lowe goes on to argue that the romanticization of China by post–May '68 French intellectuals as a utopian Other of the West ultimately permitted them to disregard France's continued exploitation of its former colonies in Africa, Asia, and the Caribbean. Perhaps the most blatant example of Kristeva's imperialist politics is found in "My Memory's Hyperbole," *New York Literary Forum* 12–14 (1984): 261–76, where she uses the story of David and Goliath to characterize the relationship between the United States and the Third World: "While the Latin American or Arab Marxist revolution is brewing on the doorstep of the United States, I feel closer to truth and liberty when I work within the space of this challenged giant, which may, in fact, be on the point of becoming a David before the growing Goliath of the Third World. I dream that our children will prefer to join this David, with his errors and impasses, armed with our erring and circling about the Idea, the Logos, the Form: in short, the old Judeo-Christian Europe" (274). For an analysis of the David and Goliath analogy, see Oliver, *Reading Kristeva*, 131.

28. Toril Moi has critiqued the individualism of Kristeva's politics in terms similar to mine, decrying what she calls Kristeva's "alarming fascination with the libertarian possibilities of American-style capitalism" (*Sexual/Textual Politics*, 168). Moi also points out that Kristeva's account of the revolutionary subject elides the question of agency, particularly as agency relates to the processes involved in collective political action. My argument diverges from Moi's, however, with regard to the reasons for Kristeva's conservative political agenda. Moi

sees a positive appeal for progressive politics in Kristeva's theorization of the materiality of language, and argues that Kristeva's conception of gender is quintessentially anti-essentialist. I, on the other hand, have attempted to show that Kristeva's political conservatism lies not just in her problematic application of an otherwise radical theory. Rather, her conservatism is grounded in the ontological and biological essentialism of the Platonic and psychoanalytic sources on which she draws for her theory of the semiotic.

29. "Affirmer la priorité de *l'être* par rapport à *l'étant*, c'est déjà se prononcer sur l'essence de la philosophie, subordonner la relation avec *quelqu'un* qui est un étant (la relation éthique) à une relation ave *l'être de l'étant* qui, impersonnel, permet la saisie, la domination de l'étant (à une relation de savoir), subordonne la justice à la liberté" (36). See Levinas, *Totalité et Infini: Essai sur l'extériorité* (The Hague: Martinus Nijhoff, 1971).

30. The Levinasian critique of ontology's suppression of the other closely allies him with Irigaray. In this sense, Irigaray and Levinas share a commitment to the primacy of the ethical relation, although Irigaray is critical of Levinas's approach, in later sections of *Totality and Infinity*, to sexual difference. See Luce Irigaray, "The Fecundity of the Caress," in *Face to Face with Levinas*, ed. Richard A. Cohen (Albany: State University of New York Press, 1986), 231–56. For an excellent overview of Levinasian ethics in relation to Irigaray, see Tina Chanter, "Levinas and the Question of the Other," in her *Ethics of Eros*, 170–224.

31. For a very different reading of Kristeva in relation to Levinasian ethics, see Ewa Ziarek, "Kristeva and Levinas: Mourning, Ethics, and the Feminine," in *Ethics, Politics, and Difference in Julia Kristeva's Writing*, 62–78. Although Ziarek's consideration of Kristeva's theory of melancholia as an ethical encounter with the maternal other is provocative, Ziarek fails to place Kristeva's description of maternal loss within the larger context of her theory of the maternal semiotic. When placed in that context, Kristevan melancholia can be viewed as part of a nostalgic structure of loss and return in which the maternal other is either hypostatized or annihilated. In either case, the result is the suppression of alterity, a suppression that occurs precisely because the other is maternalized.

32. Levinas, "Substitution," in *The Levinas Reader*, 106.

33. For an example of this feminist celebration of Kristeva, see Moi, *Sexual/Textual Politics*. Moi ultimately finds positive feminist elements in Kristeva's thought, despite her critique of Kristeva's individualism (see note 28, above). For a more recent example, see essays in Oliver, *Ethics, Politics, and Difference in Julia Kristeva's Writing*.

34. For an incisive critique of the distortions produced by the construction of "French feminism," see Delphy, "The Invention of French Feminism."

Chapter 4

An earlier version of this chapter was published in *Yale French Studies* 87 (1995): 20–41.

1. Barbara Johnson, "Poetry and Performative Language: Mallarmé and Austin," in *The Critical Difference: Essays in the Contemporary Rhetoric of Reading* (Baltimore: Johns Hopkins University Press, 1980), 57–58.

2. My analysis here is drawn primarily from the work of Judith Butler and, to a lesser degree, Eve Kosofsky Sedgwick. Butler has undeniably led the way in popularizing the notion of performativity. See especially *Gender Trouble*; "Gender Trouble, Feminist Theory, and Psychoanalytic Discourse," in *Feminism/Postmodernism*, ed. Nicholson, 324–40; "Imitation and Gender Insubordination," in *Inside/Out: Lesbian Theories, Gay Theories*, ed. Diana Fuss (New York: Routledge, 1991), 13–31; "Contingent Foundations: Feminism and the Question of 'Postmodernism,'" in *Feminists Theorize the Political*, ed. Butler and Scott, 3–21; *Bodies That Matter*; and "Endangered/Endangering: Schematic Racism and White Paranoia," in *Reading Rodney King / Reading Urban Uprising*, ed. Robert Gooding-Williams (New York: Routledge, 1993), 15–22. For Sedgwick, see especially *Epistemology of the Closet* (Berkeley: University of California Press, 1990) and *Tendencies* (Durham, N.C.: Duke University Press, 1993). Also see Andrew Parker and Eve Kosofsky Sedgwick, eds., *Performativity and Performance* (New York: Routledge, 1995); and Peggy Phelan, *Unmarked: The Politics of Performance* (New York: Routledge, 1993). For work in the social sciences, see James C. Scott, *Domination and the Arts of Resistance: Hidden Transcripts* (New Haven, Conn.: Yale University Press, 1990); Melvin Patrick Ely, *The Adventures of Amos 'N' Andy: A Social History of an American Phenomenon* (New York: Free Press, 1990); and I. M. Lewis, *Ecstatic Religion: A Study of Shamanism and Spirit Possession* (New York: Routledge, 1989). My thanks to Cathy Cohen for bringing this work in the social sciences to my attention. Finally, my understanding of performativity is crucially and most significantly indebted to the work of Luce Irigaray, especially in *Speculum* and *This Sex*.

3. The problem of what constitutes an ethical question is hardly a simple one. As Claire Nouvet points out, "we can no longer use the word 'ethics' or engage in an ethical discourse without taking note of a certain reticence. . . . The reticence to engage in an ethical discourse thus invokes another kind of ethicity, another and more imperative duty; the duty of a relentless questioning from which not even an 'ethical' discourse should be exempted" (103). See Nouvet, "An Impossible Response." My ethical critique of performativity follows Nouvet, for whom it is "the question of the other which becomes the eth-

ical question par excellence" (103). For a sociological critique of Butler, Sedgwick, and other queer theorists who fail to engage with ethical questions, see Steven Seidman, "Deconstructing Queer Theory, or the Undertheorization of the Social and the Ethical," in *Social Postmodernism: Beyond Identity Politics*, ed. Linda Nicholson and Seidman (Cambridge: Cambridge University Press, 1995), 116–41.

4. On Irigaray and ethics, see especially Whitford, *Irigaray: Philosophy in the Feminine*: "For Irigaray, epistemology without ethics is deadly" (149). Also see Grosz, *Sexual Subversions*, esp. chap. 5, "Luce Irigaray and the Ethics of Alterity"; Grosz, "The Hetero and the Homo: The Sexual Ethics of Luce Irigaray," in *Engaging with Irigaray*, ed. Burke, Schor, and Whitford, 335–50; Cornell, *Beyond Accommodation*; Spivak, "French Feminism Revisited"; and Chanter, *Ethics of Eros*. Chanter's chapter on Irigaray and Levinas ("Levinas and the Question of the Other") is particularly noteworthy for the clarity of its explanation of Levinas's influence on Irigaray's concept of ethics.

5. In both *Gender Trouble* and *Bodies That Matter*, Butler draws on Irigarayan mimesis or mimicry to develop her theory of performativity. See especially *Bodies That Matter*, 36–55. For work on Irigaray and mimicry, see Chapter 2, note 8.

6. Following J. L. Austin and Emile Benvéniste, Shoshana Felman points out that the performative is necessarily self-referential. Further, the self-referentiality of the performative links it to a structure of seduction: "Just as seductive discourse exploits the capacity of language to reflect itself, by means of the self-referentiality of performative verbs, it also exploits in parallel fashion the self-referentiality of the interlocutor's narcissistic desire, and his (or her) capacity to produce in turn a reflexive, specular illusion" (31). See Shoshana Felman, *The Literary Speech Act: Don Juan with J. L. Austin, or Seduction in Two Languages*, trans. Catherine Porter (Ithaca, N.Y.: Cornell University Press, 1983).

7. Much has been made of this term in contemporary debates about poststructuralism and postmodernism. In his early formulation of the concept of "play" (*le jeu*), Jacques Derrida makes no claim to it ever being "free"; rather, he takes pains to demonstrate the relationship between "play" and the structure that constrains it. See especially "Structure, Sign and Play" in *Writing and Difference*, trans. Alan Bass (Chicago: University of Chicago Press, 1978), 278–93; and his response to Gerald Graff in *Limited Inc.* (Evanston, Ill.: Northwestern University Press, 1988), esp. 115–16.

8. My use of the term "foundation" is quite deliberate here. Butler argues against an essentializing foundationalism (in "Contingent Foundations") because of the ontological claims upheld by any foundationalist argument. I fol-

low Levinas here in asserting the necessity of ethics, and *not* ontology, as a "first philosophy." As such, ethics accounts for an always prior sociality that subtends ontology, thereby constituting a legitimate, non-essentializing foundation for discourse and politics. We should not annihilate the other, for it is precisely the question of the other that puts "us" into question. That is a foundationalist claim which bases itself on the necessity of being put into question. See especially Levinas, "Ethics as First Philosophy," in *The Levinas Reader*, 75–87, as well as the first section of *Totality and Infinity*.

9. As Butler herself admits: "That the identity-sign I use now has its purposes seems right, but there is no way to predict or control the political uses to which that sign will be put in the future" ("Imitation," 19). Similarly, Butler asserts that "the effects of an action always supersede the stated intention or purpose of the act" ("Contingent Foundations," 10). However, she nonetheless makes liberatory claims for a performativity that would suit *her* purposes ("a very different performative purpose" ["Imitation," 24]), that is, the parodic subversion of heterosexual identity. What keeps Butler's purposeful redeployment from being, yet again, redeployed, with perhaps drastically different purposes? Nothing, we all admit, since iterability as repetition is precisely the point. Which is precisely why performativity alone is inadequate as political theory.

10. Patricia Hill Collins's work toward developing a black feminist epistemology can be seen as a model here. In *Black Feminist Thought*, Collins examines two contrasting epistemologies, a traditional "epistemology of separation" and "an epistemology of connection in which truth emerges through care" (217). While Collins's absolute division between separation and connection is problematic, her call for an ethic of care questions the very process by which knowledge claims are legitimated. This ethical stance does not deny the possibility of truth, but offers a challenge to "what has been taken to be true" (219) by opening a dialogue with those who have been silenced..

11. My thanks to Valerie Smith, whose lecture at Yale (fall 1993) on the two versions of the film *Imitation of Life* pushed me to rethink the terms of that opposition between performance and narrative.

12. Benhabib, *Situating the Self*, 219.

13. Nancy Fraser and Linda J. Nicholson, "Social Criticism without Philosophy," *Feminism/Postmodernism*, ed. Nicholson, 33.

14. See Lyotard, *The Postmodern Condition*. For a critique of Lyotard's "ethnological" view of a "prereflexive" or "primitive" narrative of the other, see Benhabib, *Situating the Self*, esp. 233n19.

15. Andrew Parker and Eve Kosofsky Sedgwick, "Introduction: Performativity and Performance," in *Performativity and Performance*, 5.

16. Indeed, Butler herself acknowledges this danger in her essay on hate speech, "Burning Acts—Injurious Speech," in *Performativity and Performance*, ed. Parker and Sedgwick, 197–227.

17. See Levinas on Martin Buber's *I and Thou* (1923) in "Martin Buber and the Theory of Knowledge" (1958), in *The Levinas Reader*, 59–74.

18. In a related argument, Leonard Harris asserts that postmodernism is grounded on "a vision which makes invisible the immiserated and renders 'the subject' devoid of the traits of agency associated with resisting oppression" (367). See Leonard Harris, "Postmodernism and Utopia, an Unholy Alliance," in *I Am Because We Are*, ed. Hord (Mzee Lasana Okpara) and Lee, 367–82.

19. Butler herself reads the violent effects of white police brutality on the black body of Rodney King in "Endangered/Endangering." Butler illustrates the twisted logic through which the jury read the videotaped scene of aggression; in that reading, white racism provides a context for the jury's interpretation of the video "performance," one that claimed to "see" Rodney King as the source of violence. Butler reads that reversal as a projection of white racist violence onto Rodney King, who in the jury's view becomes the "black" aggressor, his body the site for the displacement of "white" aggression. The self-legitimating reversal of that reading of a particular "performance" demonstrates precisely what Butler's theory of performativity lacks: the need for an ethical frame within which to ask about reading.

20. See especially Patricia J. Williams, "Alchemical Notes: Reconstructing Ideals from Deconstructed Rights," *Harvard Civil Rights–Civil Liberties Law Review* 22 (1987): 401–33. Williams challenges the Critical Legal Studies movement's rejection of rights-based theory, arguing that "for the historically disempowered, the conferring of rights is symbolic of all the denied aspects of humanity" (416). "The concept of rights," Williams concludes, "is the marker of our citizenship, our participatoriness, *our relation to others*" (431; my emphasis). For a similar rights-based argument, see Mari Matsuda, "Looking to the Bottom: Critical Legal Studies and Reparations," *Harvard Civil Rights–Civil Liberties Law Review* 22 (1987): 323–99. Also see Elizabeth M. Schneider, "The Dialectic of Rights and Politics: Perspectives from the Women's Movement," *New York University Law Review* 61 (October 1986): 589–652. Many thanks to Carla Kaplan for bringing this work to my attention.

21. Levinas: "The effort of this book is directed toward apperceiving in discourse a non-allergic reaction with alterity, toward apperceiving Desire—where power, by essence murderous of the other, becomes, faced with the other and 'against all good sense,' the impossibility of murder, the consideration of the other, or justice" (*Totality and Infinity*, 47).

22. See Plato's *Republic*, book 10, for the exclusion of imitation from philosophy: "Then the imitator, I said, is a long way off the truth, and can do all things because he lightly touches on a small part of them, and that part an image" (365).

23. The twelve lectures collected under the title *How to Do Things with Words* were delivered by Austin at Harvard University in 1955. The printed text was constituted from Austin's notes for these lectures. See J. L. Austin, *How to Do Things with Words*, ed. J. O. Urmson and Marina Sbisà (Cambridge, Mass.: Harvard University Press, 1962).

24. Timothy Gould, "The Unhappy Performative," in *Performativity and Performance*, ed. Parker and Sedgwick, 40. In his critique of Derrida's reading of Austin, Stanley Cavell emphasizes that Austin never divorced truth from the category of the performative: "Austin's introduction of an idea of force, his 'substitution' of something about force for something about truth is meant not as a revelation of truth as illusion or as will to power . . . , but rather as specifying the extent to which what may be called the value of truth—*call it an adequation of language and reality*, or a discovering of reality—is on the contrary as essential to performative as to constative utterances" (80; my emphasis). Cavell further points out that "what Austin 'substitutes' for the logically defined concept of truth is *not force but 'felicity'*" (81). Therefore, Cavell argues, constatives, "*if adequate to reality*, are true, *if not*, false" (81; my emphasis). Performatives, "*if adequate to reality*, are felicitous, *if not*, then, in specific ways, infelicitous" (81; my emphasis). While I agree with Cavell that the value of truth applies both to constatives and performatives, Austin's introduction of the concept of "illocutionary force" clearly justifies discussing performatives within a discourse that links language and power. See Stanley Cavell, "Counter-Philosophy and the Pawn of Voice," in *A Pitch of Philosophy: Autobiographical Exercises* (Cambridge, Mass.: Harvard University Press, 1994), 53–128. For a shorter version of the same argument, see Stanley Cavell, "What Did Derrida Want of Austin?" and "Seminar on 'What Did Derrida Want of Austin?'" in *Philosophical Passages: Wittgenstein, Emerson, Austin, Derrida* (Oxford: Blackwell, 1995), 42–65 and 66–90.

25. Sedgwick lists other examples of "queer" identity: "(among other possibilities) pushy femmes, radical faeries, fantasists, drags, clones, leatherfolk, ladies in tuxedoes, feminist women or feminist men, masturbators, bulldaggers, divas, Snap! queens, butch bottoms, storytellers, transsexuals, aunties, wannabes, lesbian-identified men or lesbians who sleep with men, or . . . people able to relish, learn from, or *identify* with such" (*Tendencies*, 8; my emphasis).

26. As Felman puts it: "The scandal [of the performative seduction] con-

sists in the fact that the act cannot *know what it is doing* (96). Felman calls this scandal Austin's "radical negativity," thus aligning him with thinkers such as Nietzsche and Lacan: "Thus Austin, like Lacan, like Nietzsche, like others still, instigators of the historical scandal, Don Juans of History, are in reality *bequeathing* us what they do not have: their *word*, their authority, their promise. . . . Modern Don Juans, they know that *truth is only an act*" (150). While I agree with Felman that the absolute authority of the word is put into question by the very terms of the utterance itself, it seems important to make distinctions between the relative levels of authority that are accorded particular discourses within historically constituted structures of power.

27. On the collapsing of difference into the self-identical sameness of philosophical truth, see Irigaray, *Speculum*. Also see my analysis in Chapter 2.

28. Levinas: "Critique does not reduce the other to the same as does ontology, but calls into question the exercise of the same. A calling into question of the same—which cannot occur within the egoist spontaneity of the same—is brought about by the other. We name this calling into question of my spontaneity by the presence of the Other ethics. The strangeness of the Other, his irreducibility to the I, to my thoughts and my possessions, is precisely accomplished as a calling into question of my spontaneity, my ethics" (*Totality and Infinity*, 43).

29. On the opposition between truth-value and the value of force in Austin, see Derrida, *Limited Inc*, 13. On the seductive force of the performative, see Felman, *The Literary Speech Act*.

30. Steven Seidman makes a similar critique of Sedgwick and Butler when he asks: "What ethical guidelines would permit such sexual innovation while being attentive to considerations of power and legitimate normative regulation? . . . [There is] a refusal on the part of many queer theorists to articulate their own ethical and political standpoint and to imagine a constructive social project" (136). See his "Deconstructing Queer Theory."

31. Stanley Cavell makes much of Austin's concern for morality, especially in Austin's discussion of Euripides, intention, and the danger of using metaphysics "to get out of the moral of the ordinary" ("Seminar," 75). However, Cavell fails to acknowledge the political and social structures that define what he calls "the ordinary" as a system of power in which some are privileged and others are not.

32. Unless otherwise noted, the quotes in this dialogue are taken from Irigaray's *Speculum of the Other Woman*, 43, 60, and 72 (translation modified); from her *This Sex Which Is Not One*, 76, 205, 206, 208, 209, 210, and 212; and from *Ce sexe qui n'en est pas un*, 217.

33. Felman: "To seduce is to produce felicitous language" (28). And further: "I had better declare at once that I am *seduced* by Austin" (73). See her *Literary Speech Act*.

34. On Irigaray and mimicry or mimesis, see especially Moi, *Sexual/Textual Politics*; Gallop, *Thinking Through the Body*; Grosz, *Sexual Subversions*; Schor, "This Essentialism Which Is Not One"; Christine Holmlund, "I Love Luce: The Lesbian, Mimesis and Masquerade in Irigaray, Freud and Mainstream Film," *New Formations* 9 (winter 1989): 105–23; Berg, "Irigaray's 'Contradictions'"; Braidotti, *Patterns of Dissonance*; Whitford, *Irigaray: Philosophy in the Feminine*; and Cornell, *Beyond Accommodation*.

35. Audre Lorde, "The Master's Tools Will Never Dismantle the Master's House," in *Sister Outsider*, 110–13.

36. See Judith Herman, *Trauma and Recovery* (New York: Basic Books, 1992), on the connection between hysteria and sexual abuse. Freud's publication of *The Aetiology of Hysteria* (1896), which describes that connection, was met with disbelief and ridicule by his colleagues. He subsequently abandoned what has now become known as the seduction theory. On the link between Freud's abandonment of the seduction theory and the development of his theory of the Oedipus complex, see Brenkman, *Straight Male Modern*. As Brenkman puts it: "By concluding that his women patients had not after all been 'seduced' by a male relative, but had rather fantasized such scenes of seduction based on their *own* repressed wishes, Freud attributed the basis of neurosis to children's incestuous wishes rather than adults' incestuous acts. He simultaneously accorded the 'psychic reality' of fantasy the same import as the 'material reality' of remembered events. The paradigm shift was not complete, however, until the emerging concept of the Oedipus complex could be modeled on the *male* child's fantasies rather than the little girl's experience whether real or imagined" (87).

37. Humor is a funny thing, as Freud and others have noted. A case in point is Felman's reading of Austin's humor, which she highlights in order to emphasize the subversive, self-deprecating impulse underlying Austin's speech act theory. However, to what extent does such a reading of subversion depend on a shared cultural code? Indeed, as outsiders to a hegemonic masculinist code of laughter, feminists are often accused of having no sense of humor. Conversely, those who do not share the marginal or "lesbian" code of Irigaray's labial play may not find her essay funny. In that regard, I would like to thank Galen Sherwin for our illuminating discussions about Irigaray's "inside" jokes. James Scott points to a similar dynamic of shared humor as part of a culture of resistance in *Domination and the Arts of Resistance*. See also Sigmund Freud,

"Jokes and Their Relation to the Unconscious," in *The Standard Edition of the Complete Psychological Works*, vol. 8, ed. and trans. James Strachey (London: Hogarth Press, 1961).

38. J. L. Austin: "Accuracy and morality alike are on the side of the plain saying that *our word is our bond*" (*How to Do Things with Words*, 10).

39. See Pierre Fontanier, *Les figures du discours* (Paris: Flammarion, 1977), 189; and Warminski, *Readings in Interpretation*, liii and lix. Also see Spivak, "French Feminism Revisited," who argues that we must "accept the risk of catachresis" because the "*political* use of words, like the use of words, is irreducibly catachrestic" (72).

40. See Marilyn Frye, "To See and Be Seen," in *The Politics of Reality: Essays in Feminist Theory* (Trumansburg, N.Y.: The Crossing Press, 1983), 152–74. Frye compares phallocratic reality to a play where the actors are men and the stagehands are women; women exist as such by "*loving* the actors and taking actors' interests and commitments unto themselves as their own" (169). For Frye, lesbianism means a shift of attention from the actors to the stagehands: "If the lesbian sees the women, the woman may see the lesbian seeing her. With this, there is a flowering of possibilities" (172).

41. There is much critical disagreement regarding my implicit assertion here that Irigaray provides an alternative, antinostalgic, *lesbian* model of relation. Diana Fuss, for example, proclaims Irigaray to be among "those feminist theorists . . . who have perhaps done the most to valorise 'lesbian' in contemporary critical theory" (*Essentially Speaking*, 111). Annamarie Jagose, on the other hand, sees the Irigarayan lesbian as both "remedy" and "poison": "Superfluous and necessary, dangerous and redemptive, (female) homosexuality is both that of which and by which heterosexuality must be cured" (39). Although Jagose's argument is compelling, I disagree with her underlying interpretation of the Irigarayan "relations of mimeticism between women" as "structured by trajectories of identification rather than desire" (35). On the contrary, I would argue that the "lips" essay in particular constitutes a veritable enactment of lesbian desire. See Annamarie Jagose, "Irigaray and the Lesbian Body: Remedy and Poison," *Genders* 13 (1992): 30–42.

42. "I love you is always something of a quotation, as many lovers have attested" (Jonathan Culler, *On Deconstruction: Theory and Criticism After Structuralism* [Ithaca, N.Y.: Cornell University Press, 1982], 120). More radically, see Paul de Man on the figure of the erotic: "Rather than being a heightened version of sense experience, the erotic is a figure that makes such experience possible. We do not see what we love but we love in the hope of confirming the illusion that we are indeed seeing anything at all" ("Hypogram and Inscription," in *The*

Resistance to Theory [Minneapolis: University of Minnesota Press, 1986], 53n23).
In a similar vein, Catherine Belsey asks: "How can we, unique and autonomous
as we long to be, capture the extraordinary experience of desire in the repeti-
tion of this worn-out commonplace, this blank performative . . . ?" (685). See
Catherine Belsey, "Postmodern Love: Questioning the Metaphysics of Desire,"
New Literary History 25 (1994): 683–705.

43. Lacan: "the phallus can only play its role as veiled" (82). See Jacques
Lacan, "The Meaning of the Phallus," in *Feminine Sexuality: Jacques Lacan and
the école freudienne*, ed. Juliet Mitchell and Jacqueline Rose, trans. Jacqueline
Rose (New York: Norton, 1982).

Chapter 5

An earlier version of this chapter appeared in *Yale French Studies* 90 (1996):
95–114.

1. See Scott, *Domination and the Arts of Resistance*.

2. Hélène Cixous is famous for drawing on female biology in order to contrast a liberatory *écriture féminine*, or "feminine writing," with traditional forms
of masculine artistic production. As she puts it in "The Laugh of the Medusa":
"There is always within her at least a little of that good mother's milk. She
writes in white ink" (251). Reprinted in *New French Feminisms*, ed. Marks and
Courtivron, 245–64; translation of "Le Rire de la Meduse," *L'Arc* 61 (1975):
39–54. On *écriture féminine*, also see my Introduction, note 30.

3. Monique Wittig, *The Lesbian Body*, trans. David Le Vay (New York: Morrow, 1975), 26; translation of *Le Corps lesbien* (Paris: Minuit, 1973).

4. For a detailed examination of this heritage, especially in the French literary tradition, see Joan DeJean, *Fictions of Sappho: 1546–1937* (Chicago: University of Chicago Press, 1989).

5. Grahn, *The Highest Apple*, 5.

6. As one lesbian critic puts it: " 'Lesbian' is a word written in invisible ink,
readable when held up to a flame and self-consuming, a disappearing trick before my eyes where the letters appear and fade into the paper on which they
are written, like a field which inscribes them. An unwriting goes on as quickly
as the inscription takes (its) place. Not the erasure of time's vast conspiratorial
silence, that invisibility censoriously imposed on us, but an un-writing as care-
fully prepared and enacted as the act of lesbian: composition itself. Lesbian"
(18). See Elizabeth A. Meese, *(Sem)erotics: Theorizing Lesbian Writing* (New York:
New York University Press, 1992).

7. Adrienne Rich, "Cartographies of Silence," in *The Dream of a Common
Language*, 17.

8. Nicole Brossard, *Lovhers*, trans. Barbara Godard (Montreal: Guernica, 1986), 20; translation of *Amantes* (Montreal: Editions Quinze, 1980).

9. Lynne Huffer, "Interview with Nicole Brossard," *Yale French Studies* 87 (1995): 119–20.

10. Brossard, *French Kiss, or A Pang's Progress*, trans. Patricia Claxton (Toronto: Coach House Press, 1986), 13; translation of *French Kiss: Etreinte/Exploration* (Montreal: Editions Quinze, 1980).

11. "La lettre aérienne, c'est ce qu'il advient de moi (par écrit) lorsque lentement se met à l'oeuvre une émotion qui m'ouvre à d'autres formes existentielles que celles qui me sont connues par la pratique anecdotique que j'ai des moeurs politiques, culturelles, sexuelles ou sensuelles. Lettre aérienne, c'est le fantasme qui me donne à lire et à écrire en trois dimensions, c'est mon laser. . . . Ainsi l'écriture telle que je la conçois avec ses lettres aériennes est-elle ce qui me permet d'avoir à la fois un oeil ouvert sur l'anecdote historique (de laquelle d'ailleurs je dépends) ainsi que sur ce qui me développe une vision globale: cortex et peau, de toute mémoire gyn/écologique" (65–66). See Brossard, *La lettre aérienne* (Montreal: Remue-ménage, 1985).

12. Brossard, *These Our Mothers, Or: The Disintegrating Chapter*, trans. Barbara Godard (Toronto: Coach House Press, 1983), 29; translation of *L'Amèr, ou le chapitre effrité* (Montreal: Editions Quinze, 1977).

13. Pierre Nepveu, "BJ/NBJ: Difficile modernité," *Voix et images* 10/2 (1985): 163, as translated and cited in Karen Gould, *Writing in the Feminine: Feminism and Experimental Writing in Quebec* (Carbondale: Southern Illinois University Press, 1990), 58.

14. See Chapter 1, "Blanchot's Mother," for a detailed analysis of Blanchot's concept of "neutrality." Blanchot describes the act of writing as a paradoxical movement of approach and separation, a reaching toward the referent—the object-to-be-written—which becomes nothing more than a point of absence that moves away the more closely it is approached. The space of literature is therefore a space of pure reflection, a movement of tropes in which language merely mirrors itself. Blanchot uses the term "neutrality" to describe this self-reflective realm of poetic communication that displays its own removal from a world of meanings and relative values. See especially Blanchot, *L'Espace littéraire* and *Le Livre à venir* (Paris: Gallimard, 1959).

15. Brossard, "Ce que pouvait être, ici, une avant-garde," *Voix et images* 10/2 (1985): 80, as translated and cited in Gould, *Writing in the Feminine*, 57.

16. In *La Lettre aérienne*, Brossard asks: "Mais qui sont ces femmes qui me donnent du texte à penser, de l'espace à conquérir, du temps pour renaître en chacun de leurs textes? Je les appelle urbaines radicales" (58).

17. Brossard describes the "fabular subject" (*le sujet fabuleux*) as the fictional construction of an empowered female subject: "Sujet inadmissible, le sujet féminin semble n'être réel que dans l'écriture de fiction qui le fait advenir. C'est en effet dans ce lieu (la fiction), là où le sens ordinaire est continuellement déçu, déjoué, contourné, défait et trompé par la façon (la manière de dire), que l'épreuve du sens peut véritablement avoir lieu. C'est là même où il y a 'illusion référentielle' que théoriquement nous, femmes, traversons l'opaque réalité sémantique et que le sujet fabuleux que nous sommes devient opérant" (*La Lettre aérienne*, 138–39).

18. In her translation of *Amantes*, Barbara Godard explains that *ma* designates both the possessive pronoun, feminine gender in French and, as *mâ*, the Japanese term for space.

19. Brossard, *La Nuit verte du parc labyrinthe* (Montreal: Trois, 1992), 41 (my translation).

20. Caughnawaga, Quebec, is the name of a Mohawk reservation on the Saint Lawrence River just south of present-day Montreal. The name Caughnawaga comes from the Mohawk *kahnawâ.ke*, which means "at the rapids." Originally the name of one of several Mohawk villages in the Mohawk Valley in what is now upstate New York, the name was later given to the settlement on the Saint Lawrence established by the Mohawks in the seventeenth century, many of whom came from the Mohawk Valley after their villages were destroyed by the European invaders. Today the Caughnawaga Reserve is located at the Lachine Rapids across the river from Montreal.

21. "Et au parmy d'icelles champaignes, est scitué[e] et assise ladicte ville de Hochelaga, près et joignant vne montaigne, qui est, à l'entour d'icelle, labourée et fort fertille, de dessus laquelle on voyt fort loing" (*French Kiss*, original version, 157).

22. See Bruce G. Trigger, "Hochelaga: History and Ethnohistory," in *Cartier's Hochelaga and the Dawson Site*, ed. James F. Pendergast and Trigger (Montreal: McGill-Queen's University Press, 1972), 1–93. Also see Trigger, *Natives and Newcomers: Canada's "Heroic Age" Reconsidered* (Montreal: McGill-Queen's University Press, 1985).

23. Brossard, *Picture Theory*, trans. Barbara Godard (New York: Roof Books, 1990); translation of *Picture Theory* (Montreal: L'Hexagone, 1989).

Afterword

1. See especially Benhabib, *Situating the Self*; Claudia Card, ed., *Feminist Ethics* (Lawrence: University of Kansas Press, 1990); Chanter, *Ethics of Eros*; Eve Browning Cole and Susan Coultrap-McQuin, eds., *Explorations in Feminist*

Ethics: Theory and Practice (Bloomington: Indiana University Press, 1992); Collins, *Black Feminist Thought*; Cornell, *Beyond Accommodation*; Moira Gatens, *Imaginary Bodies: Ethics, Power, and Corporeality* (New York: Routledge, 1996); Gilligan, *In a Different Voice*; Sarah Hoagland, *Lesbian Ethics: Toward New Value* (Palo Alto, Calif.: Institute of Lesbian Studies, 1988); Irigaray, *An Ethics of Sexual Difference*; Mary Jeanne Larrabee, ed., *An Ethic of Care: Feminist and Interdisciplinary Perspectives* (New York: Routledge, 1993); Lilian Mohin, ed., *An Intimacy of Equals: Lesbian Feminist Ethics* (London: Onlywomen Press, 1996); Martha Nussbaum, "Human Functioning and Social Justice: In Defense of Aristotelian Essentialism," *Political Theory* 20 (1992): 202–46; Susan Moller Okin, *Justice, Gender, and the Family* (New York: Basic Books, 1989); Elisabeth J. Porter, *Women and Moral Identity* (North Sydney: Allen and Unwin, 1991); Joan Tronto, *Moral Boundaries: A Political Argument for an Ethic of Care* (New York: Routledge, 1993); Iris Marion Young, *Justice and the Politics of Difference* (Princeton, N.J.: Princeton University Press, 1990). For a critique of the contemporary feminist "hunger for ethics" as a desire to maintain race and class privilege by being "good," see Marilyn Frye, "A Response to *Lesbian Ethics*: Why Ethics?" in *Willful Virgin: Essays in Feminism, 1976–1992* (Freedom, Calif.: The Crossing Press, 1992), 138–46.

2. This is not to imply that these conversations have not occurred. In *Feminist Contentions*, Judith Butler and Seyla Benhabib engage in a debate about feminism, postmodernism, and ethical questions. While some aspects of this exchange are useful for feminist theory, in this particular conversation Butler and Benhabib appear to be talking past each other. This does not mean, in my view, that feminist "postmodernists" and "universalists" cannot speak to each other; rather, it highlights the difficulty of such conversations. See Seyla Benhabib, Judith Butler, Drucilla Cornell, and Nancy Fraser, eds., *Feminist Contentions: A Philosophical Exchange* (New York: Routledge, 1995).

3. See Lyotard, *The Postmodern Condition*.

4. See Hannah Arendt, *The Life of the Mind* (New York: Harcourt Brace Jovanovich, 1978). Also see Hannah Arendt, "Thinking and Moral Considerations: A Lecture," *Social Research* 38 (1971), 417–46.

5. Butler, "Gender Trouble, Feminist Theory, and Psychoanalytic Discourse," 339.

6. This is not to suggest that Benhabib is an idealist. Rather, her approach to human communication is ultimately pragmatic: "There will always be a discrepancy between what we mean and what we say; but we engage in communication, theoretical no less than everyday communication, to gain some basis of mutual understanding and reasoning" (*Situating the Self*, 216). For a critique of

Habermas's commitment to reason (to the exclusion of private desire, need, and feeling), see Young, *Justice and the Politics of Difference*, esp. 118. For an interesting reading of Habermas that incorporates the evaluative and interpretive pluralism of art and literary criticism, see Georgia Warnke, "Discourse Ethics and Feminist Dilemmas of Difference," in *Feminists Read Habermas: Gendering the Subject of Discourse*, ed. Johanna Meehan (New York: Routledge, 1995), 247–62.

7. See Cathy Caruth, *Unclaimed Experience: Trauma, Narrative, and History* (Baltimore: Johns Hopkins University Press, 1996).

8. See especially Shoshana Felman and Dori Laub, M.D., *Testimony: Crises of Witnessing in Literature, Psychoanalysis, and History* (New York: Routledge, 1992). In the face of the "historical unspeakability" of the Holocaust and our collective sacralization of that silence, Felman and Laub call on our ability to listen to the survivors, "the bearers of the silence," in order "to enact the *liberation of the testimony* from the bondage of the secret" (xix).

Abel, Elizabeth. "Narrative Structure(s) and Female Development." In *The Voyage In: Fictions of Female Development*, ed. Abel, Marianne Hirsch, and Elizabeth Langland. Hanover, N.H.: University Press of New England, 1983.

Alta. "Euridice." In *I Am Not a Practicing Angel*. Freedom, Calif.: The Crossing Press, 1975.

Amsberg, Kiki, and Aafke Steenhuis. "Interview with Luce Irigaray." *Hecate: A Women's Interdisciplinary Journal* 9/1, 2 (1983): 192–202.

Arendt, Hannah. *The Life of the Mind*. New York: Harcourt Brace Jovanovich, 1978.

———. "Thinking and Moral Considerations: A Lecture." *Social Research* 38 (1971), 417–46.

Asante, Molefi Kete. *The Afrocentric Idea*. Philadephia: Temple University Press, 1987.

———. *Afrocentricity*. Trenton: Africa World Press, 1988.

———. *Kemet, Afrocentricity, and Knowledge*. Trenton: Africa World Press, 1990.

Austin, J. L. *How to Do Things with Words*. Ed. J. O. Urmson and Marina Sbisà. Cambridge, Mass.: Harvard University Press, 1962.

Barthes, Roland. *Image/Music/Text*. Trans. Stephen Heath. New York: Noonday Press, 1977.

Beauvoir, Simone de. *The Second Sex*. Trans. Howard Madison Parshley. New York: Random House, 1952.

Belsey, Catherine. "Postmodern Love: Questioning the Metaphysics of Desire." *New Literary History* 25 (1994): 683–705.

Benhabib, Seyla. *Situating the Self: Gender, Community and Postmodernism in Contemporary Ethics*. New York: Routledge, 1992.

Benhabib, Seyla, Judith Butler, Drucilla Cornell, and Nancy Fraser, eds. *Feminist Contentions: A Philosophical Exchange*. New York: Routledge, 1995.

Benjamin, Jessica. *The Bonds of Love: Psychoanalysis, Feminism, and the Problem of Domination*. New York: Pantheon, 1988.

Benstock, Shari. *Textualizing the Feminine: On the Limits of Genre*. Norman: University of Oklahoma Press, 1991.

Berg, Maggie. "Luce Irigaray's 'Contradictions': Poststructuralism and Feminism." *Signs: Journal of Women in Culture and Society* 17/1 (1991): 50–70.

Bersani, Leo. *Homos*. Cambridge, Mass.: Harvard University Press, 1995.

Blanchot, Maurice. *L'Arrêt de mort*. Paris: Gallimard, 1948. Trans. Lydia Davis as *Death Sentence*. Barrytown, N.Y.: Station Hill Press, 1978.

———. *L'Écriture du désastre*. Paris: Gallimard, 1980. Trans. Ann Smock as *The Writing of the Disaster*. Lincoln: University of Nebraska Press, 1986.

———. *L'Entretien infini*. Paris: Gallimard, 1969. Trans. Susan Hanson as *The Infinite Conversation*. Minneapolis: University of Minnesota Press, 1993.

———. *L'Espace littéraire*. Paris: Gallimard, 1955. Trans. Ann Smock as *The Space of Literature*. Lincoln: University of Nebraska Press, 1982.

———. *La Folie du jour*. Montpellier: Fata Morgana, 1973. Trans. Lydia Davis as *Madness of the Day*. Barrytown, N.Y.: Station Hill Press, 1981.

———. *The Gaze of Orpheus and Other Literary Essays*. Trans. Lydia Davis, ed. P. Adams Sitney. Barrytown, N.Y.: Station Hill Press, 1981.

———. *Le Livre à venir*. Paris: Gallimard, 1959.

Braidotti, Rosi. *Nomadic Subjects: Embodiment and Sexual Difference in Contemporary Feminist Theory*. New York: Columbia University Press, 1994.

———. *Patterns of Dissonance: A Study of Women in Contemporary Philosophy*. Trans. Elizabeth Guild. New York: Routledge, 1991.

Brenkman, John. *Straight Male Modern: A Cultural Critique of Psychoanalysis*. New York: Routledge, 1993.

Brossard, Nicole. *Amantes*. Montreal: Editions Quinze, 1980. Trans. Barbara Godard as *Lovhers*. Montreal: Guernica, 1986.

———. *L'Amèr ou le Chapitre effrité*. Montreal: Editions Quinze, 1977. Trans. Barbara Godard as *These Our Mothers, Or: The Disintegrating Chapter*. Toronto: Coach House Press, 1983.

———. *French Kiss: Etreinte/Exploration*. Montreal: Editions Quinze, 1980. Trans. Patricia Claxton as *French Kiss, or A Pang's Progress*. Toronto: Coach House Press, 1986.

———. *La Lettre aérienne*. Montreal: Remue-ménage, 1985.

———. *La Nuit verte du parc labyrinthe*. Montreal: Trois, 1992.

———. *Picture Theory*. Montreal: L'Hexagone, 1989. Trans. Barbara Godard as *Picture Theory*. New York: Roof Books, 1990.

———. "The Textured Angle of Desire." In *Another Look, Another Woman: Retranslations of French Feminism*, ed. Lynne Huffer, *Yale French Studies* 87 (1995): 105–14.

Bühler, Karl. *Theory of Language: The Representational Function of Language*. Trans. Donald Fraser Goodwin. Philadelphia: J. Benjamins, 1990.

Burke, Carolyn. "Romancing the Philosophers: Luce Irigaray." In *Seduction and Theory: Readings of Gender, Representation, and Rhetoric*, ed. Dianne Hunter. Urbana: University of Illinois Press, 1989.

Burke, Carolyn, Naomi Schor, and Margaret Whitford, eds. *Engaging with Irigaray*. New York: Columbia University Press, 1994.

Busia, Abena P. A. "What is Your Nation? Reconnecting Africa and Her Diaspora Through Paule Marshall's *Praisesong for the Widow*." In *Changing Our Own Words: Essays on Criticism, Theory, and Writing by Black Women*, ed. Cheryl A. Wall. New Brunswick, N.J.: Rutgers University Press, 1989.

Butler, Judith. *Bodies That Matter: On the Discursive Limits of "Sex"*. New York: Routledge, 1993.

———. "Burning Acts—Injurious Speech." In *Performativity and Performance*, ed. Andrew Parker and Eve Kosofsky Sedgwick. New York: Routledge, 1995.

———. "Contingent Foundations: Feminism and the Question of 'Postmodernism.'" In *Feminists Theorize the Political*, ed. Butler and Joan W. Scott. New York: Routledge, 1992.

———. "Endangered/Endangering: Schematic Racism and White Paranoia." In *Reading Rodney King / Reading Urban Uprising*, ed. Robert Gooding-Williams. New York: Routledge, 1993.

———. *Gender Trouble: Feminism and the Subversion of Identity*. New York: Routledge, 1990.

———. "Gender Trouble, Feminist Theory, and Psychoanalytic Discourse." In *Feminism/Postmodernism*, ed. Linda J. Nicholson. New York: Routledge, 1990.

———. "Imitation and Gender Insubordination." In *Inside/Out: Lesbian Theories, Gay Theories*, ed. Diana Fuss. New York: Routledge, 1991.

Butler, Judith, and Joan W. Scott, eds. *Feminists Theorize the Political*. New York: Routledge, 1992.

Card, Claudia, ed. *Feminist Ethics*. Lawrence: University of Kansas Press, 1990.

Caruth, Cathy. *Unclaimed Experience: Trauma, Narrative, and History*. Baltimore: Johns Hopkins University Press, 1996.

Cavell, Stanley. *Philosophical Passages: Wittgenstein, Emerson, Austin, Derrida*. Oxford: Blackwell, 1995.

———. *A Pitch of Philosophy: Autobiographical Exercises*. Cambridge, Mass.: Harvard University Press, 1994.

Césaire, Aimé. *Notebook of a Return to My Native Land*. Trans. Mireille Rosello with Anne Pritchard. Newcastle upon Tyne: Bloodaxe Books, 1995.

Chanter, Tina. *Ethics of Eros: Irigaray's Rewriting of the Philosophers*. New York: Routledge, 1995.

Chisholm, Dianne. "Irigaray's Hysteria." In *Engaging with Irigaray*, ed. Carolyn Burke, Naomi Schor, and Margaret Whitford. New York: Columbia University Press, 1994.

Chodorow, Nancy. *The Reproduction of Mothering: Psychoanalysis and the Sociology of Gender*. Berkeley: University of California Press, 1978.

Cixous, Hélène. *Illa*. Paris: Editions des femmes, 1980.

———. *Manna: For the Mandelstams, For the Mandelas*. Trans. Catherine A. F. MacGillivray. Minneapolis: University of Minnesota Press, 1994.

———. "Le Rire de la Méduse." *L'Arc* 61 (1975): 39–54. Trans. as "The Laugh of the Medusa." *Signs: Journal of Women in Culture and Society* 1/4 (1976): 875–93. Reprinted in *New French Feminisms*, ed. Elaine Marks and Isabelle de Courtivron. New York: Schocken, 1981, 245–64.

Clark, Timothy. *Derrida, Heidegger, Blanchot: Sources of Derrida's Notion and Practice of Literature*. Cambridge: Cambridge University Press, 1992.

Cohen, Richard A., ed. *Face to Face with Levinas*. Albany: State University of New York Press, 1986.

Cole, Eve Browning, and Susan Coultrap-McQuin, eds. *Explorations in Feminist Ethics: Theory and Practice*. Bloomington: Indiana University Press, 1992.

Collins, Patricia Hill. *Black Feminist Thought: Knowledge, Consciousness, and the Politics of Empowerment*. New York: Routledge, 1991.

Conley, Verena Andermatt. *Hélène Cixous: Writing the Feminine*. Lincoln: University of Nebraska Press, 1984.

Cornell, Drucilla. *Beyond Accommodation: Ethical Feminism, Deconstruction, and the Law*. New York: Routledge, 1991.

Culler, Jonathan. *On Deconstruction: Theory and Criticism After Structuralism*. Ithaca, N.Y.: Cornell University Press, 1982.

Davidson, Cathy N., and E. M. Broner, eds. *The Lost Tradition: Mothers and Daughters in Literature*. New York: Frederick Ungar, 1980.

DeJean, Joan. *Fictions of Sappho: 1546–1937*. Chicago: University of Chicago Press, 1989.

De Lauretis, Teresa. *The Practice of Love: Lesbian Sexuality and Perverse Desire*. Bloomington: Indiana University Press, 1994.

Delphy, Christine. "The Invention of French Feminism: An Essential Move." In *Another Look, Another Woman: Retranslations of French Feminism*, ed. Lynne Huffer, *Yale French Studies* 87 (1995): 190–221.

De Man, Paul. *Allegories of Reading: Figural Language in Rousseau, Nietzsche, Rilke, and Proust.* New Haven:Yale University Press, 1979.

———. *The Resistance to Theory.* Minneapolis: University of Minnesota Press, 1986.

———. *The Rhetoric of Romanticism.* New York: Columbia University Press, 1984.

———. "Tropes (Rilke)," in *Allegories of Reading: Figural Language in Rousseau, Nietzsche, Rilke, and Proust.* New Haven, Conn.:Yale University Press, 1979, 48.

Derrida, Jacques. *L'Écriture et la différence.* Paris: Seuil, 1967.

———. *Khôra.* Paris: Galilée, 1993.

———. "The Law of Genre." *Glyph* 7 (1980): 202–32.

———. *Limited Inc.* Evanston, Ill.: Northwestern University Press, 1988.

———. *Marges de la philosophie.* Paris: Minuit, 1972.

———. "Otobiographies:The Teaching of Nietzsche and the Politics of the Proper Name." Trans. Avital Ronell. In *The Ear of the Other: Otobiography, Transference, Translation,* ed. Christie McDonald. Lincoln: University of Nebraska Press, 1985.

———. *Parages.* Paris: Galilée, 1986.

———. *Spurs: Nietzsche's Styles / Eperons: Les Styles de Nietzsche.* Trans. Barbara Harlow. Chicago: University of Chicago Press, 1987.

———. "White Mythology." *New Literary History* 6 (1974): 5–74.

———. *Writing and Difference.* Trans. Alan Bass. Chicago: University of Chicago Press, 1978.

Djebar, Assia. *Women of Algiers in Their Apartments.* Trans. Marjolijn de Jager. Charlottesville: University Press of Virginia, 1992.

Doan, Laura, ed. *The Lesbian Postmodern.* New York: Columbia University Press, 1994.

Doane, Janice, and Devon Hodges. *Nostalgia and Sexual Difference:The Resistance to Contemporary Feminism.* New York: Methuen, 1987.

Doane, Mary Ann. "Cyborgs, Origins, and Subjectivity." In *Coming to Terms: Feminism, Theory, and Politics,* ed. Elizabeth Weed. New York: Routledge, 1989.

Eisenstein, Hester, and Alice Jardine, eds. *The Future of Difference.* Boston: G. K. Hall, 1980.

Ellman, Mary. *Thinking About Women.* New York: Harcourt, Brace and World, 1968.

Ely, Melvin Patrick. *The Adventures of Amos 'N' Andy: A Social History of an American Phenomenon.* New York: Free Press, 1990.

Essieu-Udom, Essien Udosen. *Black Nationalism: A Search for Identity in America*. Chicago: University of Chicago Press, 1962.

Felman, Shoshana. "Beyond Oedipus: The Specimen Story of Psychoanalysis." *Modern Language Notes* 95 (1983): 1021–53.

———. *The Literary Speech Act: Don Juan with J. L. Austin, or Seduction in Two Languages*. Trans. Catherine Porter. Ithaca, N.Y.: Cornell University Press, 1983.

Felman, Shoshana, and Dori Laub, M.D. *Testimony: Crises of Witnessing in Literature, Psychoanalysis, and History*. New York: Routledge, 1992.

Fontanier, Pierre. *Les figures du discours*. Paris: Flammarion, 1977.

Foucault, Michel. "Maurice Blanchot: The Thought from the Outside." Trans. Brian Massumi. In *Foucault/Blanchot*. New York: Zone Books, 1987.

———. "What Is an Author?" In *Textual Strategies*, ed. Josué Harari. Ithaca, N.Y.: Cornell University Press, 1979.

Fraser, Nancy. "Introduction: Revaluing French Feminism." In *Revaluing French Feminism: Critical Essays on Difference, Agency, and Culture*, ed. Fraser and Sandra Lee Bartky. Bloomington: Indiana University Press, 1992.

Freud, Sigmund. *The Standard Edition of the Complete Psychological Works*. Ed. and trans. James Strachey. London: Hogarth Press, 1961.

Frye, Marilyn. *The Politics of Reality: Essays in Feminist Theory*. Trumansburg, N.Y.: The Crossing Press, 1983.

———. "A Response to *Lesbian Ethics*: Why Ethics?" In *Willful Virgin: Essays in Feminism, 1976–1992*. Freedom, Calif.: The Crossing Press, 1992.

Fuss, Diana. *Essentially Speaking: Feminism, Nature, and Difference*. New York: Routledge, 1989.

———, ed. *Inside/Out: Lesbian Theories, Gay Theories*. New York: Routledge, 1991.

Gallop, Jane. *The Daughter's Seduction: Feminism and Psychoanalysis*. Ithaca, N.Y.: Cornell University Press, 1982.

———. *Intersections: A Reading of Sade with Bataille, Blanchot, and Klossowski*. Lincoln: University of Nebraska Press, 1981.

———. *Thinking Through the Body*. New York: Columbia University Press, 1988.

Gallop, Jane, and Carolyn Burke. "Psychoanalysis and Feminism in France." In *The Future of Difference*, ed. Hester Eisenstein and Alice Jardine. Boston: G. K. Hall, 1980.

Garvey, Marcus. *Philosophy and Opinions of Marcus Garvey*. Ed. Amy Jacques-Garvey. 2 vols. New York: Universal Publishing, 1923–25.

Gatens, Moira. *Imaginary Bodies: Ethics, Power, and Corporeality.* New York: Routledge, 1996.

Gaudin, Colette, Mary Jean Green, Lynn Anthony Higgins, Marianne Hirsch, Vivian Kogan, Claudia Reeder, and Nancy Vickers, eds. *Feminist Readings: French Texts / American Contexts. Yale French Studies* 62 (1981).

Gilbert, Sandra, and Susan Gubar. *The Madwoman in the Attic: The Woman Writer and the Nineteenth-Century Literary Imagination.* New Haven, Conn.: Yale University Press, 1984.

Gilligan, Carol. *In a Different Voice: Psychological Theory and Women's Development.* Cambridge, Mass.: Harvard University Press, 1982.

Gilroy, Paul. *The Black Atlantic: Modernity and Double Consciousness.* Cambridge, Mass.: Harvard University Press, 1993.

Gooding-Williams, Robert, ed. *Reading Rodney King / Reading Urban Uprising.* New York: Routledge, 1993.

Gould, Karen. *Writing in the Feminine: Feminism and Experimental Writing in Quebec.* Carbondale: Southern Illinois University Press, 1990.

Gould, Timothy. "The Unhappy Performative." In *Performativity and Performance,* ed. Andrew Parker and Eve Kosofsky Sedgwick. New York: Routledge, 1995.

Grahn, Judy. *The Highest Apple: Sappho and the Lesbian Poetic Tradition.* San Francisco: Spinsters Ink, 1985.

Greene, Gayle, and Coppélia Kahn, eds. *Changing Subjects: The Making of Feminist Literary Criticism.* New York: Routledge, 1993.

———. *Making a Difference: Feminist Literary Criticism.* London: Methuen, 1985.

Griffin, Gabriele, ed. *Outwrite: Lesbianism and Popular Culture.* London: Pluto Press, 1993.

Grosz, Elizabeth. "The Hetero and the Homo: The Sexual Ethics of Luce Irigaray." In *Engaging with Irigaray,* ed. Carolyn Burke, Naomi Schor, and Margaret Whitford. New York: Columbia University Press, 1994.

———. *Sexual Subversions: Three French Feminists.* Sydney: Allen and Unwin, 1989.

Habermas, Jürgen. *The Philosophical Discourses of Modernity.* Trans. Frederick G. Lawrence. Cambridge, Mass.: MIT Press, 1987.

Harari, Josué, ed. *Textual Strategies.* Ithaca, N.Y.: Cornell University Press, 1979.

Haraway, Donna Jeanne. "A Manifesto for Cyborgs: Science, Technology and Socialist Feminism in the 1980's." In *Coming to Terms: Feminism, Theory, and Politics,* ed. Elizabeth Weed. New York: Routledge, 1989.

Harris, Leonard. "Postmodernism and Utopia, an Unholy Alliance." In *I Am*

Because We Are: Readings in Black Philosophy, ed. Fred Lee Hord (Mzee Lasana Okpara) and Jonathan Scott Lee. Amherst: University of Massachusetts Press, 1995.

Hartman, Geoffrey. *Beyond Formalism: Literary Essays 1958–1970*. New Haven, Conn.: Yale University Press, 1970.

Hedges, Elaine, and Shelley Fisher Fishkin, eds. *Listening to Silences: New Essays in Feminist Criticism*. New York: Oxford University Press, 1994.

Heidegger, Martin. *An Introduction to Metaphysics*. Trans. Ralph Mannheim. New Haven, Conn.: Yale University Press, 1959.

Herman, Judith. *Trauma and Recovery*. New York: Basic Books, 1992.

Hirsch, Marianne. *The Mother/Daughter Plot: Narrative, Psychoanalysis, Feminism*. Bloomington: Indiana University Press, 1989.

———. "Mothers and Daughters." *Signs: Journal of Women in Culture and Society* 7/1 (1981): 200–222.

Hirsch, Marianne, and Evelyn Fox Keller, eds. *Conflicts in Feminism*. New York: Routledge, 1990.

Hoagland, Sarah. *Lesbian Ethics: Toward New Value*. Palo Alto, Calif.: Institute of Lesbian Studies, 1988.

Holmlund, Christine. "I Love Luce: The Lesbian, Mimesis and Masquerade in Irigaray, Freud and Mainstream Film." *New Formations* 9 (Winter 1989): 105–23.

———. "The Lesbian, the Mother, the Heterosexual Lover: Irigaray's Recordings of Difference." *Feminist Studies* 17/2 (1991): 283–308.

Hord, Fred Lee (Mzee Lasana Okpara), and Jonathan Scott Lee. *I Am Because We Are: Readings in Black Philosophy*. Amherst: University of Massachusetts Press, 1995.

Howe, Susan. *The Europe of Trusts*. Los Angeles: Sun and Moon Press, 1990.

Huffer, Lynne. *Another Colette: The Question of Gendered Writing*. Ann Arbor: University of Michigan Press, 1992.

———. "Interview with Nicole Brossard." In *Another Look, Another Woman*, ed. Huffer, *Yale French Studies* 87 (1995): 115–21.

———. "Luce *et veritas*: Toward an Ethics of Performance." In *Another Look, Another Woman*, ed. Huffer, *Yale French Studies* 87 (1995): 20–41.

———, ed. *Another Look, Another Woman: Retranslations of French Feminism*. *Yale French Studies* 87 (1995).

Hunter, Dianne, ed. *Seduction and Theory: Readings of Gender, Representation, and Rhetoric*. Urbana: University of Illinois Press, 1989.

Ingarden, Roman. *The Literary Work of Art: An Investigation on the Borderlines of*

Ontology, Logic and Theory of Literature. Trans. George Grabowicz. Evanston, Ill.: Northwestern University Press, 1973.

Irigaray, Luce. *Amante marine, de Friedrich Nietzsche*. Paris: Minuit, 1980. Trans. Gillian C. Gill as *Marine Lover of Friedrich Nietzsche*. New York: Columbia University Press, 1991.

———. "And the One Doesn't Stir Without the Other." Trans. Hélène Vivienne Wenzel. *Signs: Journal of Women in Culture and Society* 7/1 (1981): 60–67.

———. *Ce sexe qui n'en est pas un*. Paris: Minuit, 1977. Trans. Catherine Porter with Carolyn Burke as *This Sex Which Is Not One*. Ithaca, N.Y.: Cornell University Press, 1985.

———. *Le Corps-à-corps avec la mère*. Montreal: Editions de la pleine lune, 1981.

———. *Ethique de la différence sexuelle*. Paris: Minuit, 1984. Trans. Carolyn Burke and Gillian Gill as *An Ethics of Sexual Difference*. Ithaca, N.Y.: Cornell University Press, 1993.

———. *Et l'une ne bouge pas sans l'autre*. Paris: Minuit, 1979.

———. "The Fecundity of the Caress." In *Face to Face with Levinas*, ed. Richard A. Cohen. Albany: State University of New York Press, 1986.

———. *Speculum de l'autre femme*. Paris: Minuit, 1974. Trans. Gillian C. Gill as *Speculum of the Other Woman*. Ithaca, N.Y.: Cornell University Press, 1985.

Jacobus, Mary. *First Things: Reading the Maternal Imaginary*. New York: Routledge, 1995.

———. "Freud's Mnemonic: Women, Screen Memories, and Feminist Nostalgia." In *Women and Memory*, ed. Margaret A. Lourie, Domna C. Stanton, and Martha Vicinus, *Michigan Quarterly Review* 26 (1987): 117–39.

———. "Madonna: Like a Virgin; or, Freud, Kristeva, and the Case of the Missing Mother." *Oxford Literary Review* 8 (1986): 35–50.

Jagose, Annamarie. "Irigaray and the Lesbian Body: Remedy and Poison." *Genders* 13 (1992): 30–42.

———. *Lesbian Utopics*. New York: Routledge, 1994.

Jakobson, Roman. "Linguistics and Poetics." In *Style in Language*, ed. Thomas A. Sebeok. Cambridge, Mass.: MIT Press, 1960.

Jardine, Alice. *Gynesis: Configurations of Woman and Modernity*. Ithaca, N.Y.: Cornell University Press, 1985.

Jardine, Alice, and Paul Smith, eds. *Men in Feminism*. New York: Methuen, 1987.

Johnson, Barbara. *The Critical Difference: Essays in the Contemporary Rhetoric of Reading*. Baltimore: Johns Hopkins University Press, 1980.

―――. *A World of Difference*. Baltimore: Johns Hopkins University Press, 1987.

Jones, Ann Rosalind. "Imaginary Gardens with Real Frogs in Them: Feminist Euphoria and the Franco-American Divide, 1976–88." In *Changing Subjects: The Making of Feminist Literary Criticism*, ed. Gayle Greene and Coppélia Kahn. New York: Routledge, 1993.

―――. "Inscribing Femininity: French Theories of the Feminine." In *Making a Difference: Feminist Literary Criticism*, ed. Gayle Greene and Coppélia Kahn. London: Methuen, 1985.

―――. "Writing the Body: Toward an Understanding of *l'écriture féminine*." *Feminist Studies* 7/2 (1981): 247–63. Reprinted in Elaine Showalter, *Feminist Criticism: Essays on Women, Literature, and Theory*. New York: Pantheon, 1985.

Jones, Serene. "Divining Women: Irigaray and Feminist Theologies." In *Another Look, Another Woman: Retranslations of French Feminism*, ed. Lynne Huffer, *Yale French Studies* 87 (1995): 42–67.

―――. "This God Which Is Not One: Irigaray and Barth on the Divine." In *Transfigurations: Theology and the French Feminists*, ed. C. W. Maggie Kim, Susan M. St. Ville, and Susan M. Simonaitis. Minneapolis: Fortress Press, 1993.

Kamuf, Peggy. "Replacing Feminist Criticism." *Diacritics* 12 (1982): 42–47.

―――. *Signature Pieces: On the Institution of Authorship*. Ithaca, N.Y.: Cornell University Press, 1988.

―――. "Writing Like a Woman." In *Women and Language in Literature and Society*, ed. Sally McConnell-Ginet, Ruth Borker, and Nelly Furman. New York: Praeger, 1980.

Kamuf, Peggy, and Nancy K. Miller. "Parisian Letters: Between Feminism and Deconstruction." In *Conflicts in Feminism*, ed. Marianne Hirsch and Evelyn Fox Keller. New York: Routledge, 1990.

Kaplan, Carla. *The Erotics of Talk*. Oxford: Oxford University Press, 1996.

―――. "Reading Feminist Readings: Recuperative Reading and the Silent Heroine of Feminist Criticism." In *Listening to Silences: New Essays in Feminist Criticism*, ed. Elaine Hedges and Shelley Fisher Fishkin. New York: Oxford University Press, 1994.

Kim, C. W. Maggie, Susan M. St. Ville, and Susan M. Simonaitis, eds. *Transfigurations: Theology and the French Feminists*. Minneapolis: Fortress Press, 1993.

Klein, Richard. "In the Body of the Mother." *Enclitic* 7/1 (1983): 66–75.

Kofman, Sarah. *L'Énigme de la femme: La femme dans les textes de Freud.* Paris: Galilée, 1980.

Kristeva, Julia. *Des Chinoises.* Paris: Editions des femmes, 1974. Trans. Anita Barrows as *About Chinese Women.* London: Marion Boyars, 1977.

———. *Desire in Language: A Semiotic Approach to Literature and Art.* Ed. Leon S. Roudiez, trans. Thomas Gora, Alice Jardine, and Roudiez. New York: Columbia University Press, 1980.

———. *Histoires d'amour.* Paris: Denoël, 1983.

———. *The Kristeva Reader.* Ed. Toril Moi. New York: Columbia University Press, 1986.

———. "My Memory's Hyperbole." *New York Literary Forum* 12–14 (1984): 261–76.

———. *Polylogue.* Paris: Seuil, 1977.

———. *La Révolution du langage poétique.* Paris: Seuil, 1974. Trans. Margaret Waller as *Revolution in Poetic Language.* New York: Columbia University Press, 1984.

———. *Tales of Love.* Trans. Leon S. Roudiez. New York: Columbia University Press, 1987.

Lacan, Jacques. *Feminine Sexuality: Jacques Lacan and the école freudienne.* Ed. Juliet Mitchell and Jacqueline Rose, trans. Jacqueline Rose. New York: Norton, 1982.

———. *Le Séminaire XI: Les quatre concepts fondamentaux de la psychanalyse.* Paris: Seuil, 1973.

Lanser, Susan S. "Feminist Criticism, 'The Yellow Wallpaper,' and the Politics of Color in America." *Feminist Studies* 15/3 (1989): 415–41.

Larrabee, Mary Jeanne, ed. *An Ethic of Care: Feminist and Interdisciplinary Perspectives.* New York: Routledge, 1993.

Lechte, John. *Julia Kristeva.* London: Routledge, 1990.

Levinas, Emmanuel. *The Levinas Reader.* Ed. Seán Hand. Oxford: Blackwell, 1989.

———. *Totalité et infini: Essai sur l'extériorité.* The Hague: Martinus Nijhoff, 1971. Trans. Alphonso Lingis as *Totality and Infinity: An Essay on Exteriority.* Pittsburgh: Duquesne University Press, 1979.

Lewis, I. M. *Ecstatic Religion: A Study of Shamanism and Spirit Possession.* New York: Routledge, 1989.

Lorde, Audre. *Sister Outsider: Essays and Speeches.* Freedom, Calif.: The Crossing Press, 1984.

Lourie, Margaret A., Domna C. Stanton, and Martha Vicinus, eds. *Women and Memory. Michigan Quarterly Review* 26 (1987).

Lowe, Lisa. "*Des Chinoises*: Orientalism, Psychoanalysis, and Feminine Writing." In *Ethics, Politics, and Difference in Julia Kristeva's Writing*, ed. Kelly Oliver. New York: Routledge, 1993.

Lukacher, Maryline. *Maternal Fictions: Stendhal, Sand, Rachilde, and Bataille*. Durham, N.C.: Duke University Press, 1994.

Lyotard, Jean-François. *The Postmodern Condition: A Report on Knowledge*. Trans. Geoff Bennington and Brian Massumi. Minneapolis: University of Minnesota Press, 1984.

Marks, Elaine, and Isabelle de Courtivron, eds. *New French Feminisms: An Anthology*. New York: Schocken Books, 1981.

Matsuda, Mari. "Looking to the Bottom: Critical Legal Studies and Reparations." *Harvard Civil Rights–Civil Liberties Law Review* 22 (1987): 323–99.

McConnell-Ginet, Sally, Ruth Borker, and Nelly Furman, eds. *Women and Language in Literature and Society*. New York: Praeger, 1980.

McDonald, Christie, ed. *The Ear of the Other: Otobiography, Transference, Translation*. Lincoln: University of Nebraska Press, 1985.

Meese, Elizabeth A. *(Sem)erotics: Theorizing Lesbian Writing*. New York: New York University Press, 1992.

Mehlman, Jeffrey. *Legacies of Anti-Semitism in France*. Minneapolis: University of Minnesota Press, 1983.

Miller, Nancy K. *Subject to Change: Reading Feminist Writing*. New York: Columbia University Press, 1988.

————. "The Text's Heroine: A Feminist Critic and Her Fictions." *Diacritics* 12 (1982): 48–53.

————, ed. *The Poetics of Gender*. New York: Columbia University Press, 1986.

Moers, Ellen. *Literary Women*. New York: Anchor Books, 1977.

Mohin, Lilian, ed. *An Intimacy of Equals: Lesbian Feminist Ethics*. London: Onlywomen Press, 1996.

Moi, Toril. *Sexual/Textual Politics: Feminist Literary Theory*. London: Routledge, 1985.

Mykata, Larysa. "Vanishing Point: The Question of the Woman in the Works of Maurice Blanchot." Ph.D. diss., State University of New York at Buffalo, 1980.

Nicholson, Linda, ed. *Feminism/Postmodernism*. New York: Routledge, 1990.

Nicholson, Linda, and Steven Seidman, eds. *Social Postmodernism: Beyond Identity Politics*. Cambridge: Cambridge University Press, 1995.

Nietzsche, Friedrich. *Friedrich Nietzsche on Rhetoric and Language*. Ed. and trans. Sander L. Gilman, Carole Blair, and David J. Parent. New York: Oxford University Press, 1989.

Nouvet, Claire. "An Impossible Response: The Disaster of Narcissus." In *Literature and the Ethical Question*, ed. Nouvet, *Yale French Studies* 79 (1991): 103–34.

———, ed. *Literature and the Ethical Question. Yale French Studies* 79 (1991).

Nussbaum, Martha. "Human Functioning and Social Justice: In Defense of Aristotelian Essentialism." *Political Theory* 20 (1992): 202–46.

Okin, Susan Moller. *Justice, Gender, and the Family*. New York: Basic Books, 1989.

Oliver, Kelly. *Reading Kristeva: Unraveling the Double-Bind*. Bloomington: Indiana University Press, 1993.

———, ed. *Ethics, Politics, and Difference in Julia Kristeva's Writing*. New York: Routledge, 1993.

Parker, Andrew, and Eve Kosofsky Sedgwick, eds. *Performativity and Performance*. New York: Routledge, 1995.

Payne, Michael. *Reading Theory: An Introduction to Lacan, Derrida, and Kristeva*. Oxford: Blackwell, 1993.

Pendergast, James F., and Bruce G. Trigger, eds. *Cartier's Hochelaga and the Dawson Site*. Montreal: McGill-Queen's University Press, 1972.

Pérez, Emma. "Irigaray's Female Symbolic in the Making of Chicana Lesbian *Sitios y Lenguas* (*Sites and Discourses*)." In *The Lesbian Postmodern*, ed. Laura Doan. New York: Columbia University Press, 1994.

Phelan, Peggy. *Unmarked: The Politics of Performance*. New York: Routledge, 1993.

Plato. *The Republic: The Complete and Unabridged Jowett Translation*. New York: Random House, 1991.

———. *The Timaeus of Plato*. Ed. and trans. R. D. Archer-Hind. New York: Arno Press, 1973.

Porter, Elisabeth J. *Women and Moral Identity*. North Sydney: Allen and Unwin, 1991.

Rich, Adrienne. *The Dream of a Common Language: Poems 1974–1977*. New York: Norton, 1978.

———. *Of Woman Born: Motherhood as Experience and Institution*. New York: Norton, 1976.

Rose, Jacqueline. *Sexuality in the Field of Vision*. London: Verso, 1986.

Ruddick, Sara. *Maternal Thinking: Toward a Politics of Peace*. Boston: Beacon Press, 1989.

Saussure, Ferdinand de. *Course in General Linguistics*. Trans. Wade Baskin. New York: Philosophical Library, 1959.

Schneider, Elizabeth M. "The Dialectic of Rights and Politics: Perspectives from the Women's Movement." *New York University Law Review* 61 (October 1986): 589–652.

Schor, Naomi. *Breaking the Chain: Women, Theory, and French Realist Fiction.* New York: Columbia University Press, 1985.

———. "Dreaming Dissymmetry: Barthes, Foucault, and Sexual Difference." In *Men in Feminism*, ed. Alice Jardine and Paul Smith. New York: Methuen, 1987.

———. "Previous Engagements: The Receptions of Irigaray." In *Engaging with Irigaray*, ed. Carolyn Burke, Naomi Schor, and Margaret Whitford. New York: Columbia University Press, 1994.

———. *Reading in Detail: Aesthetics and the Feminine.* New York: Methuen, 1987.

———. "This Essentialism Which Is Not One: Coming to Grips with Irigaray." *Differences: A Journal of Feminist Cultural Studies* 1/2 (1989): 38–58.

Scott, James C. *Domination and the Arts of Resistance: Hidden Transcripts.* New Haven, Conn.: Yale University Press, 1990.

Sebeok, Thomas A., ed. *Style in Language.* Cambridge, Mass.: MIT Press, 1960.

Sedgwick, Eve Kosofsky. *Epistemology of the Closet.* Berkeley: University of California Press, 1990.

———. *Tendencies.* Durham, N.C.: Duke University Press, 1993.

Seidman, Steven. "Deconstructing Queer Theory, or the Undertheorization of the Social and the Ethical." In *Social Postmodernism: Beyond Identity Politics*, ed. Linda Nicholson and Seidman. Cambridge: Cambridge University Press, 1995.

Showalter, Elaine. *A Literature of Their Own.* Princeton, N.J.: Princeton University Press, 1977.

———, ed. *Feminist Criticism: Essays on Women, Literature, and Theory.* New York: Pantheon, 1985.

Silverman, Kaja. *The Acoustic Mirror: The Female Voice in Psychoanalysis and Cinema.* Lincoln: University of Nebraska Press, 1983.

Smock, Ann. "'Où est la loi?': Law and Sovereignty in *Aminadab* and *Le Très-haut*." *Sub-stance* 14 (1976): 99–116.

Spacks, Patricia Meyer. *The Female Imagination.* New York: Avon Books, 1972.

Spivak, Gayatri Chakravorty. "French Feminism in an International Frame." In *Feminist Readings: French Texts / American Contexts*, ed. Colette Gaudin, Mary Jean Green, Lynn Anthony Higgins, Marianne Hirsch, Vivian Kogan, Claudia Reeder, and Nancy Vickers, *Yale French Studies* 62 (1981): 154–84.

———. "French Feminism Revisited: Ethics and Politics." In *Feminists Theorize the Political*, ed. Judith Butler and Joan W. Scott. New York: Routledge, 1992.

Sprengnether, Madelon. *The Spectral Mother: Freud, Feminism, and Psychoanalysis.* Ithaca, N.Y.: Cornell University Press, 1990.

Stanton, Domna C. "Difference on Trial: A Critique of the Maternal Metaphor in Cixous, Irigaray, and Kristeva." In *The Poetics of Gender*, ed. Nancy K. Miller. New York: Columbia University Press, 1986.

———. "Language and Revolution: The Franco-American Dis-Connection." In *The Future of Difference*, ed. Hester Eisenstein and Alice Jardine. Boston: G. K. Hall, 1980.

Swan, Jim. "*Mater* and Nannie: Freud's Two Mothers and the Discovery of the Oedipus Complex." *American Imago* 31/1 (1974): 1–64.

Tong, Rosemary. *Feminist Thought: A Comprehensive Introduction.* Boulder, Colo.: Westview Press, 1989.

Trigger, Bruce G. *Natives and Newcomers: Canada's "Heroic Age" Reconsidered.* Montreal: McGill-Queen's University Press, 1985.

Tronto, Joan. *Moral Boundaries: A Political Argument for an Ethic of Care.* New York: Routledge, 1993.

Ungar, Steven. *Scandal and Aftereffect: Blanchot and France Since 1930.* Minneapolis: University of Minnesota Press, 1995.

Wall, Cheryl A., ed. *Changing Our Own Words: Essays on Criticism, Theory, and Writing by Black Women.* New Brunswick, N.J.: Rutgers University Press, 1989.

Warminski, Andrzej. *Readings in Interpretation: Hölderlin, Hegel, Heidegger.* Minneapolis: University of Minnesota Press, 1987.

Warnke, Georgia. "Discourse Ethics and Feminist Dilemmas of Difference." In *Feminists Read Habermas: Gendering the Subject of Discourse*, ed. Johanna Meehan. New York: Routledge, 1995.

Weed, Elizabeth, ed. *Coming to Terms: Feminism, Theory, and Politics.* New York: Routledge, 1989.

Wellek, René, and Austin Warren. *Theory of Literature.* New York: Harcourt Brace Jovanovich, 1977.

Whitford, Margaret. *Luce Irigaray: Philosophy in the Feminine.* London: Routledge, 1991.

Williams, Patricia J. "Alchemical Notes: Reconstructing Ideals from Deconstructed Rights." *Harvard Civil Rights–Civil Liberties Law Review* 22 (1987): 401–33.

Winterson, Jeanette. *Sexing the Cherry.* New York: Random House, 1989.

Wiseman, Mary Bittner. "Renaissance Paintings and Psychoanalysis: Julia Kristeva and the Function of the Mother." In *Ethics, Politics, and Difference in Julia Kristeva's Writing*, ed. Kelly Oliver. New York: Routledge, 1993.

Wittig, Monique. *Le Corps lesbien*. Paris: Minuit, 1973. Trans. David Le Vay as *The Lesbian Body*. New York: Morrow, 1975.

Wittig, Monique, and Sande Zeig. *Lesbian Peoples: Material for a Dictionary*. Trans. Wittig and Zeig. New York: Avon, 1979.

Young, Iris Marion. *Justice and the Politics of Difference*. Princeton, N.J.: Princeton University Press, 1990.

Ziarek, Ewa. "Kristeva and Levinas: Mourning, Ethics, and the Feminine." In *Ethics, Politics, and Difference in Julia Kristeva's Writing*, ed. Kelly Oliver. New York: Routledge, 1993.

Zimmerman, Bonnie. *The Safe Sea of Women: Lesbian Fiction, 1969–1989*. Boston: Beacon Press, 1990.

INDEX

In this index, "f" after a number indicates a separate reference on the next page, and "ff" indicates separate references on the next two pages. A continuous discussion over two or more pages is indicated by a span of page numbers, e.g., "57–59." *Passim* is used for a cluster of references in close but not consecutive sequence.

Abel, Elizabeth, 14
Absence, 1, 3f, 10, 25f, 31, 41f, 59, 61, 131
ACT-UP, 104f, 107
Africa, 16, 121
Agamemnon, 159
Agency, 88, 98, 102, 163
AIDS, 105
Alta, 35
Antifoundationalism, 137, 166
Arendt, Hannah, 137–38
Aristotle, 135, 162
Austin, J. L., 97, 103–10, 114, 166–72 *passim*
Authorship, 12, 152

Barre du jour, 125
Barthes, Roland, 37f
Beauvoir, Simone de, 7–10, 11–15 *passim*, 21–24 *passim*, 28, 89, 143, 150, 156
Belsey, Catherine, 173
Benhabib, Seyla, 100, 135–39, 176
Benvéniste, Emile, 166
Berg, Maggie, 24, 157
Bersani, Leo, 162
Blanchot, Maurice, 1, 3, 28f, 35–54, 125, 153ff, 174; *The Space of Literature*, 29, 35–40, 42, 50, 155
Bloom, Harold, 145
Body, 22f, 150
Brenkman, John, 14, 17, 146, 148, 171

Brossard, Nicole, 1–4 *passim*, 10–12, 14f, 19–24 *passim*, 28–31 *passim*, 122–33, 139, 174f; *L'Amèr*, 6, 10–12, 14, 24, 122, 131
Burke, Carolyn, 151
Butler, Judith, 25f, 31, 97–102, 104–111 *passim*, 134–38 *passim*, 165–68 *passim*, 176

Cartier, Jacques, 129–30, 175
Caruth, Cathy, 139
Catachresis, 2, 64, 67, 87, 113, 157, 172
Caughnawaga, 127, 129ff, 175
Cavell, Stanley, 103, 106, 110, 169
Césaire, Aimé, 121
Chanter, Tina, 166
Charcot, Jean Martin, 112
Chawaf, Chantal, 150
Chodorow, Nancy, 147
Chora, 30, 74–88, 91–97 *passim*, 148, 160ff
Cixous, Hélène, 21, 24, 52, 119, 148, 150, 155, 173
Clark, Timothy, 38
Clytemnestra, 69, 159
Colette, 121
Collins, Patricia Hill, 167
Combat, 155
Community, 14, 28, 133, 139
Condé, Maryse, 121
Conley, Verena Andermatt, 150
Cornell, Drucilla, 139

Coward, Rosalind, 162
Culler, Jonathan, 172

Death, 7f, 42–43, 49–55 passim, 91, 95, 131, 154, 159
Deconstruction, 2f, 9, 13, 134
De Lauretis, Teresa, 149
Delphy, Christine, 21ff
De Man, Paul, 50, 158, 172
Demeter, 18, 148
Derrida, Jacques, 38f, 49, 54, 80f, 105, 151–54 passim, 161, 166, 169
Desire, 15–22 passim, 29, 36–43 passim, 68, 98, 125f, 162, 166ff, 173, 177; lesbian, 19, 62, 113–14, 126, 149, 172
Différance, 2, 9, 143
Difference, 14, 19–22 passim, 27–32 passim, 56–68 passim, 84, 90f, 98, 107, 134–39 passim, 156–68 passim, 170; sexual, 30, 52f, 57–63 passim, 76, 86, 90, 94f, 134, 145, 152, 157, 164
Djebar, Assia, 21, 108, 150
Doane, Janice, 145
Don Juan, 98, 106, 110, 114, 170
Drag, 26, 99, 102
Duras, Marguerite, 150

Echo, 73–75, 89
Ecriture féminine, 22, 150, 173
Eidos, 64ff, 157
Electra, 17, 159
Epistemology, 29, 39, 55–62 passim, 75–87 passim, 91ff, 97–100 passim, 134ff, 166f
Essentialism, 22ff, 30, 74, 84, 88, 94, 150, 161–66 passim
Ethics, 14, 25–31 passim, 76–80 passim, 84–97 passim, 101–2, 107–13 passim, 134–39, 152, 162–70 passim, 176
Eurydice, 29, 35ff, 39–54, 75

Fabular subject, 126
Fascination, 46–49
Felman, Shoshana, 98, 106, 148, 166, 169ff, 177

Female authorship, 13, 17
Feminine (le féminin), 10, 21, 47–59 passim, 65f, 75f, 86, 90, 95, 152, 161
Feminism, 2, 6, 12, 54–57 passim, 94, 100, 125f, 134–37 passim, 164–67 passim, 176; French, 13, 21–24 passim, 57, 74, 149f, 164
Feminist criticism, 12, 17, 38, 53, 153
Feminist politics, 14, 19f, 29, 47, 68, 76–83 passim, 89f, 94–100 passim, 125, 132, 149, 167, 176
Feminist theory, 2, 17–23 passim, 56–59 passim, 67, 99, 134f, 167, 176
Foucault, Michel, 37–38
Freedom, 88–95 passim, 106, 164
Freud, Sigmund, 15–20 passim, 29f, 39, 57–63 passim, 69, 85, 112, 146f, 154–59 passim, 171
Frye, Marilyn, 172, 176
Fuss, Diana, 172
Future, 19, 31, 55, 65, 68, 105, 127–29 passim, 133–39 passim, 167

Gagnon, Madeleine, 150
Gallop, Jane, 24, 158
Gender, 9–15 passim, 22–25 passim, 29, 38f, 47–57 passim, 99ff, 109ff, 134ff, 143
Gilbert, Sandra, 145
Gilligan, Carol, 134–35
Godard, Barbara, 175
Gould, Karen, 125
Gould, Timothy, 103
Grahn, Judy, 120
Gubar, Susan, 145

Habermas, Jürgen, 135, 138, 154, 177
Hartman, Geoffrey, 38, 154
Hébert, Anne, 121
Heidegger, Martin, 80, 93, 151, 155
Herman, Judith, 171
Heteronormativity, 20, 108, 134, 149
Heterosexuality, 16f, 50f, 62, 75, 99, 104, 151, 157, 167, 172
Hochelaga, 129–32 passim, 175
Hodges, Devon, 145

Holmlund, Christine, 24, 151
Hologram, 19, 31, 127–32, 139
Homer, 121, 127, 148
Howe, Susan, 55, 69
Humor, 66–67, 112, 171
Husserl, Edmund, 91
Hustera, 30, 60f, 74–85 *passim*, 95, 161
Hysteria, 61–65 *passim*, 111f, 157–61
    passim, 171
Hyvrard, Jeanne, 150

Identity, 26, 97–101 *passim*, 106f, 125–38
    passim, 153, 167; logic of, 59–62, 82ff,
    89ff, 107, 136, 156, 158
Identity politics, 100, 126, 167
Imperialism, 30, 74ff, 88–95 *passim*, 128,
    163
Insurgé, 155
Irigaray, Luce, 1–4 *passim*, 21–30 *passim*,
    56–79, 83ff, 96ff, 110ff, 134ff, 150ff,
    156–66 *passim*, 170ff; *This Sex Which
    Is Not One*, 25ff, 64–68 *passim*, 96, 98,
    151, 156–61 *passim*, 165, 171; *Specu-
    lum of the Other Woman*, 29, 56–69
    passim, 76–79, 84f, 111, 151f, 156–59
    passim, 165, 170
Iterability, 80, 87, 155

Jacobus, Mary, 17f, 20, 145–49 *passim*,
    154
Jagose, Annamarie, 172
Jeffreys, Sheila, 159
Johnson, Barbara, 97, 107
Jouissance, 23, 66, 111
Justice, 88f, 92–97 *passim*, 102, 134f, 164,
    168

Kamuf, Peggy, 152
Kant, Immanuel, 135
Kaplan, Carla, 19, 149f
Klein, Richard, 10, 73, 91
Kofman, Sarah, 158
Kristeva, Julia, 1f, 21–24 *passim*, 28–31
    passim, 73–97, 107, 150, 159–64 *pas-
    sim*; *Revolution in Poetic Language*, 30,
    77, 80–89 *passim*, 93, 162

Lacan, Jacques, 24, 77, 154, 170, 173
Language, 2, 23–31 *passim*, 49ff, 64, 77ff,
    86, 90, 97f, 103, 164; as reflection, 2,
    44ff, 48–52 *passim*, 61, 64f, 83ff, 89,
    166, 174; and binary logic, 3, 12–13,
    28–31 *passim*, 42f, 48–53 *passim*, 63,
    128, 131, 139
Laub, Dori, 177
Lautréamont, Comte de, 92
Leclerc, Annie, 150
Lesbianism, 1–4 *passim*, 16–20 *passim*,
    24, 62, 111–21 *passim*, 125–28 *passim*,
    149f, 171ff
Lesbian mother, 1–5 *passim*, 118–21
    passim, 133, 139
Lesbian writing, 31, 119ff, 125f, 129ff,
    173
Lesbos, 31, 119–21, 125f
Levinas, Emmanuel, 30, 88–95 *passim*,
    102, 107, 151, 164–70 *passim*
Liberation, 16, 29–32 *passim*, 57, 68, 76,
    87f, 93–97 *passim*, 102, 119ff, 133,
    148, 167, 177
Lips, 24–31 *passim*, 64–67, 97f, 110–14
    passim, 123, 151, 157, 171f
Literary authority, 13, 17, 52, 152
Literary space, 29, 35–39 *passim*, 44–51,
    125, 153, 174
Lorde, Audre, 112
Lowe, Lisa, 163
Lyotard, Jean-François, 39, 137, 167

MacGillivray, Catherine, 150
Mallarmé, Stephane, 38, 92
Marginalization, 92, 101, 137, 139
Marx, Karl, 93
Maternal metaphor, 24, 47f, 57–61
    passim, 75, 84
Matricide, 69
Meese, Elizabeth, A., 173
Memory, 17–20 *passim*, 43ff, 69, 78, 94,
    127–32 *passim*, 137ff, 148, 154, 174
Metaphor, 28, 61–67 *passim*, 75, 84f, 91,
    157
Miller, Nancy K., 152
Mimicry, 25ff, 31, 44, 52, 58–68 *passim*,

74, 78–84 *passim*, 91, 96ff, 104–7
    passim, 111f, 156, 166, 171f
Moi, Toril, 90, 150, 160–64 *passim*
Montreal, 122–31 *passim*, 175
Mother, 6–12 *passim*, 23–40 *passim*,
    46–54 *passim*, 58–65, 69–79 *passim*,
    83–96 *passim*, 133–36 *passim*, 146–51
    passim, 155, 159–64 *passim*, 173; and
    daughter, 1, 3ff, 12, 18, 118, 121, 144
Mutuality, 4, 6, 27, 139
Mykata, Larysa, 153

Narcissus, 75, 85, 89, 93, 95, 162
Narrative, 98–102 *passim*, 110, 114, 132f,
    137ff
Negativity, 10, 37, 44, 84, 153, 162, 170
Neutrality, 29, 47f, 51ff, 125f, 174
Nietzsche, Friedrich, 59, 151, 158, 170
Nostalgia, 1–6 *passim*, 13–31 *passim*, 35,
    39–53 *passim*, 58, 68f, 76, 89–97 *pas-
    sim*, 120, 125–39 *passim*, 145–49 *pas-
    sim*, 162ff
Nouvet, Claire, 165

Oedipus, 15–17, 29, 39f, 146ff, 154, 159,
    171
Oliver, Kelly, 89, 163
Ontology, 30, 75–89, 91–94, 107, 134ff,
    164–70 *passim*
Orestes, 69, 159
Orientalism, 163
Origin, 9, 15–19 *passim*, 26–31 *passim*,
    41–46 *passim*, 52f, 58–65 *passim*,
    74–84 *passim*, 89–99 *passim*, 119f,
    125–33 *passim*, 145, 160
Orpheus, 29, 35–37, 39–53, 75, 81
Other, 15–21 *passim*, 27–30 *passim*, 47,
    63, 69, 75, 79, 88–98 *passim*, 102, 107,
    135–39, 162–70 *passim*

Parisis, Jean-Marc, 155
Parker, Andrew, 101
Parody, 26, 167
Particularity, 2, 25–28 *passim*, 56, 80, 94,
    99f, 105, 135ff
Paternal authority, 12, 15, 84, 109

Payne, Michael, 162
Performance, 30, 61, 66, 99f, 105ff, 112,
    137, 168
Performative utterance, 101–4 *passim*,
    110, 166–73 *passim*
Performativity, 25ff, 31, 96–108 *passim*,
    138, 165ff
Persephone, *see* Demeter
Phallus, 24, 111, 173
Phenomenology, 91
Philosophy, 29, 56–61 *passim*, 68f, 74–79
    passim, 83–87 *passim*, 91–96 *passim*,
    102f, 138, 156f, 164, 169f
Plato, 29, 45, 56–63 *passim*, 69, 73–95
    passim, 102, 156–64 *passim*, 169; *The
    Timaeus*, 30, 74–84, 160–62 *passim*;
    and the cave, 58ff, 63ff, 73ff, 84f, 95,
    156f, 161; *The Republic*, 74–79, 83f,
    156f, 159, 169
Plotinus, 111
Poetic communication, 35–52 *passim*,
    77, 87, 154, 174
Postfeminism, 56f
Postmodernism, 25, 39, 55f, 66, 95–100
    passim, 135–38 *passim*, 166, 176
Prague Structuralists, 153f
Pre-Oedipal phase, 17–19, 77, 144–48
    passim
Proust, 121
Psychoanalysis, 3, 9, 15, 19–22 *passim*,
    29, 39f, 57–62 *passim*, 77, 146–50
    passim, 164

Queer Nation, 104
Queer theory, 26, 97, 101–6 *passim*, 162,
    166–70 *passim*

Rawls, John, 135
Referent, 37–42 *passim*, 46–51 *passim*,
    85, 161, 166, 174f
Representation, 55–64 *passim*, 77–86,
    98, 103
Reproduction, 15, 17, 24, 60, 86, 94
Rich, Adrienne, 20, 24, 120f, 131, 144
Rochefort, Christiane, 150
Ruddick, Sarah, 143

Same, logic of, 28ff, 55f, 58–64, 67, 84, 91–94 *passim*, 107, 136–39 *passim*, 156–61 *passim*, 170
Sappho, 9, 16, 31, 119–21, 125–27
Sartre, Jean-Paul, 38, 106
Saussure, Ferdinand de, 9, 143
Schor, Naomi, 150
Scott, James, 171
Sedgwick, Eve Kosofsky, 101, 106, 165, 169f
Seidman, Steven, 166, 170
Semblant, 67, 86f, 113f, 158, 161
Semiotic (*le sémiotique*), 30f, 74–78 *passim*, 84–88, 91f, 94, 161, 164
Sexuality, 26, 62, 101, 111, 159
Silence, 1, 3f, 10, 26, 31, 52f, 114, 119–21, 133, 139, 155, 167, 173, 177
Sisters, 6, 28, 69, 139, 148
Sitney, P. Adams, 38
Sociality, 27, 30, 76f, 89, 162f, 167
Socrates, 78, 84
Speech act theory, 100–4 *passim*, 109f
Spivak, Gayatri Chakravorty, 163, 172
Sprengnether, Madelon, 149
Stanton, Domna, 24
Storytelling, 80, 99–102, 110, 114, 127, 132f, 137–39
Subject, 23ff, 37ff, 44, 51–58 *passim*, 77, 85–100 *passim*, 106f, 111, 125, 135, 175
Subjectivity, 15–17, 27, 31, 38, 58, 90, 98, 138
Supplementarity, 61ff
Swan, Jim, 146
Symbolic (*le symbolique*), 77f, 88f

Testimony, 177

Third kind (*triton genos*), 82, 157, 161
Topos, 87, 91
Trauma, 139
Trope, 41f, 48–53 *passim*, 57, 61–66 *passim*, 75, 80–91 *passim*, 113, 157, 174
Truth, 44–66 *passim*, 78, 83f, 95–98 *passim*, 102f, 107–14 *passim*, 154ff, 162, 167–70 *passim*

Universalism, 56, 136, 176
Urban radical, 123–31 *passim*, 174
Utopia, 4, 12, 18f, 68, 80, 125, 131, 148, 163

Valéry, Paul, 154
Violence, 31, 68f, 91f, 98–102 *passim*, 106–14 *passim*, 123, 128–33 *passim*, 138f, 158, 168
Visibility, 45, 79ff, 119f, 131ff, 173

Warnke, Georgia, 177
Whitford, Margaret, 166
Williams, Patricia J., 168
Winterson, Jeanette, 11, 117–21 *passim*, 132f
Wittig, Monique, 4, 21, 119
Woman, 56–65, 69, 75, 90, 99–102 *passim*, 111, 125f, 131, 134–39 *passim*, 156f
Womb, 10–11, 16, 28, 60, 74–79 *passim*, 97, 146, 157–62 *passim*
Writing, 37, 41, 49, 78, 123f, 127–33

Yale French Studies, 38
Young, Iris Marion, 177

Ziarek, Ewa, 164

Library of Congress Cataloging-in-Publication Data

Huffer, Lynne

  Maternal pasts, feminist futures : nostalgia, ethics, and the
question of difference / Lynne Huffer.

     p. cm.

  Includes bibliographical references and index.

  ISBN 0-8047-3025-3. — ISBN 0-8047-3026-1 (pbk.)

  1. French literature—20th century—History and criticism.
2. Mothers in literature. 3. Nostalgia in literature. I. Title.

PQ305.H84   1998

840.9'3520431—dc21   97-41231

                                              CIP

Original printing 1998

Last figure below indicates year of this printing:

07 06 05 04 03 02 01 00 99 98